AND GOD
SPOKE THESE
WORDS

AND GOD SPOKE THESE WORDS

The Ten Commandments and Contemporary Ethics

RIFAT SONSINO

URJ PRESS
New York, New York

All rights reserved. No part of this book may be reproduced, stored in a retrieval system, or transmitted without express written permission from URJ Press. This excludes brief quotations used only for the purpose of review.

For permission to reprint, please contact:
URJ Press
633 Third Avenue
New York, NY 10017-6778
212-650-4120
press@urj.org

Library Of Congress Cataloging-In-Publication Data is available for this title.

Printed on acid-free paper
Copyright © 2014 Rifat Sonsino

Text design and composition by John Reinhardt Book Design
Manufactured in the United States of America
10 9 8 7 6 5 4 3 2 1

*Dedicated to the memory of my parents,
Albert and Victoria Sonsino,
and my in-laws,
Israel ("Isidoro") and Juana ("Chiqui") Goldstein*

Contents

Acknowledgments ix
Abbreviations xi
The Ten Words xiii
Preface xix

Torah and Law in Judaism 1
Text and Context 13

The Decalogue

The First Word: God 31
The Second Word: Idolatry 47
The Third Word: Misuse of God's Name 63
The Fourth Word: The Sabbath 77
The Fifth Word: Honoring Parents 95
The Sixth Word: Homicide 113
The Seventh Word: Adultery 133
The Eighth Word: Stealing 151

The Ninth Word: False Witness 169
The Tenth Word: Coveting 185
Legislation and Commandment 201

Notes 205
Bibliography 221

Acknowledgments

Unless otherwise indicated, the translation of Pentateuchal texts was taken from *The Torah: A Modern Commentary*, revised edition, edited by W. Gunther Plaut (New York: Union for Reform Judaism, 2005). The rest of biblical texts come from *JPS Hebrew-English Tanakh* (Philadelphia: Jewish Publication Society, 1999).

I wish to thank my colleagues Rabbis Neil Kominsky, Michele Lenke, Carl Perkins, Jay Perlman, and Don Splansky for providing me with valuable suggestions and comments. Also, my gratitude to Michael Goldberg, editor-in-chief of URJ Press, for his encouragement in writing this book.

A note about transliteration: It is not always easy to transliterate Hebrew texts into English, because Hebrew contains certain letters that cannot be easily reproduced by the English alphabet. In scholarly publications in the United States, it is customary to use the system created by the *Journal of Biblical Literature*. There is no unanimity among authors and editors of more popular books on this subject. In this book, I have attempted to render the Hebrew words as an English-speaking reader would understand. However, in order to distinguish between the Hebrew letters ח (*chet*) and כ (*khaf*), I have used *ch* for the first and *kh* for the second. Thus, for example, in the word for "month," *chodesh*, the first letter, *chet*, should be pronounced like the last two consonants of the German word *buch* or the name of the musician Bach, and not as "sh" like *chien* (French for "dog") or as "tch" like "charity." Similarly, *zakhor* ("remember"), with *khaf*, should be pronounced as *zahor* in Spanish or Latin.

A word about the title: "God spoke" (*vay'dabeir Elohim*) comes from Exod. 20:1, with which the biblical text introduces the Ten Commandments. Some Rabbis, taking the text literally, said that God, to be better understood, addressed the Israelites coming out of Egypt in the language they spoke in the country, namely, in ancient Egyptian (see *Tanchuma* B, #16). Most Jews, however, echoing the teachings of many ancient and medieval Jewish sages, argue that "God spoke" must be taken figuratively (see, for example, *Sifrei*, Numbers 112; *Guide of the Perplexed* 1:46), "as if" God had spoken like a human being. For many Reform Jewish teachers, this expression means that divine revelation is progressive and must be acknowledged "whether shining from the annals of ancient revelations or reaching us through the seers of our own time" (*Union Prayerbook*, 1959, 34). For me, "God spoke" implies that the teachings of the Ten Commandments are so important and so compelling in our lives that they are worthy of attribution to the highest we know, God.

Abbreviations

ANET .... *Ancient Near Eastern Texts Relating to the Old Testament* (ed. James B. Pritchard)
Ant .... *Antiquities* (by Josephus)
BT .... Babylonian Talmud
CCAR .... Central Conference of American Rabbis
Chron .... Chronicles
Dan .... Daniel
Deut ...... Deuteronomy
Eccles ..... Ecclesiastes
Eph .... Ephesians
Exod ...... Exodus
Ezek .... Ezekiel
Gen .... Genesis
Hab .... Habakkuk
Hos .... Hosea
Isa .... Isaiah
Jer .... Jeremiah
Josh .... Joshua
JPS .... Jewish Publication Society
JT .... Jerusalem Talmud
Judg .... Judges
Lam .... Lamentations
Lev .... Leviticus
Mal .... Malachi
Matt .... Matthew
Mic .... Micah
Neh .... Nehemiah
NJPS ...... New (version of) Jewish Publication Society
NRSV .... New Revised Standard Version
Num ...... Numbers
Prov .... Proverbs
Ps .... Psalm
Pss .... Psalms
Rom .... Romans
RSV .... Revised Standard Version
Sam .... Samuel
URJ .... Union for Reform Judaism
Zech ...... Zechariah

The Ten Words

Exodus 20:2-14

2] I the Eternal am your God who brought you out of the land of Egypt, the house of bondage:

3] You shall have no other gods besides Me.

4] You shall not make for yourself a sculptured image, or any likeness of what is in the heavens above, or on the earth below, or in the waters under the earth.

5] You shall not bow down to them or serve them. For I the Eternal your God am an impassioned God, visiting the guilt of the parents upon the children, upon the third and upon the fourth generations of those who reject Me,

6] but showing kindness to the thousandth generation of those who love Me and keep My commandments.

7] You shall not swear falsely by the name of the Eternal your God; for the Eternal will not clear one who swears falsely by God's name.

8] Remember the sabbath day and keep it holy.

9] Six days you shall labor and do all your work,

10] but the seventh day is a sabbath of the Eternal your God: you shall not do any work—you, your son or daughter, your male or female slave, or your cattle, or the stranger who is within your settlements.

11] For in six days the Eternal made heaven and earth and sea—and all that is in them—and then rested on the seventh day; therefore the Eternal blessed the sabbath day and hallowed it.

12] Honor your father and your mother, that you may long endure on the land that the Eternal your God is assigning to you.

13] You shall not murder. You shall not commit adultery. You shall not steal. You shall not bear false witness against your neighbor.

14] You shall not covet your neighbor's house: you shall not covet your neighbor's wife, nor male nor female slave, nor ox nor ass, nor anything that is your neighbor's.

שמות כ:ב-יד

ב אָנֹכִי יְהֹוָה אֱלֹהֶיךָ אֲשֶׁר הוֹצֵאתִיךָ מֵאֶרֶץ מִצְרַיִם מִבֵּית עֲבָדִים:

ג לֹא־יִהְיֶה לְךָ אֱלֹהִים אֲחֵרִים עַל־פָּנָי:

ד לֹא־תַעֲשֶׂה לְךָ פֶסֶל וְכָל־תְּמוּנָה אֲשֶׁר בַּשָּׁמַיִם מִמַּעַל וַאֲשֶׁר בָּאָרֶץ מִתָּחַת וַאֲשֶׁר בַּמַּיִם מִתַּחַת לָאָרֶץ:

ה לֹא־תִשְׁתַּחֲוֶה לָהֶם וְלֹא תָעָבְדֵם כִּי אָנֹכִי יְהֹוָה אֱלֹהֶיךָ אֵל קַנָּא פֹּקֵד עֲוֹן אָבֹת עַל־בָּנִים עַל־שִׁלֵּשִׁים וְעַל־רִבֵּעִים לְשֹׂנְאָי:

ו וְעֹשֶׂה חֶסֶד לַאֲלָפִים לְאֹהֲבַי וּלְשֹׁמְרֵי מִצְוֹתָי:

ז לֹא תִשָּׂא אֶת־שֵׁם־יְהֹוָה אֱלֹהֶיךָ לַשָּׁוְא כִּי לֹא יְנַקֶּה יְהֹוָה אֵת אֲשֶׁר־יִשָּׂא אֶת־שְׁמוֹ לַשָּׁוְא:

ח זָכוֹר אֶת־יוֹם הַשַּׁבָּת לְקַדְּשׁוֹ:

ט שֵׁשֶׁת יָמִים תַּעֲבֹד וְעָשִׂיתָ כָּל־מְלַאכְתֶּךָ:

י וְיוֹם הַשְּׁבִיעִי שַׁבָּת לַיהֹוָה אֱלֹהֶיךָ לֹא־תַעֲשֶׂה כָל־מְלָאכָה אַתָּה וּבִנְךָ וּבִתֶּךָ עַבְדְּךָ וַאֲמָתְךָ וּבְהֶמְתֶּךָ וְגֵרְךָ אֲשֶׁר בִּשְׁעָרֶיךָ:

יא כִּי שֵׁשֶׁת־יָמִים עָשָׂה יְהֹוָה אֶת־הַשָּׁמַיִם וְאֶת־הָאָרֶץ אֶת־הַיָּם וְאֶת־כָּל־אֲשֶׁר־בָּם וַיָּנַח בַּיּוֹם הַשְּׁבִיעִי עַל־כֵּן בֵּרַךְ יְהֹוָה אֶת־יוֹם הַשַּׁבָּת וַיְקַדְּשֵׁהוּ:

יב כַּבֵּד אֶת־אָבִיךָ וְאֶת־אִמֶּךָ לְמַעַן יַאֲרִכוּן יָמֶיךָ עַל הָאֲדָמָה אֲשֶׁר־יְהֹוָה אֱלֹהֶיךָ נֹתֵן לָךְ:

יג לֹא תִרְצָח לֹא תִנְאָף לֹא תִגְנֹב לֹא־תַעֲנֶה בְרֵעֲךָ עֵד שָׁקֶר:

יד לֹא תַחְמֹד בֵּית רֵעֶךָ לֹא־תַחְמֹד אֵשֶׁת רֵעֶךָ וְעַבְדּוֹ וַאֲמָתוֹ וְשׁוֹרוֹ וַחֲמֹרוֹ וְכֹל אֲשֶׁר לְרֵעֶךָ:

Deuteronomy 5:6-18

6] I the Eternal am your God who brought you out of the land of Egypt, the house of bondage:

7] You shall have no other gods beside Me.

8] You shall not make for yourself a sculptured image, or any likeness of what is in the heavens above, or on the earth below, or in the waters below the earth.

9] You shall not bow down to them or serve them. For I the Eternal your God am an impassioned God, visiting the guilt of the parents upon the children, upon the third and upon the fourth generations of those who reject Me,

10] but showing kindness to the thousandth generation of those who love Me and keep My commandments.

11] You shall not swear falsely by the name of the Eternal your God; for the Eternal will not clear one who swears falsely by God's name.

12] Observe the sabbath day and keep it holy, as the Eternal your God has commanded you.

13] Six days you shall labor and do all your work,

14] but the seventh day is a sabbath of the Eternal your God; you shall not do any work—you, your son or your daughter, your male or female slave, your ox or your ass, or any of your cattle, or the stranger in your settlements, so that your male and female slave may rest as you do.

15] Remember that you were a slave in the land of Egypt and the Eternal your God has commanded you to observe the sabbath day.

16] Honor your father and your mother, as the Eternal your God has commanded you, that you may long endure, and that you may fare well, in the land that the Eternal your God is assigning to you.

17] You shall not murder. You shall not commit adultery. You shall not steal. You shall not bear false witness against your neighbor.

18] You shall not covet your neighbor's wife. Likewise, none of you shall crave your neighbor's house, or field, or male or female slave, or ox, or ass, or anything that is your neighbor's.

דברים ה:ו-יח

ו אָנֹכִי יְהֹוָה אֱלֹהֶיךָ אֲשֶׁר הוֹצֵאתִיךָ מֵאֶרֶץ מִצְרַיִם מִבֵּית עֲבָדִים:

ז לֹא־יִהְיֶה לְךָ אֱלֹהִים אֲחֵרִים עַל־פָּנָי:

ח לֹא־תַעֲשֶׂה לְךָ פֶסֶל כָּל־תְּמוּנָה אֲשֶׁר בַּשָּׁמַיִם מִמַּעַל וַאֲשֶׁר בָּאָרֶץ מִתַּחַת וַאֲשֶׁר בַּמַּיִם מִתַּחַת לָאָרֶץ:

ט לֹא־תִשְׁתַּחֲוֶה לָהֶם וְלֹא תָעָבְדֵם כִּי אָנֹכִי יְהֹוָה אֱלֹהֶיךָ אֵל קַנָּא פֹּקֵד עֲוֺן אָבוֹת עַל־בָּנִים וְעַל־שִׁלֵּשִׁים וְעַל־רִבֵּעִים לְשֹׂנְאָי:

י וְעֹשֶׂה חֶסֶד לַאֲלָפִים לְאֹהֲבַי וּלְשֹׁמְרֵי מִצְוֺתָי:

יא לֹא תִשָּׂא אֶת־שֵׁם־יְהֹוָה אֱלֹהֶיךָ לַשָּׁוְא כִּי לֹא יְנַקֶּה יְהֹוָה אֵת אֲשֶׁר־יִשָּׂא אֶת־שְׁמוֹ לַשָּׁוְא:

יב שָׁמוֹר אֶת־יוֹם הַשַּׁבָּת לְקַדְּשׁוֹ כַּאֲשֶׁר צִוְּךָ יְהֹוָה אֱלֹהֶיךָ:

יג שֵׁשֶׁת יָמִים תַּעֲבֹד וְעָשִׂיתָ כָּל־מְלַאכְתֶּךָ:

יד וְיוֹם הַשְּׁבִיעִי שַׁבָּת לַיהֹוָה אֱלֹהֶיךָ לֹא־תַעֲשֶׂה כָל־מְלָאכָה אַתָּה וּבִנְךָ־וּבִתֶּךָ וְעַבְדְּךָ־וַאֲמָתֶךָ וְשׁוֹרְךָ וַחֲמֹרְךָ וְכָל־בְּהֶמְתֶּךָ וְגֵרְךָ אֲשֶׁר בִּשְׁעָרֶיךָ לְמַעַן יָנוּחַ עַבְדְּךָ וַאֲמָתְךָ כָּמוֹךָ:

טו וְזָכַרְתָּ כִּי עֶבֶד הָיִיתָ בְּאֶרֶץ מִצְרַיִם וַיֹּצִאֲךָ יְהֹוָה אֱלֹהֶיךָ מִשָּׁם בְּיָד חֲזָקָה וּבִזְרֹעַ נְטוּיָה עַל־כֵּן צִוְּךָ יְהֹוָה אֱלֹהֶיךָ לַעֲשׂוֹת אֶת־יוֹם הַשַּׁבָּת:

טז כַּבֵּד אֶת־אָבִיךָ וְאֶת־אִמֶּךָ כַּאֲשֶׁר צִוְּךָ יְהֹוָה אֱלֹהֶיךָ לְמַעַן יַאֲרִיכֻן יָמֶיךָ וּלְמַעַן יִיטַב לָךְ עַל הָאֲדָמָה אֲשֶׁר־יְהֹוָה אֱלֹהֶיךָ נֹתֵן לָךְ:

יז לֹא תִרְצָח וְלֹא תִנְאָף וְלֹא תִגְנֹב וְלֹא־תַעֲנֶה בְרֵעֲךָ עֵד שָׁוְא:

יח וְלֹא תַחְמֹד אֵשֶׁת רֵעֶךָ וְלֹא תִתְאַוֶּה בֵּית רֵעֶךָ שָׂדֵהוּ וְעַבְדּוֹ וַאֲמָתוֹ שׁוֹרוֹ וַחֲמֹרוֹ וְכֹל אֲשֶׁר לְרֵעֶךָ:

Preface

Samuel Sandmel, the author of *The Hebrew Scriptures*, wrote, "More people praise the Bible than read it. More read it than understand it, and more understand it than conscientiously follow it."[1] The same judgment, I think, applies to the Ten Commandments (also referred to as "the Decalogue," Greek for "Ten Words"). Even though most people think that the Ten Commandments contain the basic principles of morality in our society, only a few seem to have a clear understanding of what they mean. This is borne out in many surveys on this subject. For example, in 1997, a poll conducted by the *Sunday Times* in England revealed that only 17 percent of the Anglican clergy were able to cite all of the Ten Commandments.[2] Similarly, a 2007 survey by Kelton Research found that more Americans could recall the seven ingredients of a McDonald's Big Mac than could name any of the injunctions of the Decalogue.[3]

It is popularly believed that the so-called Golden Rule, "Treat others as you want to be treated," is included in the Ten Commandments or that one of the Ten Words of the Decalogue is "You shall love your neighbor as yourself." In reality, the Decalogue does not include the Golden Rule; it is derived from a saying attributed to Rabbi Hillel (first century CE) in the Talmud (BT *Shabbat* 31a) and is also quoted in the New Testament in Matt. 7:12. Similarly, the teaching about "loving your neighbor" comes from Lev. 19:18, not from the Decalogue.

The Ten Commandments have long inspired artists, but their work is rarely reliable, either historically or linguistically. In film, many have seen movies portraying the revelation of the Decalogue, such as the classic *Ten*

Commandments directed by Cecil B. DeMille in 1956 (regularly shown on TV around Easter, a remake of his 1923 silent movie), have heard about a 1988 Polish movie on the same subject directed by Krzysztof Kieslowski, or even laughed at Mel Brooks's rendition of this episode in *History of the World, Part One* in 1981. The Decalogue has also fired the imagination of poets, like Arthur Hugh Clough (1819–1861) and Ambrose Bierce (1842–1913), and many modern comedians, like George Carlin. Similarly, the "Ten Words" have appeared in paintings by artists as diverse as Lucas Cranach the Elder (1472–1553) and Philippe de Champaigne (1648) in the Middle Ages to Marc Chagall (1887–1985) in the modern period.

In addition to the world of art, the Decalogue has played a central role in Judaism and Christianity for a very long time and been considered the highest expression of the religious values in both religions. There are textual references to indicate that they were well-known during biblical times, for they are invoked in some prophetic writings (Hos. 4:1; Jer. 7:9; Ps. 50:18) and, later on, alluded to in the New Testament (Mark 10:17–22; Matt. 19:16–22; Luke 18:18–23; Rom. 13:8–10).

Many Christians view the Decalogue as central to their concept of morality. As David Flusser points out, "From the time of the earliest Fathers of the Church, Christians assigned an even more exalted position to the Decalogue than Judaism did."[4] Many Christians consider its broad and universal focus as the literal word of the living God and, therefore, more important than the detailed laws of Judaism, which are not deemed as binding. In fact, a contemporary Christian theologian writes, "If we may apply the term 'Christian' thus retrospectively to the Decalogue, we should say, what it contains is not general but Christian ethics."[5] The Protestant reformer Martin Luther dedicated nearly half of the one hundred pages of his book *Large Catechism* (1529) to this subject. Many Christian thinkers in our time still consider the Decalogue as the rock of Christian ethics.

In the last two decades, the belief that the Ten Commandments stands for God and religion has spilled over into our legal courts in a dramatic way. In August 2001, Chief Justice Roy S. Moore of the Alabama Supreme Court put up a 5,280-pound monument of the Decalogue in the lobby of the Alabama Judicial Building. A year passed and Judge Myron H. Thomson, a federal district judge, ruled that the display violated the "separation of Church and State" and threatened to make Judge Moore pay five thousand dollars for every day that the Ten Commandments remained in public view. Judge Moore responded by saying, "It is a sad day in our country when the moral foundation of our laws and the acknowledgment of God have to be hidden," and refused to comply with Judge Thomson's request. Immediately after, eight associate judges of Alabama's supreme court overruled Judge Moore and ordered him to remove the monument. Judge Moore remained defiant; "I must obey God," he retorted and turned to the U.S. Supreme Court. On August 20, the Supreme Court rejected his appeal. This decision led to many protests around the country in support of Judge Moore. But it was of no avail, because two days later a judicial panel suspended Judge Moore and gave him thirty days to respond. Finally, on November 13, 2003, a special ethics panel ousted the judge from the bench altogether.

The same issue surfaced later in many parts of the country, such as Texas and Kentucky, where community leaders tried to exhibit the Decalogue in public domains. Finally, in June 2005, the Supreme Court ruled on this issue and, by a 5–4 decision, upheld its display on government property under limited circumstances. It stated that if it promotes religion, it is not acceptable, but if it has a "secular purpose" (such as educational or historical), the Ten Commandments can be set up. Thus, the court said that Texas could keep the Ten Commandments because the monument has stood for decades on its capitol grounds, presumably for historical reasons, whereas two Kentucky counties had to take the Decalogue down because they were erected in 1999 in their courthouses in order to promote religion. This court decision may have resolved the legal issue for the moment but left dissatisfied a great many. In fact, the monument that Judge Moore tried to put up about a decade ago was sent around the country to innumerable religious institutions as a way to promote his cause, and presently, for many religious conservatives, it continues to be a reminder of a concerted effort by liberals to erase any mention of God and religion from the public arena in America.

In Judaism, the "Ten Words" has a prominent place within the Torah. For the Greek-Jewish philosopher Philo of Alexandria (first century CE), given the fact that God revealed many other laws besides the Decalogue, the "Ten Words" represent "general legal categories" (*The Decalogue*, 19). In Rabbinic Judaism, the Decalogue stands for the entire Torah and the covenant between God and the Jewish people. As the author of *M'norat HaMaor* states, "The Ten Commandments are the foundation of our faith."[6] It is also the main scriptural reading for the festival of Shavuot ("Weeks"), which recalls the revelation of the Torah on Mount Sinai and is considered the source of all the biblical and Rabbinic laws. As Rashi, the great medieval Jewish commentator, states, "All the 613 commandments are included in the Decalogue" (see his comments to Exod. 24:12). Similarly, the *Zohar*, the classic text of Jewish mysticism (thirteenth century), declares, "The Ten Words contains the essence of all the [613] commandments, the essence of all celestial and terrestrial mysteries, the essence of the Ten Words of Creation."[7]

For centuries, these Ten Commandments have been studied by scholars and popularizers from different perspectives. In the Jewish world, Solomon Goldman collected most of the Rabbinic teachings in his book *The Ten Commandments* (1963). In 1990, the Hebrew University of Jerusalem issued a scholarly study titled *The Ten Commandments in History and Tradition*, which included articles dealing with many aspects of the Decalogue. Rachel Mikva edited a spiritually oriented book on this subject called *Broken Tablets* (1999). Dennis S. Ross, in 2000, published a short book entitled *The Ten Commandments: From the Shadow of Eden to the Promise of Canaan*, based on a conceptual approach to the text through the eyes of Rabbi Abraham bar Hiyyah, who lived in Spain in the eleventh century. Simon Glustrom published his *Timeless Tablets* in 2006, where he discusses some of the general Jewish issues dealing with the Decalogue. The most recent Jewish analysis of this subject is by David Hazony, *The Ten Commandments; How Our Most Ancient Moral Text Can Renew Modern Life* (2010), which deals with some of the religious and ethical values related to the Decalogue. To my knowledge, however, presently there is no book on the Ten Commandments in Judaism that studies each commandment using a critical-historical method that also deals with traditional Jewish values as well as contemporary ethics. The present book plans to fill this gap.

In our study of each command of the Decalogue, we will use the following methodology: First, we will discuss some of the key Hebrew terms in the biblical text by looking at other biblical material that employ the same expressions in an effort to grasp their original meaning. At times, we will refer to other languages spoken in the Mediterranean basin or Mesopotamia to look for cognates, knowing full well that clear nuances exist even within the same family of Semitic idioms. Next, we will study the Ten Commandments within the biblical context to ascertain what they probably meant, and then we will look at the early Rabbinic literature to see how the Rabbis understood the Decalogue in their own time and if or how they enlarged the focus of these divine words because of the necessities of the Mishnaic and Talmudic periods. Finally, following the line of development, we will try to see what each commandment means or could mean today, including their ethical implication for the present world. This will enable us to read the ancient "words" in our own contemporary setting with meanings that are more compatible with our present views.

In our time, scholars will continue to analyze the text of the Ten Commandments critically in light of new archaeological discoveries as well as contemporary anthropological and linguistic studies. This book will benefit from the researchers' insights but will represent my personal reading of the sacred texts, highlighting for readers the ethical and practical aspects of the Decalogue in our daily life. Ultimately, if the Ten Commandments have any relevance today, it is because they are meaningful and compelling to us in our interaction with others.

Torah and Law in Judaism

We affirm that Torah is the foundation of Jewish life.
("A Statement of Principles for Reform Judaism," 1999)

The Ten Commandments and Torah

The Ten Commandments represent certain basic legal and moral foundations of Judaism. They are considered part of "Torah." However, they do not cover all the contingencies of daily Jewish life, past or present. For that, we need to turn to other legal compendia found in different parts of the Pentateuch and in the Rabbinic literature. Yet the Decalogue, with its special form and content, stands alone as a unique text in the entirety of Jewish literature.

Jewish tradition tells us that Moses received the Torah on Mount Sinai (*Pirkei Avot* 1:1), and the Ten Commandments are considered as either the only text of revelation or, as later rabbis affirmed, the most important component of it. Obviously the Decalogue and Torah are related. The question is, how? The answer may be found in the meaning that the words "Torah" and "Decalogue" assumed through the ages. In the following chapters we shall study this development. We begin now with the word "Torah."

The Word "Torah"

"Torah" is one of the three pillars of Judaism—along with "God" and "Israel"—and, as with the other pillars, carries multiple layers of meaning. Coming from the Hebrew root *y-r-h* ("to throw" or "to teach"), an appropriate literal translation for it might be "instruction" in general and "religious instruction" in particular.

On the one hand, the word "Torah" can refer to a physical object. In the synagogue, when a holy scroll containing the Five Books attributed to Moses is taken out of the ark, the prayer leader proclaims, "This is the Torah that Moses placed before the Children of Israel." Here "Torah" clearly means the parchment on which the Pentateuch is written. On the other hand, "Torah," used in the broadest sense of the word, may (and often does) mean the combination of all the Jewish wisdom taught by the sages of our people throughout the ages. Thus, for instance, when people get together to study ancient or modern texts coming out of the Jewish sacred literature, they are, in fact, "studying Torah." These texts may include the Bible, the Mishnah, the Talmud, or modern Bible commentaries.

The foundational text of Judaism, the Hebrew Bible—though mostly composed in Hebrew, it also has a number of passages in Aramaic—was written in the language of its own time, with some parts being even older than the others. The Bible's Hebrew is often very different from Rabbinic and Modern Hebrew, in terms of grammatical structure as well as the meaning of some of the words used in it. Therefore, it is appropriate to ask, what did the Hebrew word *Torah* mean in the Bible?

The Term *Torah* in the Bible

In the Pentateuch, the Hebrew word *Torah* was associated with oracular teachings of the priests. In the ancient Near East, people used different magical methods to determine gods' will, including throwing lots, analyzing the viscera of animals, or observing the shape of oil in a water container. Ancient Israelites resorted to dreams or prophecy as means to find out what God wanted, but it was the "Urim and Thummim" employed by the priests that played the fundamental role, especially in the older periods (see I Sam. 28:6). It was the primary responsibility of these Temple professionals to impart and teach Torah (e.g., Lev. 11; Deut. 33:10) by means of the Urim and Thummim (e.g., Exod. 28:30; Lev. 8:8; Deut. 33:8; or *tamim*, as in I Sam. 14:41); these objects were kept on their breastplates. The meaning of these two words is obscure. The Talmud connects "Urim" with *or*, "light," and "Thummim" with *tam*, "perfect" (BT *Yoma* 73b). Most likely, the Urim and Thummim were small stones or sacred lots, each in the shape of a die, which was cast to the ground (implied in the original meaning of the word *torah*, "to throw") in order to answer specific questions addressed to them. The response often took the form of "yes" or "no." Jacob Milgrom (1923–2010), a modern biblical scholar, suggests that it is also possible that these two obscure words referred to the twenty-two letters of the Hebrew alphabet, and the priests could somehow extract a meaning by relying on the special nature of the Hebrew language, which is based on three root consonants.[1] In modern times, the words *Urim v'Thummim* appear (in Hebrew) on Yale University's insignia, rendered in Latin as "Lux et Veritas" ("Light and Truth"). However, the most probable translation is "lights and perfections."[2]

We find a few examples of the use of the Urim and Thummim in the Hebrew Bible. In the First Book of Samuel, during the reign of King Saul, the Urim and Thummim are used to discover the real culprit who had committed the grave sin of consuming blood. King Saul asks the priests to find out who was the guilty party and says, "Show Thammim [*sic*]" (I Sam. 14:41). The Hebrew text here is cryptic. However, the Septuagint, the ancient Greek translation of the Hebrew Bible (third century BCE, Alexandria), gives us a fuller account: "If the iniquity was due to my son Jonathan or to me, O Eternal, God of Israel, show Urim; and if you say it was due to Your people Israel, show Thummim." Another example comes again regarding King Saul. It appears that before engaging the Philistines in battle at Gilboa, at the Valley of Jezreel, the king wants to know how to proceed. So, the Bible tells us, "Saul inquired of the Eternal [through priests], but the Eternal did not answer him either by dreams or by Urim or by prophets" (I Sam. 28:6). Consequently, the king calls in a woman from En-Dor who consults ghosts, and he seeks God's will by asking her to bring up the ghost of Samuel, his mentor, from the netherworld. She does, and Samuel, not pleased that he has been disturbed, delivers Saul a grim message from God. Here only "Urim" are mentioned, but this may be a shorter form of "Urim and Thummim," like Num. 27:21, where "Urim" appears by itself. These two objects are not mentioned again after the reign of King David. According to Ezra 2:63, they were not used during the Second Temple period, for certain priests were told "not to eat of the most holy things until a priest with Urim and Thummim should appear." The Mishnah states, "When the first prophets died, the Urim and Thummim ceased" (*Mishnah Sotah* 9:12).

As religious practices evolved, the term *Torah* assumed a wider meaning and began to refer to specific religious instructions, such as the "*Torah* of the Meal Offering" (Lev. 6:7) or "*Torah* of the Nazirite" (Num. 6:21). In the biblical wisdom literature, like the Books of Proverbs and Ecclesiastes, which deal with human virtue and social ethics, the word *Torah* was equated with human wisdom; for example, "Hear, my son, the discipline of your father and do not forsake the instruction [*torah*] of your mother" (Prov. 1:8). In the postexilic period (sixth to fifth century BCE and beyond), "Torah" described the basic substance of the Pentateuch, the Five Books of Moses (Neh. 8:8; Ezra 3:2). By the second century BCE, the term referred to the whole Pentateuch, as distinguished from the Prophets and other sacred material. In the postbiblical period, "Torah" not only referred to the Pentateuch, but became the equivalent of the entire Hebrew Bible, *Tanakh*, as represented by the Pentateuch (*Torah*), Prophets (*N'vi-im*), and Writings (*K'tuvim*).

The Term "Torah" in the Rabbinic Literature

During the biblical period, God's will was transcribed into writing, in stages, by the teachers and wise people of their time. For them, the term "Torah" meant the "Written Torah" and comprised the three parts of the *Tanakh*. However, in the first century BCE, the nature of "Torah" became a matter of controversy within the Jewish community. Whereas some Jews believed that only the "Written Torah" (*Torah Shebikhtav*) was revealed on Mount Sinai/Horeb, others maintained that in addition to the Written Torah, an "Oral Torah" was revealed to Moses on the same spot. Among those who followed the first path were the members of the Jewish sect called Sadducees, which included conservative priests and perhaps some of the wealthy landowners who supported them. They maintained that only the Written Torah was authoritative and binding, and not the later elaborations made by subsequent sages. Other Jews, however, took a totally different position. The Pharisees, the pious Jews of the time who were committed to ritual purity and sanctity in Jewish practice, argued that in addition to this Written Torah, Moses received oral instructions regarding the application and amplification of the rules, regulations, and teachings found in the written texts. They called these compendia of material *Torah Sheb'al Peh*, "Oral Torah" (e.g., BT *Shabbat* 31a; *B'midbar Rabbah*, *Naso*, 14:10). The Rabbis who are mentioned in the Mishnah (second century CE) emerged out of the earlier Pharisaic movement. They differentiated between the *Torah Shebikhtav* and *Torah Sheb'al*

Peh but gave the same religious weight to both teachings. They stated that the Oral Torah was transmitted faithfully from one generation to another by word of mouth: "Moses received the [oral] Torah from Sinai, and he delivered it to Joshua, and Joshua to the elders, and the elders to the prophets, and the prophets delivered it to the men of the Great Synagogue" (*Pirkei Avot* 1:1).

To understand God's will, the Rabbis of the Mishnah (called *Tannaim*) and, later on, the Rabbis of the Talmud (called *Amoraim*) taught that it is necessary to refer to this oral tradition in order to determine the correct meaning of the divine instructions (see, for example, how the Rabbis reinterpreted the talion law, in "The Sixth Word: Homicide") and, in fact, insisted that without the validity of the Oral Torah it would be impossible to understand the implication of some of the Torah's teachings. Thus, for example, when the Torah says, "Bind them [God's instructions] as a sign on your hand and let them serve as a symbol on your forehead; inscribe them on the doorposts of your house and on your gates" (Deut. 6:8–9), the references to "hand" and "forehead" are left unclear. How do you bind the instructions on your hand or on your forehead? The same applies to placing them on the doorpost. Where do you put them, and how? In the biblical text, these references may have been figures of speech emphasizing the importance of observing diligently the divine teachings. But for the Rabbis, they also referred to physical objects: "binding them on the hand" meant the phylacteries (i.e., small black leather boxes containing parchments inscribed with biblical verses) placed on the arm (*t'fillin shel yad*), and "placing them on the head" referred to the phylacteries placed on the head (*t'fillin shel rosh*). And the instructions about the "doorpost" (*m'zuzah*) meant writing down these teachings (the Rabbis identified them as Deut. 6:4–9 and 11:13–21) on a parchment and then placing the parchment in a small container affixed to the doorpost of the house in a particular way, namely, on the right-hand side of the door, in the upper third section.

Hermeneutical Rules

How did the Rabbis come up with these specific interpretations? They believed that the divinely revealed written text already contained the meaning that was received from the oral tradition. All the ancient Sages had to do was to develop an appropriate methodology to derive such interpretations for their time. One version of these hermeneutical rules, called *midot*, are expounded in greater detail in the *Baraita D'Rabbi Yishmael* (second century CE), which serves as an introduction to the tannaitic commentary to the Book of Leviticus, called *Sifra*. One example: From the similarity of words used in two different biblical passages, the Rabbis inferred that what is expressed in one text also applies to the other (this is called *g'zeirah shavah* in Hebrew). Thus, the expression "Hebrew slave" in Exod. 21:2, though ambiguous in Exodus in that it could mean either a heathen slave owned by a Hebrew or a slave who is a Hebrew, can be correctly understood to mean a slave who is a Hebrew, because in a parallel text in Deut. 15:12, there is a reference to "your Hebrew brother who is sold to you." Another example: An inference can be drawn from a minor statement to a major one, or vice versa (this is called *kal vachomer*). If, for example, a particular activity is forbidden during an ordinary festival, it is all the more so forbidden during Yom Kippur, which is the most important holy day in the Jewish calendar; or, vice versa, if an act is permitted on Yom Kippur, it stands to reason that it would be permitted during other ordinary festivals.[3]

In our time, many Orthodox Jews still maintain that the ancient Rabbis' interpretation is derived from the correct understanding of the oral tradition through the application of specific hermeneutical rules, whereas most liberal Jews argue that the Oral Torah simply represents the customs, traditions, and practices developed over a long period of time. Divine revelation, they say, is progressive; it was not frozen at Mount Sinai, and we continue to attach new meaning to old teachings. Words, institutions, and concepts change over the years. The same word may mean one thing at one point, another later on. What is needed is to trace its development in time in order to have a better understanding of the Hebrew Bible as a whole. What the Rabbis actually did, liberal Jews note, is to give legitimacy and primacy to the practices and rules that were prevalent in their days or those they had created for their contemporaries. This liberal position seems to be reflected in the writings of Josephus, the first-century-CE Jewish historian, who states, "The Pharisees have made many ordinances among the people, according to the tradition of their fathers, where there is nothing written in the laws of Moses, for which cause they are rejected by the sect of the Sadducees, who affirm that they ought to keep the written ordinances, and not to observe those that are grounded upon the tradition of the fathers" (*Ant*. XIII, 10:6). Therefore, just as the ancient Rabbis adapted the Written Torah to the conditions of their own time, we, too, as liberal Jews, following in the same tradition, can read into the text the needs of our own days and come up with newer interpretations and novel applications of old instructions. As Reform Judaism's Centenary Perspective of 1976 states, "The creation of Torah has not ceased and Jewish creativity in our time is adding to the chain of tradition."

The Codification of the Oral Torah

For a long time the oral tradition was kept alive by Rabbinic sages, and among them, some teachers even became specialists in certain areas of Jewish life, committing large bodies of information to memory, but the massive size of the tradition and the local differences that emerged from community to community necessitated the codification of some of the major rules and regulations dealing with daily life. Thus, beginning with Rabbi Akiva (second century CE), a new trend began among the ancient Rabbis to start collecting some of these oral teachings. In the days of Y'hudah HaNasi (early third century CE), who was considered to be the religious and political leader of the Jewish community in Judea, it was finally decided to edit them in order to preserve them, over the objections of some dissenters (e.g., BT *T'murah* 14b; BT *Gittin* 60b). A few texts were added later after Y'hudah's death. This collection is called Mishnah.

The Mishnah is divided into six major volumes: *Z'raim* (Seeds), *Mo-eid* (Festivals), *Nashim* (Women), *N'zikin* (Damages), *Kodashim* (Holy Things), and *Tohorot* (Purifications). The collection is primarily made up of legal matters, but it does contain a tractate dealing with religious ethics (namely, *Pirkei Avot* in *N'zikin*). The text was produced in Judea primarily in Hebrew, with a number of words in Greek, reflecting the cultural domination of the country by the Greeks at the time. Altogether it contains sixty-three tractates. Around the year 300 CE, a number of parallel and at times supplementary texts (called *baraitot*) were compiled in a collection named *Tosefta* (meaning "additions").

The Sages continued to comment upon the texts of the Mishnah. These discussions, recorded in the colloquial Aramaic, are called Gemara. In time, the Mishnah and the Gemara were combined, and this formed the Talmud. On the surface, the Gemara ("the commentary") gives the impression that all the discussions are taking place around the table at a given historical time, but very often, the opinion of one sage is recorded as a reaction to the teaching of another who lived centuries before. The teachers of the Talmud were not ordained rabbis like their predecessors in the Mishnah. They called themselves "Rav" (Master), but they were no less erudite and no less influential.

There are two versions of this enormous collection. The Talmud of the Land of Israel (often called the Jerusalem Talmud) was completed around 450 CE. The Babylonian Talmud, created by the sages of the prominent Rabbinic academies in Sura and Pumpedita in Babylon, was completed around 500 CE.

In addition to the legal material contained in the Mishnah and the Talmud, a body of literature called midrash emerged as a result of Rabbinic creativity. In Hebrew, the word *midrash* (pl. *midrashim*) refers to scriptural exegesis, and the collection of midrashim contains stories, homilies, and folklore as well as exegesis of scriptural verses.

There are two types of midrash: *midrash halakhah*, midrash that deals with legal matters; and *midrash aggadah*, midrash that covers nonlegal issues. The most important collections of halakhic midrashim are the *M'khilta* (a commentary on Exodus), the *Sifra* (on Leviticus), the *Sifrei* (on Numbers), and *Sifrei D'varim* (on Deuteronomy). Among the aggadic midrashim are the *Tanchuma*, *P'sikta Rabbati*, *Pirkei D'Rabbi Eliezer*, *Midrash T'hillim*, and *Midrash Rabbah*. These collections were produced between 200 CE and medieval times.

Along with the legal and nonlegal material, the ancient and medieval Rabbis wrote and edited mystical literature (the Kabbalah), created legal codes to regulate daily life (like the *Shulchan Arukh* by Joseph Caro of Safed, sixteenth century), completed commentaries on the Bible and the Talmud, and produced response literature (*sh'eilot ut'shuvot*, "questions and answers") and liturgical texts.

In our time, in addition to modern commentaries on the Bible (e.g., *The JPS Torah Commentary*; *The Torah: A Modern Commentary*, by URJ Press; *The Torah: A Women's Commentary*, by URJ Press) and creative liturgy prepared by many religious denominations (e.g., *Mishkan T'filah*, 2007, by the Reform Movement; Mahzor Lev Shalem, 2010, by the Conservative Movement), many individual Jews or institutions continue to write to prominent rabbinic sages of our time asking guidance regarding Jewish religious life. The answers (responsa) are often published in book form or made available online (see, for example, the *t'shuvot* by the CCAR Responsa Committee or the Conservative Movement's Committee on Law and Standards).

Torah and Law

The Hebrew Bible includes a number of law collections, such as the Book of the Covenant (Exodus 21–23), the Holiness Code (Leviticus 19–27), and the Deuteronomic laws (Deuteronomy 12–28), but it also contains other literary genres such as poetry, historical narratives, fables, wisdom sayings, and others. The same applies to the Rabbinic literature. As we noted above, *Torah* means "[religious] instruction," and not only legal norms. However, in the Septuagint, the translators used the term *nomos*, a Greek word primarily meaning "law," for the Hebrew expression *Torah*, thus restricting its focus. The first-century Jewish historian Josephus, too, uses the term *nomos* predominantly in reference to the laws given by God to Moses (*Ant.* 3:205; 4:209ff.). The writers/editors of the New Testament, using the Septuagint as their source, also rendered *Torah* as "law," and from then on, the concept dominated Western cultural understandings of Torah.

The consequence of this mistranslation has been very damaging to Judaism. As Louis I. Rabinowitz writes, "The designation of the Torah by *nomos*, and by its Latin successor *lex* (whence, "the Law"), has historically given rise to the sad misunderstanding that Torah means legalism."[4] Regrettably, this mistranslation also appears in some Jewish sources of our time, such as the translation of Psalm 19, read just before the Torah service, in the Reform prayer book *Gates of Prayer*—"The law of the Lord [*torat Adonai*] is perfect, restoring the soul"[5]—or in the paraphrase of the prayer called *Ahavah Rabbah* ("[With] great love") in the Rosh HaShanah morning service of the Reform *machzor* (High Holy Day prayer book) *Gates of Repentance*—"The Law has been our garden of delight"[6]—even though, in both cases, the Hebrew text speaks of "Torah." The new Reform prayer book, *Mishkan T'filah*, corrects the mistake in Psalm 19 and properly reads, "God's Torah is perfect, reviving the soul."[7]

In the Hebrew Bible, given the diversity of literary genres, it is almost impossible to draw a clear distinction between moral teachings and legal norms because they are both formulated in the same way. Therefore, it is not easy to identify what we would now call "law." Unlike the *Tanakh*, Roman legal texts differentiated between *ius* (human law) and *fas* (divine law); Mesopotamian texts also contained separate collections for laws (*dinu*), wisdom sayings (*kibsu*), and priestly injunctions (*parsu*). Not so in the Bible. Even within the so-called collections of "laws" in the Hebrew Scriptures, divine commands of all kinds are referred to by various names: *mitzvot* (commandments), *chukim* (decrees), *mishpatim* (rules), *eidot* (stipulations), and *d'varim* (words); for example, "These are the decrees [*chukim*] and rules [*mishpatim*] that you must carefully observe" (Deut. 12:1; cf. 4:1, 5:1). The Bible itself does not give us enough information to identify what they are or how to separate one from the other in the context of its own time.

The term *mitzvah* (pl. *mitzvot*) is generally translated as "commandment." For the Rabbis of the Mishnah and Talmud, *mitzvah* meant a law, whether biblical or Rabbinic, derived from God as ordained at Mount Sinai. Even though many people today translate *mitzvah* as "the right thing to do," the concept itself implies an obligation. A good deed is voluntary, whereas a commandment is binding. The question for us this: if *mitzvah* is a commandment, who is the commanding authority? For some Jews, the authority of the mitzvah comes from the actual word of God found in sacred texts; for others, like me, the commander is the ongoing Jewish tradition, which is reflected in the practices of Sephardic and Ashkenazic cultures.

The ancient Rabbis identified 613 mitzvot and divide them in various ways: some mitzvot are between God and the individual (*bein adam LaMakom*) and others between one human being and another (*bein adam lachaveiro*); 249 of them are positive commandments ("You shall do…") and 365 are negative ("You shall not do…"); some derive from the Torah directly (*d'oraita*) and others from the Sages themselves (*d'rabanan*). In modern times not all 613 commandments can be carried out in our daily life; some referred to the ritual in the Temple of Jerusalem, others can only be practiced in the Land of Israel. Today only about two hundred mitzvot can be observed by practicing Jews.

The Rabbis also regarded mitzvot as either *mishpatim* or *chukim*. *Mishpatim* refer to those commandments that regulate normal social behavior in society, perhaps functioning as precedents for the future, such as the laws against theft and murder; their meaning is clearly understood by the human mind. *Chukim*, on the other hand, are commandments whose main object is to instill obedience in the human heart and establish discipline in society, even though their real purpose has been withheld from us, as Maimonides writes, "because of the incapacity of our intellects or the deficiency of our knowledge" (*Guide of the Perplexed* 3:26). Among these are the laws that prohibit eating nonkosher food, the laws about *shaatneiz* (prohibiting wearing clothing containing both wool and linen [Lev. 19:19; Deut. 22:11]), and the law about the red cow (Num. 19:1–10); they are all named *chukim* because we cannot understand their purpose.

Where do the Ten Commandments fit in this division? Are they to be considered *mishpatim* or *chukim*? First, it is noteworthy that the Decalogue, though included in the Torah, is not identified as "law" or "rule" at all, but simply as "words" (*d'varim*), in the sense of "divine words" (see "Text and Context"). Do "words" have the same weight as "laws"? Is the Decalogue to be viewed as law at all? Furthermore, it is known that laws, both past and present, contain a penalty clause in order to be operative in society. The Decalogue does not. So, how can they be applied to everyday situations? One Rabbinic answer is that the Decalogue states the norm, but the punishment is found elsewhere in the Bible. For example, "Do not kill/murder" is punishable by death because of what we find in Exod. 21:12, "One who fatally strikes another person shall be put to death" (cf. Gen. 9:6; Num. 35:30). However, this interpretation is forced, because it does not answer the question of how the ten "words" were applied to everyday situations.

Furthermore, in the Bible some instructions appear as ad hoc commands given in a particular historical situation and others as laws that are to be kept in the future, having the force of binding rules (or, in the worlds of the Bible, *l'chukat olam*, "forever"; e.g., Lev. 16:29; Num. 19:10). How can we separate one category from the other? This is not an easy task. Some biblical narratives, such as the death penalty imposed upon the wood-gatherer on the Sabbath during the wilderness period (Num. 15:32–36), appear to have legal force, even though the text does not contain a recognized form of a legal injunction. It is clear, however, that it is meant as a legal precedent and therefore should be considered a law for the future.[8]

Similar to laws, the Hebrew Bible also contains wisdom sayings formulated as conditional sentences or second-person commands. The Book of Proverbs has plenty of examples: "When you sit down to dine with a ruler, consider well who is before you" (Prov. 23:1); "Do not devise harm against your fellow" (Prov. 3:29). The content and nature of the literature, however, make it clear that we are dealing here with moral teachings and not positive laws.

The Decalogue as Law

Clearly, formal structures alone cannot determine whether or not instructions have the force of law; the content and context have to be considered as well. The Decalogue, as we saw before, shares the same formal expressions as other divine instructions. Are the Ten Commandments then to be viewed as ad hoc commands, laws, wisdom teachings, or ancient tribal norms?

The formulation of the Ten Words strongly suggests that they represent a combination of ritual and moral instructions. Unlike laws, they lack a penalty clause, and some of the actions, like "belief in God," "not coveting," or "honoring one's parents," take place in secret, in one's heart, or even beyond the reach of the law enforcers, which makes the act hard to prove and almost impossible to prosecute. Yet, Jewish tradition and many contemporary non-Jewish thinkers today consider them as norms that have the strength of law.

It seems most likely that what gives the Ten Commandments the weight of law is that they are ultimately attributed to God. And, throughout the centuries, many people believed that these instructions by God are authoritative and binding. They are Torah, revealed by God at Mount Sinai/Horeb, even though it is still undetermined to what extent these rules played a role in the realities of legal practice during biblical times.

Today, the big debate among religious thinkers is whether or not the *Tanakh*, which includes the Decalogue, is to be viewed as the exact words of God, and therefore immutable, or a sacred text inspired by the Divine but written by human hands, and therefore fallible. Orthodox Jews and many Christians support the first proposition, whereas liberal Jews and other Christians, the second. No matter what position one takes—and in this book, I have followed the liberal line—the Decalogue remains a collection of religious teachings of great importance in the Western world, thus representing some of the highest ideals worthy of pursuit in our daily life.

Mainstream Jewish tradition considers the Decalogue as a set of basic legal norms, above the *mishpatim* and *chukim*. It also views them as fundamental legal principles that are given to the Jewish people and, through them, to all humanity as laws and commandments for all time.

In the next few chapters, after we cover a few preliminaries dealing with form and context, we will discuss how each of the Ten Commandments was understood in the past and what impact they now have on our religious beliefs and ethical behavior. Do they motivate us to act more humanely and empathically toward the others? How do they help us understand the sanctity of human life, the importance of marital fidelity, the necessity to curb our excessive desires, the need to sanctify a day during the week, the proper channel to worship God by turning away from what we would now consider idolatrous practices? It is to these and other similar topics of contemporary concern that we shall turn for further study and analysis.

Text and Context

The Text

The Decalogue appears in two parallel versions in the Hebrew Bible: Exod. 20:2–14 and Deut. 5:6–18. Some scholars argue that another version of the Ten Commandments exists in Exod. 34:10–26, which deals with the worship of other gods, religious festivals, and certain ritual matters. They call this one the "Yahwist Decalogue" because of the exclusive use of *YHVH* for the name of God. They also claim that whereas Exodus 20 represents an "ethical Decalogue," Exodus 34 is considered a "ritual Decalogue." However, the distinction between "ethical" and "ritual" is foreign to biblical thinking. Besides, it is difficult to identify in Exodus 34 a set of ten norms. Most likely Exodus 34 represents another short collection of laws unrelated to our Decalogue.[1]

Terminology

The Hebrew Bible refers to the Decalogue (from the Greek *deka*, "ten," and *logos*, "word") as *Aseret HaD'varim*, "the Ten Words" (Exod. 34:28; Deut. 10:4). In the Talmud we find the expression *Aseret HaDib'rot* (BT *B'rakhot* 12a; BT *Shabbat* 86b), where the singular *dibeir* is a technical term for divine speech (see Jer. 5:13). The term "Decalogue" was applied to our text by a Greek church father, Clement of Alexandria, about 200 CE. In contemporary writings, the English terms "Decalogue," "Ten Commandments," and "Ten Words" refer to the same text in Exodus 20 and Deuteronomy 5.

Versions

Outside of the Hebrew Bible, the text of the Decalogue is found in other ancient texts with slightly different wording, indicating that it remained fluid for a long time until it was finally edited in its present form. One version appears in the Samaritan Pentateuch (ca. fourth century BCE). The Samaritans were a Jewish sect that emerged around the eighth century BCE when the Assyrians, who had destroyed the Northern Kingdom of Israel, brought into Israelite territory many colonists from Assyria. These people intermarried with the local population, and allegedly the Samaritans are the product of this mixture. For them only the Pentateuch is sacred. They also consider Mount Gerizim as holy, instead of Jerusalem. The text of their Five Books of Moses contains a version of the Decalogue that is similar to the one found in our Hebrew Bible, but with a few differences; for example, the Sabbath commandment in Exodus starts with the word "Remember," like the Deuteronomic text of the Hebrew Scripture.[2] Another version of the Decalogue appears in the Nash Papyrus (second century BCE), a collection of four different Jewish texts, where it is closely related to the Septuagint's version of Exodus 20.[3] The Decalogue found among the Dead Sea Scrolls (ca. first century BCE) reads like the version found in our Book of Deuteronomy.

As we shall see in the following chapters, there are a number of textual differences between the two texts of the Decalogue in our Hebrew Bible. This duplication is traditionally explained by saying that both versions were simultaneously uttered by God in a manner that is impossible for humans to comprehend (BT *Sh'vuot* 20b; cf. *M'khilta D'Rabbi Ishmael, Bachodesh* 7).[4] Commenting on "All these words" (Exod. 20:1), the *M'khilta* clearly states, "God spoke the Ten Commandments with one utterance, something that is impossible for human beings to do." However, it also provides a secondary explanation: "After saying all the Ten Commandments in one utterance, God repeated them, pronouncing each commandment separately" (*Bachodesh* 4).

The ancient Rabbis were aware of the presence of these two parallel texts of the Ten Commandments and tried to come up with appropriate teachings. For example, noting that in Exodus the Sabbath commandment begins with the command "Observe [*shamor*]" whereas Deuteronomy says "Remember [*zakhor*]," the *M'khilta* provides the following explanation: *"Remember* it before it [the Sabbath] comes and *observe* it after it is gone" (*Bachodesh* 7).

The belief that the two versions were uttered simultaneously remained popular among Jews even in the late medieval times. The Sabbath hymn *L'kha*

Dodi ("Go forth to meet the bride"), which we often sing during the Friday night service, is attributed to Solomon Alkabetz (sixteenth century, Safed). It, too, states, "'Observe' and 'Remember' were spoken in one utterance." However, most modern thinkers maintain that this repetition resulted from the work of scribes and redactors over a long period of time.

There are other differences between the two versions in Exodus and Deuteronomy:

- According to Exodus, the Decalogue was given on Mount Sinai; in Deuteronomy this mountain is called Horeb.
- There are minor textual variations between the two sets in commandments 4 (Sabbath), 5 (honoring parents), and 10 (not coveting). In some cases, as in commandments 5 (honoring parents) and 10 (not coveting).
- Deuteronomy adds a few additional phrases to the text in Exodus.
- In commandment 4, dealing with the Sabbath, the motive clause for the commandment in Exodus is totally at variance with its parallel text in Deuteronomy.

These differences will be studied in greater detail in the following chapters.

Formulation of the Decalogue

The writing of legal injunctions tends to be formulaic. In the Decalogue, within only fourteen verses, we find a combination of many legal forms cited side by side and, at times, even clustered around similar phrases. For example, in Exod. 20:2–3, God speaks in the first person, but in the rest of the commandments, God is referred to in the third person. Some commandments are short, such as "You shall not murder" (Exod. 20:13; Deut. 5:17). Others, like the Sabbath commandment, are much longer. Some carry motivational clauses (e.g., about the Sabbath and honoring the parents); others do not. It is not clear if these rationales, added to some of the commandments, are original or if they were posted later on. Both positions have been argued forcefully, without any clear solution. Furthermore, only two of the commandments are expressed positively, "Honor your father and your mother..." and "Observe/ remember the Sabbath day...." The rest are in the second-person negative form, "you shall not."

In the Decalogue, God directs the commands to every individual, in the second person masculine. The reason is, some Rabbinic sources say, "so that each person would think that he alone, in the whole world, was responsible for studying, performing and upholding all the words of the Torah."[5] However, this does not mean that only men were responsible for these commandments. The obligation for women is simply implied. Otherwise, it would mean that they could murder or commit adultery without punishment. The Rabbis are quick to add that all the instructions of the Decalogue are binding on women as well. Thus, for instance, *Sefer HaChinukh* ("The Book of [Mitzvah] Education") by Rabbi Pinchas HaLevi of Barcelona (ca. thirteenth century), commenting on the first commandment regarding the belief in one God, clearly states, "It [this commandment] is in force in every place, at every time, for both man and woman."[6] It uses the same phrase with regard to the other Ten Commandments too.

The combination of different legal forms within the short text of the Decalogue raises the possibility that, at one time, the various clusters of directives found in it existed separately and were ultimately combined by an editor, or editors, in the course of history. Today, the Decalogue stands as an entity by itself.

Cardinal Numbers in Hebrew

In the past (and to a certain extent even now) certain cardinal numbers played a key role in the culture of the Jewish people. In addition to three (e.g., three patriarchs), seven (e.g., seven days of Creation) and forty (e.g., forty years in the Sinai desert), the number ten is known for its religious, cultural, legal, and perhaps even magical significance. According to the Book of Genesis, just ten righteous people could have saved the cities of Sodom and Gomorrah from divine retribution (Gen. 18:32). A group of ten individuals made up a court of law in biblical times (Ruth 4:2). The Bible recounts the ten plagues that fell upon Egypt (Exodus 7–12). Ten generations separate Adam from Noah, and another ten are listed between Noah and Abraham. According to the Book of Deuteronomy, every Israelite was expected to set aside a tenth of his produce for the poor (14:22, 26:12). In the Jewish calendar there are ten days between Rosh HaShanah and Yom Kippur. Rabbinic sages required the presence of ten adults to form a quorum (minyan) to conduct a worship service and recite certain prayers (BT *K'tubot* 7b). In the Kabbalah, God is manifested through ten *s'firot*, ten emanations. In many cases, the number "ten" seems to refer to a complete group of items, not necessarily ten (and only ten) individuals.

Given the number of direct commands in the text of our Decalogue—and there are more than ten—it is difficult to say why we have "ten" commandments. The *Zohar* surmises that because the world was created with ten divine utterances (see *Pirkei Avot* 5:1), the Ten Commandments correspond to each one of them.[7] Some modern critics suggested, perhaps facetiously, that the reason is because it is easy to count them on our ten fingers.

The Division of the Ten Words

In view of the fact that there are more than ten individual commands in the Decalogue, there are at least three major ways in which the entire unit has been divided in order to arrive at "ten" distinct norms. Most Rabbinic sages agree on the division as seen in the printed text at the beginning of this book. Others thought otherwise. For example, Philo of Alexandria (20 BCE–50 CE) as well as the Jewish historian Josephus (first century CE), and even some individual rabbis in the early Rabbinic period, considered the first half of commandment 2, "You shall have no other gods…" (Exod. 20:3; Deut. 5:7), as the *first* commandment, and the second part of commandment 2, beginning with "You shall not make for yourself…" (Exod. 20:4–6; Deut. 5:8–10), as the *second* commandment. The Protestant Reformer John Calvin (1509–1564) argued likewise.

On the other hand, Saint Augustine (354–430) and, following him, the Catholic Church and the Protestant Lutheran Church count "You shall have no other…" (Exod. 20:3–6; Deut. 5:7–10) as the *first* commandment, consider "You shall not swear falsely by the name of the Eternal…" (Exod. 20:7; Deut. 5:11) as the *second* commandment, and divide the last one on not coveting (Exod. 20:14; Deut. 5:18) into two different commandments.

In this study we shall follow the traditional Jewish division as indicated in the printed text above.

It is also noteworthy that there are two different cantillation systems that are attached to the text of our Ten Commandments. The "lower" one, recognized through special symbols placed under the consonants, divides the Hebrew text into thirteen verses. The "upper," attached to the top of the consonants, divides the text into ten units. The "upper" system is used for public reading, while the "lower" one is reserved for private study.

In traditional Jewish sources, the set of the Ten Words is also divided in terms of their content: the first half deals with relations "between God and human beings" (*bein adam LaMakom*), and the second half relations "between one person and another" (*bein adam lachaveiro*), with the commandment about honoring the parents playing the role of a bridge between the two sets. According to *Tz'ror HaMor*, a rabbinic commentary by Avraham ben Yaakov Saba (Spain, sixteenth century), "The first five of the Ten Commandments are spiritual in nature, while the last five are, as it were, material. That is why they are joined together, like body and soul, soul and body."[8]

In Rabbinic literature, the second half of the Decalogue is, at times, paired off with the first five commandments: Thus, commandment 6, "You shall not murder," corresponds to commandment 1, "I the Eternal," teaching us that murder diminishes the image of God. Commandment 7, "You shall not commit adultery," is paired with 2, "You shall have no other gods," implying that committing adultery is as grave an offense as worshiping idols. Commandment 8, "You shall not steal" is paired with 3, "You shall not swear falsely by the name of the Eternal," letting us know that stealing ultimately leads to using God's name in vain. The commandment about bearing false witness (9) corresponds to the one about the Sabbath (4), informing us that by bearing false witness against another, one would deny that God created the universe in six days. The commandment about coveting (10) corresponds to commandment 5, "Honor your father and your mother," instructing us that coveting can lead to dishonoring one's parents (see *P'sikta Rabbati* 21:18–19).

Dating

We do not know exactly when the Decalogue was formulated. The Bible attributes it to the wilderness period during the days of Moses, the dates of which are unknown. Scholarly views on this subject vary. Though some accept the biblical timeline, many place its redaction in the exilic period after the destruction of the First Temple in Jerusalem (sixth century BCE).

The Decalogue appears to have been quoted by some of the eighth-century-BCE prophets (e.g., Amos 3:1–2; Hos. 4:2; Jer. 7:9), which implies its antiquity. It is also referred to in the psalms (e.g., Ps. 50:7, 81:9–10), most of which come from after the exilic period (sixth century BCE). The word "house" used in the tenth commandment (Exod. 20:14; Deut. 5:18) implies a sedentary setting, after Israel's entry into Canaan, but it can more likely be understood as "household" and, therefore, applicable to an earlier period as well. As Moshe Weinfeld writes, "There is no proof that the Ten Commandments are older than any other laws in the Torah," and "Just as there is no proof of the special antiquity of the Decalogue, so are there no grounds for postponing it."⁹ Similarly, Moshe Greenberg argues, "While there is no proof of Mosaic origin, there is no ideological or substantive objection to the Decalogue's originating in Moses."¹⁰ It is possible, however, that the various motive clauses that accompany some of the commandments, or even the commandments themselves, were expanded by the editors of Exodus or Deuteronomy, in line with their own style. The date of the redaction of the Decalogue remains unknown.

Uniqueness

Biblical Israel was part of the ancient Near East, which included the major eastern empires in Mesopotamia (today Iraq) such as Babylon in the south and Assyria in the north, as well as the many states in the Mediterranean basin, like that of the Hittites in modern Turkey, and Egypt in the west. After their emergence in Canaan as a singular group of tribes around the thirteenth century BCE, the Israelites were surrounded by groups of people, such as the Arameans in the north and the Ammonites, Moabites, and Edomites in the immediate east. So far no collection of laws has been found in the ancient Near East that reads like our Decalogue, which is formulated in a terse language, covering both social concerns and matters of ritual, but there are some parallels. The Egyptian "Book of the Dead" (ca. sixteenth century BCE) contains a text in which an individual declares his innocence before the tribunal of the god Osiris. This negative confession, one of the most important sources of Egyptian social law, reads, in part, as follows: "I have not committed evil against men. I have not mistreated cattle. I have not committed sin in the place of truth. I have not blasphemed a god. I have not defamed a slave to his superior" (*ANET*, 34). Similarly, in ancient Babylonia, the king used to make a declaration of innocence during the new year festival that read like the Decalogue, but not exactly in the same form as our Ten Commandments: "I have not been negligent in respect to your godhead... I have not destroyed Babylon... I have not smitten the cheek of the people under (your) protection... I have not occasioned their humiliation."¹¹ Also, the Mesopotamian incantations called *shurpu*, formulated in the third person and pronounced by the priests, referred to all kinds of sins, including murder, adultery, false oaths, and tale bearing; for example, "He entered his neighbor's house; he had intercourse with his neighbor's wife; he shed his neighbor's blood."¹² However, in terms of form and content, these statements are hardly similar to our Decalogue.

In reality, as Moshe Weinfeld points out, "The Decalogue is *sui generis*. It differs from every other list of commandments. What makes it different is that it brings together a distilled short list of the basic prerequisites laid down for each member of the Israelite community who wants to be party to the special covenant of the people with its God. It serves as a sort of Israelite catechism."[13]

Function of the Decalogue

Biblical scholars have offered different views on the historical function of the Ten Commandments. One opinion is that the Decalogue constituted Israel's preexilic criminal law code given to her at Sinai. Another one is that it represents a series of prohibitions against entering an Israelite sanctuary dedicated to the worship of the God called *YHVH*. More broadly, some critics have suggested that the Ten Words are an educational and ethical ideal by which the individual Jew may be trained. Similarly, another scholar has argued that it comprises the minimal imperatives essential to the maintenance of an ordered and wholesome society. Others, acknowledging the close connection between the covenant of Sinai and the Decalogue, have maintained that the Decalogue identifies the basic conditions for inclusion in the community of Israel.

The original purpose and function of the Ten Commandments in the Bible remains obscure, and its connection to the rest of the biblical laws is also debatable.

The Larger Context—Mount Sinai

When reading the narrative about the revelation of the Torah on Mount Sinai, one gets the impression that the text of the Ten Commandments breaks the continuity of the story. One could easily go, without much interruption, from the end of Exodus 19, where God is said to have come down to address the Israelites, to Exodus 24, where Moses actually repeats to the people "all the commands of the Eternal and all the rules [*mishpatim*]" (Exod. 24:3). In fact, after writing them down, Moses reads to the people "the record of the covenant" (*sefer hab'rit*), and the people respond, "*Naaseh v'nishma*" ("We will faithfully do") (Exod. 24:7; cf. 19:8). But it is not clear what was inside "the record of the covenant." Did this "record" (*sefer*) refer to the Decalogue? Most likely the expression refers to some or all the laws of the Book of the Covenant found in Exod. 20:19–23:26. In fact, Exodus 21 is introduced by the words *eileh hamishpatim* (these are the rules), and they are much longer than the Decalogue. It also appears that the expression *Aseret HaD'varim* (Ten Words) in Exod. 34:28 originally referred to the so-called Yahwist Decalogue of Exod. 34:10–26, and only secondarily to our Ten Commandments in Exodus 20. We, therefore, need to look at the larger context within which the Decalogue has ultimately been placed by a later editor.

According to Jewish tradition, the Decalogue of Exodus 20 was revealed by God on Mount Sinai The ancient Rabbis teach that not only the Ten Commandments but the entire Torah was given to Moses on this mountain (*Pirkei Avot* 1:1), including what the prophets were to prophesy to subsequent generations and what the Rabbinic sages were to teach in their own time (*Sh'mot Rabbah* 28:6). But where is Mount Sinai? The simple answer is that we do not know. It is remarkable that the exact location of one of the most significant events in Jewish history is unknown. Furthermore, there are a number of scholars who convincingly argue that the Israelites were never in Egypt but coalesced among the tribes already living in Canaan, rendering the entire episode of Sinai as a foundational mythic experience. Even those who maintain that at least some of the tribes did, in fact, leave Egypt cannot agree on the route they took when they entered the wilderness of Sinai. There are, at least, three theories: (a) The "northern route" by the Mediterranean Sea; (b) the "central route" across the wilderness of Sinai; and (c) the "southern route," toward the southern end of the Sinai Peninsula. Each one has its pluses and minuses. The early Christians identified Mount Sinai with Jebel Musa ("The Mount of Moses") along the "southern route." In fact, the Byzantine king Justinian I dedicated a monastery there in 527 CE. However, this identification is relatively late and seriously doubtful.

The importance of the mountain of revelation is highlighted in the Bible not only by virtue of the fact that the Torah was given on it, but because God's revelation to Moses through the Burning Bush also took place there: "Now Moses, tending the flock of his father-in-law Jethro, the priest of Midian, drove the flock into the wilderness, and came to Horeb [Sinai], the mountain of God" (Exod. 3:1). Similarly, it was at the foot of Mount Sinai that Moses built an altar and set up twelve stones representing the twelve tribes of Israel (Exod. 24:4) before receiving the Ten Commandments. It was also to this place that the prophet Elijah went in order to seek God (I Kings 19:8–9).

In the biblical texts, the mountain on which the Decalogue was given is called by different names. As noted previously, in Exodus it is "Mount Sinai" (Exod. 19:20), but in Deuteronomy it is "Mount Horeb" (Deut. 4:10, 5:2).

The mountain was also called "the mountain of God" (Exod. 3:1; I Kings 19:8). It is almost certain that the terms "Mount Paran" (Deut. 33:2; cf. Hab. 3:3–4), "Mount Seir" (Deut. 33:2), and simply "the mountain" (Exod. 19:2, 24:13) refer to the same location. Many traditional commentaries, trying to resolve the problem of identification of the mountain, claim that Horeb and Sinai are the same mountain (e.g., Ibn Ezra on Deut. 5:2). Other critics disagree and say that that they refer to two different mountains, that they represent two different peaks in one range, or even that one is the name of the area whereas the other is the name of the peak. The exact location of this historic mountain remains unknown.[14]

The Revelation of the Decalogue

God's revelation to the Children of Israel is told in majestic language. However, the sequence of events as described in Exodus 19, and its parallel text in Deuteronomy 5, is rather confusing. For centuries, scholars, both old and new, have labored over these passages in order to establish a reasonable sense of order, without much success. According to Exodus 19, the Israelites arrived in the Sinai wilderness three months after they left Egypt and camped at the foot of Mount Sinai. In Exodus 19, Moses is pictured as going up and down the mountain at least three times. God's appearance is described either in terms of volcanic smoke and fire (v. 18) or with thunder and lightning (v. 16). The text of Deuteronomy also contains some internal contradictions. In Deut. 5:4 we read, "Face to face the Eternal One spoke to you on the mountain," yet in 5:5, we are told, "I [Moses] stood between the Eternal and you [the Israelites]." In addition to the problems within Exodus 19 and 20, there are a number of inconsistencies between the texts in Exodus and Deuteronomy. We have already indicated that the mountain in Exodus is called "Sinai," whereas in Deuteronomy it is "Horeb." In Deuteronomy, people are afraid of approaching the mountain because of fire: "This fearsome fire will consume us" (Deut. 5:22); whereas in Exodus 19, it is because of God's warning: "You warned us saying, 'Set bounds about the mountain'" (Exod. 19:23). In Exodus, the Sinai covenant is between God and the Israelites of the wilderness period. In Deuteronomy, however, the same covenant is between God and future generations of Israelites as well (Deut. 29:14).

Based on this analysis, it is difficult to consider these texts as historical descriptions of what may have taken place in the wilderness. We are dealing here more with poetry than with a simple prose narrative. In fact, the text in

Exodus has been described as a *shirah*, a poetic song. The language is exalted. The Israelites seem to witness the revelation with heightened sensitivity and recall it with grandeur as befits the occasion. It is, therefore, inappropriate to read the passage as a news release. As one scholar writes, here "we are dealing with standard poetic imagery to describe the awe-inspiring impact of the event upon those who experienced it."[15]

Even though the biblical description of what actually happened at Sinai/Horeb is not coherent, it is still possible to draw a broad outline of what the Israelites remembered: After their exodus from Egypt, the Israelites entered the wilderness of Sinai on the third month of the year (Exod. 19:1). In the early biblical calendar, this month was called *Aviv* ("Spring"; Exod. 13:4; 23:14).[16] On the third day of the month, God came down to Mount Sinai (Exod. 19:11), and the Israelites assembled at the foot of the mountain (Exod. 19:17). Jewish tradition says that the Torah was given during the Festival of Shavuot, which falls on the sixth of Sivan (BT *Shabbat* 86b; cf. *M'khilta, Bachodesh* 3).[17] In Rabbinic literature, Shavuot is called *z'man matan Torateinu* (time/season of the giving of our Torah) and became associated with the giving of the Decalogue after the destruction of the Second Temple in 70 CE, when it was impossible to bring the first fruits and the appropriate sacrifices to the Temple.

The Format of the Revelation

Jewish tradition records various scenarios about the format of the revelation. As noted above, according to Exodus and Deuteronomy, the Ten Commandments were verbally revealed by God on Mount Sinai/Horeb amid impressive natural phenomena: smoke and fire, or thunder and lightning. Some Rabbis, however, imagined that the Ten Words were given in total silence: "When God gave the Torah no bird twittered, no fowl flew, no ox bellowed, none of the angels (ophanim and seraphim) said, 'Holy, Holy,' the sea did not roar, the creatures did not speak, but the whole world was hushed into breathless silence, and the voice went forth: 'I the Eternal am your God'" (*Sh'mot Rabbah* 29:9).

In Exodus 34 we find a different narrative about how the Decalogue was revealed. Moses went up to Mount Sinai and remained with God forty days and forty nights: "He ate no bread and drank no water; and he wrote down on the tablets the terms of the covenant, the Ten Commandments" (v. 28). Here our text does not make it clear who was the writer: God or Moses? The context suggests it was Moses. Yet, according to Deuteronomy, the author is God (Deut. 9:10; 10:2, 10:4; cf. Exod. 31:18). On the other hand, the Bible states that the laws of the Book of the Covenant were written by Moses: "Moses then wrote down all the commands of the Eternal" (Exod. 24:4).

When Moses came down from the mountain, bearing the two tablets of stone containing the Ten Words, he found that the people had set up a golden calf for purposes of worship (see "The Second Word: Idolatry"). Furious over this incident, Moses smashed the tablets of the Decalogue, after which he ascended the mountain once again to plead forgiveness from God. Once the culprits were punished, God forgave the People of Israel and told Moses to carve two new tablets on which God then inscribed the words that were on the first tablets (Exod. 34:1). This second set was placed in the portable sanctuary in the wilderness; later on, it was transferred to the town of Shiloh and finally deposited in the First Temple in Jerusalem. The fate of these tablets is unknown. They were not present in the Second Temple in Jerusalem. According to one Rabbinic legend, they were hidden in order to save them from destruction by the Babylonians. According to another, King Josiah hid the Ark of the Covenant under a rock. Yet another suggests that an angel came down from heaven and removed it from the Temple.[18] Throughout history, wild guesses have been made regarding the fate of the Ark, including the fascinating movie *The Raiders of the Lost Ark* (1981), in which the Ark is finally found in Tanis, Egypt, rescued from the Nazis, and ultimately preserved in a sealed wooden crate among hundreds of others in a warehouse in the United States.

The variety of scenarios as well as the lack of clarity about what must have occurred on Mount Sinai gave rise to different interpretations of this singular event in the history of the Israelites. Already in the second century BCE, the *Book of Jubilees*, reflecting the practices of a sectarian Jewish group, claimed that Moses received on Mount Sinai the details of the sectarian group's own solar calendar (1:29). And Philo of Alexandria (first century CE) argued that even though the Decalogue, which was uttered by God alone, contained "general legal categories," Moses's laws were specific legal injunctions. As noted above, according to the Rabbis, not only the Decalogue, but the entire Torah was revealed on Mount Sinai.

The Rabbis speculated not only about the way in which the Decalogue was revealed but also to whom it was addressed, and here they present two distinctive perspectives. On the one hand, they argued that the Ten Words were given in public, openly in the wilderness, to all the nations, so that anyone wishing to accept it could come and live by them (*M'khilta, Bachodesh* 1). Moreover, God's voice "split up into seventy voices, into seventy languages, so that all the nations should understand" (*Sh'mot Rabbah* 5:9). Some sages even claimed that the revelation took place according to the strength of every individual: "to the old, according to their strength; to the young according to their strength; to the children, to the babies, and to the women according to their strength" (*Sh'mot Rabbah* 5:9). On the other hand, some Rabbinic sages taught that the Ten Commandments were given only to the Israelites, because only they accepted it, while the rest of the nations rejected its teachings (*M'khilta, Bachodesh* 5). There is also a Rabbinic teaching, attributed to Rabbi Avdimi ben Chama, that states that the Ten Words were imposed upon the Israelites, not willingly accepted by them: "The Holy One, blessed is He, overturned the mountain upon them like an (inverted) cast, and told them, 'If you accept the Torah, it will be well with you; if not, it shall be your burial" (BT *Shabbat* 88a).

What did the Israelites hear on Mount Sinai? Exodus states that the Israelites wanted to hear the commandments directly from Moses: "'You speak to us,' they said to Moses, 'and we will obey, but let not God speak to us, lest we die'" (Exod. 20:16). As noted above, in Deuteronomy we find two contradictory statements: on the one hand, we are told that God spoke directly to the people (Deut. 5:4), but on the other, it was Moses who related the commandments to the Israelites (Deut. 5:5). Philo of Alexandria, who could not accept that God had a mouth and tongue like any human being, wrote, "God wrought on this occasion a miracle of a truly holy kind by bidding an invisible sound to be created in the air more marvelous than all instruments...a voice so loud that it appeared to be equally audible to the farthest as well as the nearest" (*Decalogue* 9–10). In some Rabbinic texts, the Israelites, we are told, heard only the first two commandments, but "the rest of the commandments God spoke through the mouth of Moses" (*Pirkei D'Rabbi Eliezer* 41; BT *Makot* 24a).

In medieval times, the discussion about the format of the revelation continued. The great Jewish philosopher and Torah scholar Moses Maimonides (1135–1204) opined that the Israelites heard nothing but inarticulate words, which Moses had to interpret for the people. He writes in his *Guide of the Perplexed*, "Speech was addressed to Moses alone…it was he [Moses] who was spoken to and they [the people] heard the great voice, but not the articulation of speech" (2:33). Modern Jewish existentialist thinkers, like Martin Buber and Franz Rosenzweig, argued that the People of Israel experienced at Sinai only the overwhelming presence of God. The words, however, came through Moses. Mendel of Rymanov, a Chasidic teacher (eighteenth century), maintained that the only thing the Israelites heard was the *alef* (the first letter of the Decalogue). For Mordecai Kaplan (1881–1983), a religious naturalist, God's revelation was not verbal and is simply the human discovery of the moral law.

We know from the biblical text that God spoke the Ten Commandments—ancient Rabbinic sages say God spoke in Hebrew—but who transcribed them for the people? In the liturgy of the Torah service today, after the reading of the Torah in the synagogue, it is customary to raise the scroll, and the reader then says the following: "This is the Torah that Moses put before the Children of Israel, as dictated by God [*al pi YHVH*] and by the hand of Moses [*b'yad Mosheh*]." This prayer combines two texts taken from the Bible. The first half comes from Deut. 4:44, and the second from Num. 9:23. Especially the second clause creates a theological problem. What does *b'yad Mosheh* mean? Even though it means literally "by the hand of Moses," it could also be translated as "through Moses" (e.g., Exod. 9:35, 35:29). In its original context within the Book of Numbers, we are told that the Israelites moved their camp in the wilderness *al pi YHVH* ("on a sign from the Eternal" or "at the command of God") and that the action was carried out *b'yad Mosheh* ("through Moses"). The expression *b'yad Mosheh* is also found in the Book of Chronicles: "the priest Hilkiah found a *sefer Torat YHVH b'yad Mosheh*," literally, "a Torah scroll by the hand of Moses" (II Chron. 34:14). The expression "by the hand of Moses" is missing in the parallel story in II Kings 22:8. If the clause is taken literally, it could imply that even though God was the speaker, Moses was the actual writer of the Torah. Orthodox Jews reject this interpretation and argue that the liturgical passage mentioned above should be understood figuratively as "dictated by God [*al pi YHVH*] and transmitted through Moses [*b'yad Mosheh*]," inasmuch as the entire Torah is divine word, and both the wording and the authorship belong to God. Moses was only a medium. Non-Orthodox Jews, on the other hand, maintain that the clause *b'yad Mosheh* can be taken literally, namely, "through the authorship of Moses," and translated as "transcribed by Moses,"[19] for they argue that the Torah was inspired by God but edited by human beings. This accounts for the various duplications, mistakes, and repetitions in the text of the Bible. Although no one can know what really happened at Mount Sinai, I believe that the Ten Words, inspired by God, emerged out of the creative religious genius of the Israelite people, were formulated and edited over a long period of time by the sages and teachers of ancient Israel, and ultimately considered as being worthy of God's signature.

In spite of the fact that we lack information about the location as well as the format and content of God's revelation, "Mount Sinai" has become in Jewish tradition more of a concept than a specific geographic location, as the popular Rabbinic expression *Torah miSinai* (Torah from Sinai) implies, and is viewed as one of the foundational myths of Judaism. The medieval commentator Rashi noted that in Exod. 19:1, the Bible reads, "on this day [*bayom hazeh*] they [i.e., the Israelites] entered the wilderness of Sinai." He said the reason it is written "on this day" instead of "on that day" is to tell us that "the teachings of the Torah must be new to you as if they were given out today, every day." And, I would add, in every place.

The Decalogue in the Liturgy

Today it is customary to read the Ten Commandments in the synagogue during the Festival of Shavuot, which celebrates the summer harvest as well as the revelation of the Torah at Mount Sinai, and whenever the weekly Torah readings including the Decalogue (*Yitro*, Exod. 18:1–20:23; and *Va-et'chanan*, Deut. 3:23–7:11) fall in the Jewish calendar.

From the Rabbinic literature, we know that the Decalogue was originally included in the daily worship of the Second Temple. Each morning, before the daily whole-offering, the priest in charge would ask another priest, "Recite a benediction. They recited a benediction, and read the Ten Commandments, then the *Sh'ma* [Deut. 6:4–9] and 'If you obey' [Deut. 11:13–21]" (*Mishnah Tamid* 5:1). It is not clear whether this recitation was exclusive to the Temple complex, for the Nash Papyrus includes both the Decalogue and the *Sh'ma*. This may indicate that these texts were used outside the Temple as well.

At some point, the Rabbis abolished the daily recitation of the Decalogue from the liturgy outside of the sanctuary. The Talmud states, "In the Temple service, the Ten Commandments were read before the *Sh'ma*. This custom, however, was not adopted outside of the Temple, on account of the *minim* [heretics] who said that only these commandments were divinely revealed" (BT *B'rakhot* 12a). The identity of these heretics is unknown. Many believe that the reference is to some early Christian group. However, as Urbach points out, "We have no way of finding out whether the *minim* who held that only the Decalogue was revealed constituted a specific sect."[20]

Many people stand up during the formal recitation of the Decalogue in the synagogue. Some derive this custom from the biblical text, which states that when the Israelites heard the commandments at Sinai, "They took their places [*vayitzyatz'vu*] at the foot of the mountain" (Exod. 19:17; cf. Deut. 29:9, *atem nitzavim hayom*, "You are standing today"). The expression *vayitzyatz'vu* was understood as "standing up" by *P'sikta D'Rav Kahana*: "Read this chapter every year, and I will in turn count it in your favor as if you were standing in my presence at Sinai." Other midrashim reflect the same belief; for example, "When you stood [*amadtem*] at Sinai and received the Torah..." (*Sh'mot Rabbah* 32: 2). The idea of "standing up" gave rise to the Rabbinic concept of *maamad har Sinai*, "the experience of standing before Sinai during God's revelation." Others, however, argue that the Decalogue is not more or less important than the other commandments, for, as Maimonides points out in one of his responsa (#263), "If we stand, we are making a distinction between these Ten and the rest of the Torah, and behaving like Karaites, who stand when the Torah is read." Most Reform Jews stand during the reading of the Ten Commandments. Orthodox and Conservative Jews do not.

In Conclusion

The Ten Commandments form a set of basic religious and social instructions. They are formulated in a variety of styles, were promulgated in an unknown location, at a debatable historical age, in a manner that cannot be clearly reconstructed, and whose original function is obscure. Most likely, once compiled and placed within the historical context of the mutual covenant concluded between the Eternal and the People of Israel, the entire text was edited by many Israelite teachers and sages of the past over a long period of time. It was considered to be of such importance that Jewish tradition attributed it to the God of Israel, who gave it first to the Israelites, before it was ultimately appropriated by the entire Western world.

The Decalogue

The First Word: God

The Scope of the First Word

According to Jewish tradition, the First Word establishes the foundation for the belief in one God. Formally speaking, however, this First Word does not read like a commandment because it does not contain a command, such as "You must believe in the existence of one God." In spite of this, Jewish sages have viewed it as the first of the "Ten Words," whereas many Christians consider it an introduction to the entire Decalogue.

The First Word raises a number of difficult theological and ethical questions. The Bible never orders us to believe in God. Can we assume that this belief is commanded at all? Jewish teachers have offered various concepts of God in the past. What kind of God should we believe in our time? Many thinkers argue that belief in God is the prerequisite for an ethical life. Is it then possible to live a moral life if one is an agnostic or an atheist? And what does it mean to be an atheist today? Before we turn to these important questions, let us try to understand the meaning of the statement as it appears in our Hebrew Bible.

The Text of the First Word

The First Word is the same in both Exodus and Deuteronomy: "I the Eternal [*YHVH*] am your God who brought you out of the land of Egypt, the house of bondage" (Exod. 20:2; Deut. 5:6).

Structurally speaking, Exod. 20:2 is a subordinate clause, which functions as the motivation for the command that follows. As such, the text, combining verses 2 and 3, could be read as follows: "[Because] I the Eternal am your God who brought you out of the land of Egypt, the house of bondage, [therefore] you shall have no other gods...." A medieval Jewish philosopher, Joseph Albo (fifteenth century), agrees with this understanding.[1] Similarly, the Italian-Israeli scholar Umberto Cassuto (1883–1951) admits that "in this verse we have no command but only an announcement to tell you who is the speaker."[2] Some medieval rabbinic grammarians were also aware of this problem and stated, as Ibn Ezra did, "This is not a mitzvah, either positive or negative."

The dominant Jewish tradition disagrees with this evaluation. In reference to Exod. 20:2, Maimonides states in his *Mishneh Torah* that this is indeed a mitzvah by itself: "To acknowledge this truth [i.e., of the existence of the First Being] is an affirmative precept" (*Hilkhot Y'sodei HaTorah* 1:6). Another medieval Jewish commentator, Ramban, agrees with him, commenting on the verse, "This is a positive commandment." Similarly, *Sefer HaChinukh* (ca. fourteenth century) insists that Exod. 20:2 is a commandment and even provides a possible rationale for it: "Its meaning is as if He [God] said, 'You shall know and believe that the world has a God."[3] Thus, according to Jewish tradition, this commandment stands alone and is counted as the first one in the Decalogue. It is as if the text had said, "I, *YHVH*, am *to be* your God."

How did the Rabbis come to their understanding of the verse? Both the Rabbis and contemporary biblical scholars can tease endless layers of meaning from every word of the text, so to answer these questions we now turn to a detailed analysis of each word of the verse.

I [Am]

In the ancient Near East, many documents begin with a self-presentation formula, such as "[I] Hammurabi [am] the shepherd chosen by the god Enlil" (eighteenth century BCE) or "I, Mesha, [am] son of Kemosh... king of Moab" (ninth century BCE). In the same way, at the start of God's first self-revelation to Moses, the Israelite God identifies God's self generically as: "I am the God of your father [*elohe avikha*]..." Ex. 3: 6), but during a second self-revelation, God is identified by a proper name: "Ani YHVH, "I [am] the Eternal" (Exod.6: 2 ; cf. Gen. 15:7, 28:13;for an individual identifying himself, as did Joseph, see Gen. 45:4).

In biblical Hebrew, the first personal pronoun can be formulated in two related ways: *ani* or *anokhi* (in West Semitic it is *anaku*). Our text uses the second one. Why? Both mean the same thing, with *anokhi* being less frequent and found primarily in older biblical texts. However, in the midrash, the homiletic literature of the ancient Rabbis, the choice of this word is justified by saying that God's first word to the Israelites in the wilderness was formulated in the language with which they were more familiar, namely in Egyptian (*Tanchuma* Buber, *Yitro* 16, *Pesikta Rabbati* 21, 105b). It is doubtful, however, that the Rabbis knew ancient Egyptian (where *anokhi* is *'nk*). Most likely, the word *anokhi* sounded to them as being archaic and, therefore, more authentic. Some modern commentators distinguish between *ani* and *anokhi* by stating that *ani* calls attention to the speaker, whereas *anokhi* places the speaker in intimate relationship to the one spoken to. Thus, says Rabbi Moshe ben Asher, "the very first word spoken to us puts us on notice that we are to have a special, exclusive relationship with God."[4]

The Eternal—*YHVH*

In the ancient Near East, all nature was viewed as being animated by divine beings. Each carried a separate name. Thus, for example, in the Akkadian pantheon, An was the sky god, Enlil was the air-god, Enki was the deity for sweet water. Certain gods had cosmic roles, whereas other deities functioned more like household gods protecting individuals against all types of trouble. Cities or countries also had their own gods: Marduk was the god of Babylon, Ashur was the god of Assyria, and the Canaanites worshiped El or Baal.

Things were different in ancient Israel. Though the Israelites, too, went through different stages of theological development, they finally settled on the belief in one God who is invisible, ineffable, and the creator of all existence. They referred to this God using various names, including, *El, Elohim,* and *Shaddai*. But, in the mind of the Israelites, their national God bore a special personal name: *YHVH*.

God's personal name, transliterated either as *YHVH* or *YHWH*, is known as the Tetragrammaton (from the Greek *tetra*, "four," and *grammaton*, "letter") and occurs more than sixty-eight hundred times in the Bible. It is the distinctive name of the God of Israel favored by one of the four documents that make up the Pentateuch called the Yahwist documents of Judah: "Eternal One [*YHVH*] is His name" (Exod. 15:3). Though spelled out fully as *YHVH*, it also appears as an abbreviation in the form of *Yah*—"The Eternal [*Yah*] is my strength" (Exod. 15:2)—and as *Yahu* in the names of many Israelites, such as Uziyahu (Isa. 6:1), Yirm'yahu (Jer. 1:1), or, in shortened form, Uriyah (for Uriyahu; II Kings 16:16), as well as in the expression *hal'luyah* (hallelujah). Its grammatical root is perhaps related to *Ehyeh*, which is found in God's answer to Moses, "Thus shall you say to the Israelites, '*Ehyeh* sent me to you'" (Exod. 3:14).

Coming from the Hebrew root *hayah*, the name *YHVH*, in its third-person masculine imperfect form, can be most accurately translated as "Existence," "He is," "He is present," or even "He causes to be." The origin of the name is uncertain. According to one biblical tradition, it was introduced to Moses before the Exodus: "God spoke to Moses and said to him, "I am the Eternal [*YHVH*]. I appeared to Abraham, Isaac, and Jacob as *El Shaddai*, but I did not make Myself known to them by My name *YHVH*" (Exod. 6:2–3). Yet, other sources in the Book of Genesis clearly state that this name was already known before Moses's time, dating back to the time of Enosh, the grandson of Adam (Gen. 4:26; see also 14:22, 24:31). Biblical tradition insists that Moses did not introduce a new God but reaffirmed the same God who had led the patriarchs in their wanderings, though known to them only as *El Shaddai*.

Living among the Canaanites, the Israelites ascribed to *YHVH*, their patron God, many characteristics of other gods worshiped by the local people. But, *YHVH* was considered not only a deity who controlled nature but also one who showed concern for the poor and downtrodden (cf. Leviticus 19; I Sam. 2:7–9 ; Psalm 82). Though *YHVH* lives in the heavens (e.g., Ps. 123:1; Isa. 63:15), *YHVH*'s name, symbol of God's presence, dwells in Jerusalem (e.g., I Kings 11:36; II Kings 21:4), and in some priestly texts, *YHVH*'s "glory" (*kavod*; namely, God's gravitas, weight) resides in the sanctuary (e.g., Exod. 29:43; I Kings 8:11).

The name *YHVH* has been found in extra-biblical literature, such as the Moabite Stone of King Mesha of Moab (ninth century BCE), and in a tenth-century-BCE, four-tiered cult stand from Ta'anah in northern Syria, where *YHVH* is even associated with the goddess Asherah. The earliest reference to *YHVH* in the Bible is found in the Song of Deborah (Judg. 5:2–31) and in the Song of Moses (Exod. 15:1–18), both dating from about the eleventh century BCE.

The Bible provides some hints that the name could be of southern, wilderness origin, when it asserts in the final blessing of Moses, "The Eternal [*YHVH*] came from Sinai" (Deut. 33:2), or in the prophecies of Habakkuk,

"God is coming from Teman, the Holy One from Mount Paran" (3:3), all in northwestern Arabia. It is possible that the Israelites learned about *YHVH* from some of their neighbors and adopted *YHVH* as their national God. How this happened, however, is not known. Some scholars argue that Moses learned about *YHVH* from his Midianite father-in-law Jethro. Others claim that the Israelites learned about *YHVH* from the Egyptians who had a god by a similar name. All of these theories, however, are highly speculative. The truth is, we do not know how and when the Israelites first came to view *YHVH* as their God, except for what the Bible states—that *YHVH* was revealed for the first time to Abraham (Gen. 12:1), traditionally considered to be the first "monotheist."[5]

The major problem with the term *YHVH* is that there is no definitive pronunciation for this name. In some ancient Hebrew manuscripts, even though the rest of the biblical texts appear in late Aramaic script, the name *YHVH* is still written in archaic Hebrew letters without any vowels, most likely because of its sacred character. The vowels that came to be attached to this name for God are of later Rabbinic origin.

In ancient times there was a prohibition against misusing *YHVH*'s name. The Ten Commandments clearly state, "You shall not utter the name of the Eternal [*YHVH*] your God in vain [*lashav*]" (Exod. 20:7), most likely because it could be used for magical purposes. However, the meaning of this text is not totally clear. Later on, the Rabbis also feared that the holy name could be used in magical formulas (JT *Sanhedrin* 28b) (see "The Third Word: Misuse of God's Name"). Therefore, given the sacred character of the name, they discouraged people from uttering it as written.

During the Second Temple period, the name *YHVH* was pronounced with its proper vowels only by the High Priest during the *Avodah* service on Yom Kippur within the Temple (*Mishnah Yoma* 6:2) and by ordinary priests when they recited the Priestly Benediction in the Temple itself (*Mishnah Sotah* 7:6). With the passing of time, however, the correct pronunciation was lost.[6] In order to preserve the reverence for the divine name, the Rabbis substituted the word *Adonai*, meaning "Master" or "my Master." They taught, "Not as I am written, am I pronounced. I am written *YHVH*, but I am pronounced as *Adonai*" (BT *Kiddushin* 71a). They further said, "Whoever pronounces God's name according to its consonants has no share in the world-to-come" (*Avot D'Rabbi Natan* 36:6).[7]

In the Greek translation of the Pentateuch, the Septuagint, *YHVH* is translated as *kyrios* (Lord). Theodoret of Cyrus, a fourth-century church father, testifies that the Samaritans used to read it as *Yabe*. In 1278, a Spanish monk named Raymund Martini spelled it as *Yohoua*. In the early sixteenth century, a Catholic priest from Italy, Petrus Galatinus, spelled it is a *Yehoua*. The popular name "Jehovah" appears for the first time in 1530 in the English Bible by William Tyndale. Most scholars today think that that the correct pronunciation is "Yahveh." However, as one biblical scholar notes, "Most attempts at recovery [of the correct pronunciation] are conjectural."[8]

During the Rabbinic period, other names of God were created to reflect the needs of the community and the theology that was prevalent at the time. Among those are *HaShem* (the Name), *Shamayim* (Heaven), *Avinu Malkeinu* (Our Father, our King), *Melekh malkhei ham'lakhim* (the King of all kings), *HaRachaman* (the Merciful One), and *Mi she-amar v'hayah haolam* (the One who spoke and the world came into being). Medievalists added a few more: *Ilat ha-ilot* (Cause of causes), *Ilah Rishonah* (the First Cause). In Jewish mystical writings, God is often referred to as *Shekhinah* (Divine Presence). In modern times, many thinkers prefer to speak of God as "Fountain of Life," "Friend," or "the Eternal."

All of these names refer to the same ultimate reality and simply highlight different aspects of the Divine that human beings can fathom. Ultimately, all names for God are symbolic and fall short of the total existence they claim to portray.

Your God—*Elohekha*

The personal pronoun attached to the word "God" in *Elohekha* (your God) is in the second person masculine singular. This means that the First Word is addressed not to the community at large, but to each and every individual in society. This makes the command more personal and more direct. God considers each person in the community, both men and women, a partner in the covenant.

Some Rabbinic commentators extend the meaning of the First Word by saying that the expression "your God" eliminates the possibility of turning to other divinities. Thus, the *M'khilta*, for example, suggests that the reason this section of the commandments is formulated in this way is because it wishes to teach the nations of the world that they have no "excuse for saying that there are two Powers" (*Bachodesh* 8). God is the same whether appearing as a mighty hero waging war against the Egyptians (cf. Exod. 15:3) or viewed at Sinai as an old man full of mercy. Similarly, Obadiah Sforno (fifteenth century) states that *Elohekha* means "without any intermediary" (ad loc.), perhaps alluding to the Christian belief that places Jesus in that position. Others point out that "your God" means that God spoke to every individual according to his or her level of understanding, thus setting the background for a modern understanding that we all encounter God in different forms or images and using different names (*Iturei Torah*).

Who Brought You Out of the Land of Egypt

When critical modern historians write about history, they do so without consideration of God's involvement in human affairs. They evaluate the relevant documents, study the events, use their judgments, and create a credible evaluation of what must have happened. Their conclusion may be at variance with other historians' analyses, because ultimately writing history is based on personal interpretation of human actions, and that may vary from one critic to another. But God rarely (if at all) plays a role in this evaluation.

Things were very different in the ancient Near East, where divine beings were always viewed as intervening in human affairs. A military victory occurred only because of the gods' beneficent deeds. And defeat was considered as the gods' anger and punishment. Thus, for example, Sargon of Agade claims that "Enlil [the god] gave him the region from the Upper Sea (to) the Lower Sea" (*ANET*, 267). In the inscription about Naram-Sin, we are told that "the god Nergal did open up the path for the mighty Naram-Sin, and gave him Arman and Ibla" (*ANET*, 268). Similarly, Shamshi-Adad I of Assyria (seventeenth century BCE) claimed, "With the help of Ashur (and) Shamash, the great gods, my lords, I... am a conqueror (of the regions) from the Great Sea which is in the country Amurru as far as the Great Sea which is in the Nairi country" (*ANET*, 275). There are many such examples in the annals of Assyro-Babylonian history.

Being part of the ancient Near Eastern world, the biblical Israelites thought very much alike regarding God's involvement in human history. They claimed that their God was an *Ish Milchamah*, a "Warrior" (Exod. 15:3), and Master of all historical events. Thus, "Pharaoh's chariots and his army He has cast into the sea" (Exod. 15:4). God brought up "the Philistines from Caphtor and the Arameans from Kir" (Amos 9:7) and redeemed the Israelites from Egypt (e.g., Exod. 18:1; Lev. 25: 42). God even commissioned an enemy from the north (Jer. 1:15), perhaps the Babylonians, to punish Judah and its inhabitants.

The First Word highlights the redemption from Egypt. After using a self-introductory formula, our text goes on to say that God is the One "who brought you out of the land of Egypt, the house of bondage." It is noteworthy here that God is viewed not as Creator but as Redeemer. It is true that the role of Redeemer does not negate the role of Creator, but for reasons that are not clear to us, this text stresses God's involvement in human history as a power of redemption and seems to ignore or fails to mention God's creative role in the universe. The Israelites left Egypt, the text says, but they did not get out on their own. It was God who actually made this happen. The implication of the biblical assertion is that because God redeemed the People of Israel, Israel now owes gratitude and service to *YHVH*. In fact, this motif becomes the rationale for many biblical laws, including the celebration of the Festival of Passover (Exod. 23:15), the manumission of indentured servants (Deut. 15:12–15), or the generosity to be shown the downtrodden during the celebration of the Feast of Weeks, Shavuot (Deut. 16:10–12).

The idea that God is active in Jewish history is a prevalent concept in Rabbinic literature, too. The traditional Passover Haggadah, for example, does not mention Moses, the great liberator, but assigns all the glory to God. Similarly, in *Al HaNisim* ("The Miracles"), a Rabbinic blessing recited during Chanukah , the text emphasizes the spiritual over the military exploits and attributes the victory to God, not to the Maccabees who actually did the fighting: "In your great mercy You rose up with them [i.e., the People of Israel] in their time of trouble and fought in their fight, judged their cause just." This belief is highly debatable in modern time.

Also, for the author/editor of the First Word, Jewish history seems to have started with the Exodus from Egypt, not with the patriarchs of the Book of Genesis. Was this a deliberate omission or simply a matter of stressing one singular event in Jewish history? Could there have been various traditions as to the beginning of the Jewish people in the minds of the ancient Israelites? Scholars continue to debate this issue in our time, still with little result.

The Role of the First Word

As noted above, in Rabbinic literature Exod. 20:2 (Deut. 5:6) establishes the basis for the fundamental belief in the existence of God. *Sefer HaChinukh* makes it clear that according to the First Word, "the world has one God, who brought all existence into being; by His power and His will does everything come about—all that was, that is, and that will be for time eternal" (*Yitro*,

#25). It further comments that "whoever does not believe in it denies the main principle [of the One God], and has no portion or merit within the People of Israel." Furthermore, it derives other conclusions from this First Word, even though our text is silent about them, such as "to know that He is immanent, wholly perfect, without any body or physical power of a body."

Other critics, however, take a slightly different view of this verse. Joseph Albo (d. 1444), for example, argues that there are three basic fundamental dogmas in Judaism that are based on divine law: the existence of God, revelation, and reward and punishment. The first principle emerges out of the Creation story in Genesis 1. But the First Word, he adds, is only a specific command (mitzvah), not a principle of faith, because none of the Torah commandments should be counted as principles (*Ikarim* 1:14, 128). Albo seems to have a more convincing view on this matter because the belief in God is nowhere in the Bible dictated. It is simply taken for granted.

The Various Jewish Views of God

In an article titled "Man vs. God," the author and thinker Richard Dawkins (b. 1941) states that "God is not dead. He was never alive in the first place."[9] The thinking in the ancient Near East as well as in the Bible is very different. The existence of gods was taken for granted. The question then was how to relate to divine beings and how to carry out their will. After the exilic period (ca. sixth century BCE), when strict monotheism appeared in ancient Israel, the Bible proclaimed the existence of one universal and intangible God. Yet, it is remarkable that nowhere in the Bible is there a passage attempting to prove the existence of God. It is assumed. The Psalmist states, "The fool says in his heart, 'There is no God'" (Pss. 14:1, 53:2).

In line with its monotheistic teachings, the Jewish literature of the postbiblical period has consistently promoted the belief in God's unity. God is one, not two or three. It would be more accurate to say that most Jews today view God as being "alone," "unique," or "incomparable." Thus, the Plaut Torah commentary, based on the Jewish Publication Society's *Tanakh*, translates the *Sh'ma*, the watchword of the Jewish faith, as "Hear O Israel! The Eternal is our God, the Eternal alone" (Deut. 6:4).[10]

In the past, many Jewish philosophers advocated different perceptions of the Divine that were sometimes at variance with the thinking of other Jews. And that is acceptable. As Reform Judaism's "A Centenary Perspective" (1976) states, "The affirmation of God has always been essential to our people's will to survive. In our struggle through the centuries to preserve our faith we have experienced and conceived God in many ways." Similarly, "A Statement of Principles for Reform Judaism" (1999) clearly states, "We affirm the reality and oneness of God, even as we may differ in our understanding of the Divine presence." This assertion is based on the acceptance that human beings can achieve greatness but can never transcend their humanity. Human beings are finite. Their knowledge is limited. Humans can never become divine. Therefore, any theology that suggests that individuals can become god (such as the claim in Christianity that Jesus is part of the divine essence) remains outside of Judaism. In the Bible and Rabbinic writings, God is spiritual, invisible, and unfathomable. God cannot be compared to anything or anyone we know or conceive. Only God is God.

Presently, when a person says, "I believe in God," or negates the existence of the Divine by arguing, "I do not believe in God," it is most likely that he or she has in mind a particular conception of God, technically called "theism." However, given the diversity of God concepts in Judaism, the term "God" should not be exclusively used in reference to theism, where God appears as a personal God (for details, see below). This is not correct. Theism is only one of the various views about God in Judaism. On the other hand, the term "atheism" simply means "not believing in a *theistically defined* God," and not the rejection of the idea or reality of God altogether. By my definition, an atheist can subscribe to other views of God and still remain a religious person. A person who does not hold to a theistic view is, in my use of language, simply a "non-theist." What is needed is for each person to study the spectrum of all theological positions compatible with his or her religion and to choose the interpretation that is most reasonable or acceptable. Yet, it must be admitted that because of our limitations, no concept of God totally answers all our existential questions.

The major divide in theological thinking is between theism and non-theism. Let us now identify briefly other views of God that are compatible with Judaism today.[11]

Classical theism is the most popular God concept today. According to theists, God is one, and a spiritual being who expresses will, love, or concern. In other words, God is a personal God. Furthermore, God is all-powerful, supernatural and transnatural, all-good, and all-knowing. God hears our prayers and answers them, though we may not know how or when.

Medieval philosophers have designed proofs for the existence of the theistically viewed God, using various arguments. The teleological (from the Greek meaning "purpose") argument is based on the observation that if there is an order in the universe, there must be an ordering, organizing Mind, God. The moral argument supposes that if morality exists, it must have its source in the spiritual realm of being, God.[12]

Though these philosophical arguments are very convincing for many people, they also suffer from two major difficulties: (a) They may prove the necessity of the idea of God, but not God's existence; that still requires a "leap of faith." and (b) they do not resolve the problem of evil: if God is all-good and all-powerful, why is there evil in the world? Many answers have been proposed. None, however, is totally satisfactory.

Outside of classical theism, some thinkers have opted for "theistic finitism," where God, though a personal God, is not all-powerful. This allows for the presence of evil. According to these philosophers, history is a process that is moving toward a higher goal, for which God needs the help of humanity to accomplish.

Other philosophers, called religious naturalists, view God not as a personal God, but as the supreme Energy or Power, who energizes the universe from within and who acts through the laws of nature. This allows for the presence of evil in the world. The world is not perfect; it is incomplete and full of risks. Some religious people look to Kabbalah, Jewish mysticism, and maintain that God (the *Ein Sof*, "without end") is unknowable and that God relates to the world through the mediation of ten emanations (called *s'firot*) emerging from the Godhead. And religious humanists consider God only an idea, not a reality, which represents the highest image of ourselves.

As this short survey indicates, there are a number of God concepts that are valid within the broad framework of Judaism. Those mentioned above do not exhaust the list. Contemporary Jewish thinkers continue to probe new views of God, all compatible with traditional Judaism, and offer various approaches, such as "God is the enduring possibility of Being" (Alvin Reines), "God is the soul of the universe" (Jacob Agus), "God is both Supreme Being and Supreme Becoming-Panentheism" (Bernard Martin), plus Jewish feminist perspectives on the Divine as discussed by thinkers such as Judith Plaskow and Marcia Falk. No God concept in Judaism is the only true one. And every Jew is urged to probe the mystery of the Divine and come up with the one that is most satisfactory.

The variety of God concepts in Judaism has a direct impact on the way we view the world and on the way we behave in our society. A theist expects a response to prayers, while a religious naturalist does not, arguing that prayer can change only the individual who is praying, and not the world outside. A theist behaves ethically because of the belief that ethics are grounded in the belief in a (theistically) defined God. Non-theists use different criteria. The question is this: What constitutes morality, and on what is it based?

Can an Atheist Be an Ethical Person?

Many people argue that in order to be a moral person you must believe in God. In other words, ethics is grounded in God, and consequently, if you do not believe in God, you cannot be ethical. In fact, a saying is attributed to the famous Russian novelist Fyodor Dostoyevsky (1821–1881) (wrongly, I think) that "if there is no God, everything is permissible."

There are many theists who behave ethically because, they believe, God commanded them. The prophets of Israel, who stressed deed over belief, based their morality on the existence of God. Thus, for example, the prophet Micah (eighth century BCE) taught, "He has told you, O man, what is good, and what the Eternal requires of you: only to do justice and to love goodness, and to walk modestly with your God" (Mic. 6:8). God's moral teachings, the followers of this view argue, represent absolute standards against which people can measure their behavior. On the other hand, we all know that belief in God does not guarantee ethical behavior. Otherwise, how can we explain the many news reports of clergy in our time, both Jewish and Christian, who are accused of sexually unlawful behavior, or the actions of those laypeople who have been involved in illegal financial transactions even though they are religiously observant? We know from our daily interaction with people that there are many individuals in our society who deny the existence of (theistically viewed) God or are totally agnostic about religious matters and still lead an impeccable moral life.

The question is, therefore, not the belief or the denial of God, but the source of authority on which an ethical life depends. For theists, it is God; but for others, it could have another base. Given the fact that nature does not discriminate between the innocent and the virtuous, some thinkers, like Immanuel Kant (1724–1804), argue that an act can only be considered ethical if it has universal validity. Utilitarian thinkers, like John Locke (1632–1704), maintain that people attain knowledge of moral life through education, environment, or local customs. Others, like Jean Jacques Rousseau (1712–1778) even base ethics on a social contract, self-preservation, or self-interest.[13]

It is, therefore, clear that theism does not have a monopoly on ethical life and that each God concept has its ethical component. The ideal is to be truthful to one's belief in God, however conceived, and lead a moral life that is compatible with it. What about the agnostic who is still trying to figure out an appropriate belief in God? That person, too, needs to act ethically, simply because society compels it or social values determine his or her ethical behavior.

Is Belief Necessary to Be a Jew?

The Hebrew Bible, as we noted, assumes the existence of God, but nowhere does it demand that one actually believe in God. This is most likely because, in the past, the reality of God was a given, and it was rarely challenged. Even the Hebrew verb *aman*, which gives us the Modern Hebrew *emunah* (faith), simply means "confirm" or "support" in the Bible. Thus, for example, the patriarch Abraham is told by God that as part of the covenant, he will have an enduring progeny, and based on that promise, "He [Abraham] put his trust [*v'he-emin ba-YHVH*] in the Eternal, who reckoned that as loyalty to him" (Gen. 15:6). The context makes it clear that Abraham's righteous act was based on his trust in God's word. There is no reference to a theological dogma here. It is also debatable whether Rabbinic literature contains systematic dogmas outside of a belief in bodily resurrection and *Torah min hashamayim*, namely, that the Torah is of divine origin (*Mishnah Sanhedrin* 10:1).

Things changed with Maimonides, who insisted that one can become a Jew only through the acceptance of his Thirteen Principles of Faith, which include the belief in the existence of God: "The First Fundamental Principle: to believe in the existence of the Creator" (*Chelek*: *Sanhedrin* 10). (Maimonides viewed God in Aristotelian terms as the Unmoved Mover.) In creating his list of beliefs, the philosopher was probably reacting, on the one hand, to the Karaites, a Jewish sect who challenged Rabbinic thinking, and, on the other, to Muslim philosophers of his time who were in the process of systematizing the theology of Islam. However, this was a major shift in Rabbinic thinking. And, in the opinion of Menachem Kellner, this was rather "unfortunate."[14] Maimonides, argues Kellner, tried to convert Judaism into an ecclesiastical community, which, historically, stressed the performance of mitzvot. In fact, other Jewish philosophers of the medieval times, such as Hasdai Crescas, rejected the idea that the Torah contains commandments involving beliefs.

The question as to whether belief can be required is still being debated today. The Reform Jewish platform called "A Centenary Perspective" (1976) reads, "We ground our lives, personally and community, on God's reality, and remain open to new experiences and conceptions of the Divine." Similarly, the latest Reform platform, "A Statement of Principles for Reform Judaism" (1999), states, "We affirm the reality and oneness of God, even as we may differ in our understanding of the Divine presence." Others take exception to this requirement and prefer to deal only with the Rabbinic definition of "who is a Jew" that is based on biology; namely, a Jew is one who is born of a Jewish mother or duly converted to Judaism. Faith is secondary.

The implication of this debate for our time is enormous. Just as there are many Jews who believe in the existence of God, there are others who have doubts about it, and some even outright deny it. What is their place within the Jewish community? Is belief in the existence of God necessary for Jewish identity? Modern science and philosophy can only tell us that if the world is the way it is, there "could" be a God, but only a religious person, making a leap of faith, can state that God "*does* actually exist." And, what do we do with agnostic Jews? Do we throw them out of the Jewish community because of their doubts? I would say, not. Judaism is not only a religion but a culture as well, and there is room in it for both perspectives.

I maintain that belief cannot be mandated. It has to be accepted voluntarily after reflection and final assent to a proposition. What we need is an inclusive theology that accepts the reality of various God concepts in Judaism, in line with its historical attitude on admitting diversity on this subject. Obviously, there are limits: if someone claims a belief in the divinity of Jesus, the Jewish community will not accept that person as a member in good standing.

Whatever our image of God, the best that we can say is that God is a transcendental force, a Power that stands beyond us, pulling us to become the best of what we can be. The mystery that surrounds us is vast, and the human terms we use for God are simply inadequate to describe it. They are, as Maimonides taught us, all metaphors. According to Chasidic thought, God is called in the Bible *Elohei HaElohim*, "God of Gods" (Deut. 10:17), in order to demonstrate that God is higher than any idea of God of which humanity is capable of conceiving. We must search, both within ourselves and in the larger world, to come to know and understand what God is or could be.

In Conclusion

We stand in awe before the intricacies of the universe. The more we become aware of the world around us, the greater our reverence for the power, for the energy, that stands behind it. An ordinary Jew once asked the Baal Shem Tov, the founder of the Chasidic movement (seventeenth century), "Why are we told to fear the King of kings when it is known that we stand in fear of a mortal king without such a command?" He replied, "The fear we have of a mortal king is but an outer fear, a fear of losing a material thing. We, however, are instructed to have an inner reverence for God. Any person who is without such reverence is spiritually crippled."

I hope we can open our minds and hearts to the world around us, marveling at the mysterious workings of nature. We can then declare, along with the Psalmist, "How great are Your works, O Eternal, how very profound Your designs" (Ps. 92:6), always keeping in mind that we stand before the Ultimate Reality, who in biblical language, the First Word announced a Presence by saying, "I, *YHVH*, am the Eternal your God."

The Second Word: Idolatry

Idolatry Today?

A number of years ago when I visited the Westminster Abbey of London for the first time, I was struck by the number of statues that adorn the different parts of the ancient building. The Abbey, properly called "The Collegiate Church of St. Peter at Westminster," is not only a historic site where royal coronations take place and important personalities of Great Britain, such as Churchill, Allenby, Attlee, and Chamberlain are buried, but also a religious site where religious ceremonies, such as weddings, are often held. By contrast, in Jewish tradition no Jew is ever buried in a modern synagogue, nor does it feature a statue of any individual, based on the Rabbinic interpretation of the second commandment, which prohibits the presence of sculptured images in the sanctuary. For many Jews, the presence of these works of art smacks of idolatry.

The Second Word covers the making of an idol (i.e., a physical representation of a deity), the worship of such an idol, and the worship of God (*YHVH*) through pagan rites and rituals. How relevant is this commandment today? Some would argue that it is not, because not too many people worship sticks and stones anymore. Though this is mostly correct, there are some religions in the world that are, from the perspective of Judaism, considered idolatrous (see below). Furthermore, many people in our society still place their highest loyalties on money, the party, or country, which many Jewish teachers would consider worship of foreign gods as understood in its broadest and metaphoric sense. In this chapter we shall study not only the topic of idolatry in the past, but also the worship of various "idols" of our time.

The Text of the Second Word

The second commandment is one of the longest in the Decalogue. It contains four verses. Addressed to an individual and not the community as a whole, it is formulated as a direct command in the second person masculine singular:

> You shall have [*lo yihyeh l'kha*] no other gods [*elohim acheirim*] besides Me [*al panai*] [v. 3]: you shall not make for yourself a sculptured image [*pesel*], or any likeness [*t'munah*] of what is in the heavens above, or on the earth below, or in the waters under the earth [v. 4]; you shall not bow down to them or serve them—for I the Eternal am an impassioned God [*El kana*], visiting the guilt of the parents upon the children, upon the third and upon the fourth generations of those who reject me [v. 5], but showing kindness to the thousandth generation of those who love Me and keep my commandments [v. 6]. (Exod. 20:3–6; cf. Deut. 5:7–10)

In Jewish tradition these four verses represent one single commandment, namely, the second in the list of the Decalogue. The Protestant Reformer John Calvin split the commandment into two, with verse 3 being the First Word and verses 4–6, the Second Word (see "Text and Context").

Outside of the Decalogue, the prohibition of worshiping other gods and the manufacturing of idols are mentioned in the Pentateuch in Lev. 19:4: "Do not turn to idols [*elilim*] and make molten gods [*elohei maseikhah*] for yourselves." We also find a similar statement in the Book of Deuteronomy, "Be most careful . . . not to act wickedly and make for yourselves a sculptured image [*pesel*] in any likeness whatever [*t'munat kol samel*] (Deut. 4:16), and in the list of curses of Deut. 27:15, "Cursed be anyone who makes a sculptured or molten image [*fesel umaseikhah*], abhorred by the Eternal, a craftsman's handiwork, and sets it up in secret."

The View of the World: The Ancient Context

In order to understand better the meaning and implication of the Second Word, it is necessary to place it in context of the *Tanakh*'s view of the world, which is not too different from the way in which it is usually described in the ancient Near Eastern literature. For instance, according to the Babylonian Creation story (*Enuma Elish*), when Marduk began to create the world, he split the body of Tiamat (divine patron of salt water) into two, using one half to make the heavens and the other, the earth. Similarly, in the Book of Genesis, God made an expanse (*rakia*) in the midst of the cosmic waters, "separating the waters beneath the expanse from the waters above the expanse" (Gen. 1:7). In this prescientific conception of the universe, the world, being flat, is surrounded by the heavens above and the waters below. The sun, moon, and stars hover above the heavens, moving around the earth. Rain comes through the "sky's floodgates" (Gen. 7:11), which were conceived as holes or openings in the expanse of the heavens. And the multitudes of gods spread throughout the then-known universe. *YHVH* is viewed in Genesis 1 and 2 in a similar way to other ancient Near Eastern gods, except that *YHVH* works alone, without any competition. When the Second Word states that you should not make for yourself any image of a divinity that is either "in the heavens above," or "on the earth below," or even "in the waters under the earth"—in other words, everywhere—it reflects this primitive idea of the universe.

No Other Gods Besides Me

The Second Word demands the worship of only one God, but the final clause, *al panai*, seems to limit its scope. In fact, it is not clear how best to translate the expression *al panai*. While the translation in the Plaut Torah commentary renders it as "besides Me," it is also possible to translate it, as others have done, "in My presence" (like the Akkadian *ana pani*), "in defiance of Me," "to rival Me," or "outside of Me." It probably means, as it appears in the Septuagint and in the Aramaic version of Onkelos, "except Me." Irrespective of which rendition we prefer, the text does not seem to deny that other divinities are, in fact, "gods"; it simply states that the Israelites are not to worship any of them. Israel has a special bond with *YHVH* and owes its existence as a nation and its loyalty only to *YHVH*. But this is not pure monotheism as we understand it. In reality, the conception of God in the Bible has gone through many changes, moving from polytheism, to monolatry,[1] and finally to monotheism. However, these changes did not always happen one after another. Often, these phases existed simultaneously, and at times, one theological view dominated the others. How did this change take place?

Polytheism

There is much evidence to suggest that some Israelites, in the early period of their history, were polytheists and that the national god of Israel, *YHVH*, was worshiped along with other gods for a considerable period of time until pure monotheism was firmly established just before or during the exilic period in the sixth century BCE. Examples of polytheism abound in the Bible. The most famous incident of idolatry appears in the Golden Calf episode after the Exodus. According to the biblical story, when Moses came down from Mount Sinai, he found that at the insistence of the people, his brother, Aaron, had made a "golden calf" (Exodus 32) for worship purposes. However, it is not clear if this calf was another god, an image of *YHVH*, or even the pedestal on which *YHVH* sat.[2] But this is not the only recorded example of idolatry in the Hebrew Scriptures. The prophets often accused the Israelites of worshiping other gods: "They turn to other gods and love the cups of the grape" (Hos. 3:1); "[They] followed the Baalim [Canaanite gods]" (Jer. 9:13); the prophet Elijah cried out, "I am the only prophet of the Eternal left, while the prophets of Baal [functioning in the Kingdom of Israel during the reign of Ahab] are four hundred and fifty men" (I Kings 18:22). Rachel, the wife of Jacob, had her household gods (*t'rafim*) with her when she escaped from her father, Laban (Gen. 31:34). According to the Book of Numbers, "Moses made a copper serpent and mounted it on a standard; and when bitten by a serpent, anyone who looked at the copper serpent would recover" (Num. 21:9). The Israelites continued to offer sacrifices to this image, called "Nechushtan," even during the First Temple period, but it was ultimately removed by King Hezekiah of Judah (ca. seventh century BCE; II Kings 18:4). According to the Book of Judges, the mother of Micah of Ephraim had a sculptured image and a molten image made by a local smith and kept it in Micah's house, which included all kinds of idolatrous images, including various household idols (*t'rafim*) (Judg. 17:4–5). This event was probably not uncommon in its time. Toward the end of King Solomon's reign, altars were dedicated near Jerusalem to the worship of the pagan gods Chemosh and Molech (I Kings 11:7). During the nineteenth and twentieth centuries, hundreds of folk ritual objects, including many household gods and goddesses, were found in archaeological digs in ancient Israel.

Even the name of God in the Bible could support the argument that ancient Israelites engaged in polytheistic practices. The generic name of God in the Bible, *Elohim*, contains a plural ending, *-im*. In the overwhelming majority of cases, this noun is accompanied by a singular verb, which indicates that the term was viewed as singular (like the English "media is"). Yet, in a few texts *Elohim* appears in the plural, most likely a remnant of a polytheistic background. For example, in Gen. 20:13, Abraham says, "When God [*Elohim*] made me wander from my father's house"; here the verb "wander" is in the plural, *hitu*, as if to say, "When gods made me wander." Similarly, Gen. 35:7 says that after Jacob's flight from Esau, in the city of Beth El "God [*Elohim*] had been revealed to him [Jacob]"; here, too, the verb "revealed" is in the plural, *niglu*.

How rampant was polytheism in the everyday lives of the Israelites? In a detailed study of this subject, Jeffrey Tigay, without denying that polytheism existed in ancient Israel, convincingly argues that "the low representation of pagan deities in Israelite names and inscriptions indicates that—so far as our evidence goes—deities other than YHWH were not widely regarded by Israelites as sources of beneficence, blessing, protection, and justice."[3] Obviously, the other possibility is that the final editors of the Bible eliminated a number of vestiges of polytheism in the Bible. It is clear, however, that at a time that cannot be clearly determined, many Israelites started to move away from polytheism and became monolatrists.

Monolatry

"Monolatry" is a system of belief that holds that even though there are many gods, there is only one god that is worthy of worship; the rest of humanity can serve their own divinities, but we know ours is the best. The Book of Deuteronomy states that when you look up at the heavenly beings, you must not be lured into worshiping them, for "these the Eternal your God allotted to other people everywhere under heaven" (Deut. 4:19). The classic example of this monolatrist position is found in the Song at the Sea, which contains the line "Who is like You, Eternal One, among the celestials [lit. "gods"]?" (Ex. 15:11). Similarly, the Psalmist declares, "The Eternal is a great God, the great king of all divine beings" (Ps. 95:3); "You are exalted high above all divine beings" (Ps. 97:9). Here there is no unequivocal denial that there are other gods in the world, only that the Eternal is the best.

Monotheism

Eventually, some Israelites, and certainly the literati in society, adopted monotheism by affirming that what others call "gods" are not gods at all and that only *YHVH* is God. A clear expression of this belief is found prominently in the writings of the prophet called Second Isaiah, whose teachings are recorded in the second half of the Book of Isaiah. He emerged during the exilic period in Babylonia, after the destruction of the First Temple. Examples include "I am the Eternal, and there is none else" (Isa. 45:18) and "I am divine, and there is none like Me" (Isa. 46:9). It is also expressed in some of the psalms, such as "All the gods of the peoples are mere idols" (Ps. 96: 5) and "Who is God except the Eternal" (Ps. 18:32; cf. II Sam. 22:32). This may have also been the meaning of the watchword of the Jewish faith in Deut. 6:4, "Hear, O Israel! The Eternal is our God, the Eternal alone." But monotheism is a late development, and most likely a popular belief only among the intelligentsia of ancient Israel. The majority of Israel, I would argue, remained in a monolatristic stage for a very long time. Our Decalogue reflects this middle stage.

The Rabbis were pure monotheists. They taught, "Whoever acknowledges a false god denies the entire Torah" (*Sifrei D'varim* 54; cf. Maimonides, *Mishneh Torah, Hilkhot Avodat Kokhavim* 2:4). In a comment on "other gods," the *M'khilta* states, "What does the Scripture mean when it says, "other gods"? The answer is: "Merely those that others call gods" (*Bachodesh* 6).

What Is Prohibited?

The Second Word prohibits the manufacturing of a *pesel* or a *t'munah* (Lev. 19:4 adds *elohei maseikhah* as a prohibited item), bowing down to these in obeisance, and worshiping them (through sacrifices). What, exactly, do these terms mean, and what actions, precisely, are banned?

In Ugaritic, a *psl* (a cognate of the Hebrew word *pesel*) is a statue made of wood, an idol. In biblical Hebrew, this word refers to an image made of wood or metal or hewn in stone. *Elohei maseikhah* means "molten gods." The word *t'munah* ("picture" in Modern Hebrew) means "likeness," "visible form," or "visage." According to biblical law, religious art that is used for the purpose of worship is prohibited, but those not intended as objects of worship, such as of cherubim or lions, are permitted in the sanctuary. During their polytheistic phase, the Israelites are known to have made images of *YHVH*, as seen in the stone carvings found in Kuntillet Ajrud in the Sinai wilderness (eighth century BCE), where *YHVH* appears with "his *asherah*." In ancient times the term *asherah* referred either to a Canaanite goddess or to her wooden cult symbol. It is most likely that *YHVH* is featured here with his spouse.[4]

This physical representation of *YHVH* was not tolerated in the Temple of Jerusalem, but other objects were included without objection. Thus, for example, the water tank of the Temple stood on twelve oxen (I Kings 7:25), and the sanctuary contained a number of "cherubim" (*k'ruvim*) (Exod. 25:18). Unlike the round-faced infants of medieval art in the Western world, called *putti*, these biblical cherubim refer to heavenly winged beings having a human or animal face and a number of legs. Such composite beasts are well known in ancient Near Eastern art, and particularly in Assyrian art. In the Bible, the cherubim appear either as woven into fabrics or freestanding. During the Exodus period, the Tabernacle contained cherubim in the inner curtains (Exod. 26:1). In the Temple of Jerusalem, carved cherubim appeared on the walls (I Kings 6:29), on the lavers (I Kings 7:28–29), even in the Holy of Holies: "In the Shrine [*d'vir*] he made two cherubim of olive wood, each ten cubits high" (I Kings 6:23). These cherubim were not worshiped but represented the resting place or the throne of *YHVH*, as the prayer of King Hezekiah of Judah clearly indicates: "O *YHVH* of Hosts, Enthroned on the Cherubim" (II Kings 19:15). These cherubim also are listed as guardians of the Garden of Eden (Gen. 3:24).

The prophet Isaiah states that he had "seen" God in the Temple seated on a high and lofty throne, with seraphim standing in attendance (Isa. 6:2). The word "seraphim" (lit. "the burning ones") most likely refers to some unknown heavenly beings, perhaps in the form of flying serpents (cf. Isa. 14:29, 30:6). The prophet describes them as follows: "Each of them had six wings: with two he covered his face, with two he covered his legs [i.e., genitals], and with two he would fly" (Isa. 6:2). The relationship between these seraphim and the cherubim is not clear. Though some scholars argue that they are one and the same, it is most likely that they were very different from one another. The cherubim had only one set of wings, whereas the seraphim had six. Furthermore, the seraphim appear as flying, whereas the cherubim remain by the side of the divinity. Hans Wildberger suggests that seraphim were probably demons in the form of snakes who were members of the heavenly host.[5] The closest parallel we have would be the Egyptian "fabulous winged creature," as portrayed in a grave at Beni Hasan, about fifteen miles to the south of modern-day Minya, in Middle Egypt.

In postbiblical times, the second commandment was at times strictly observed and at times more liberally interpreted. Thus, while making images, even of animals, was frowned upon during the Maccabean era, the practice was relaxed in the following centuries. For example, in the Dura-Europos synagogue in eastern Syria (third century CE), one of the panels has a group of Philistines depicted as contemporary Persian soldiers. The fifth-century synagogue in Sepphoris, in central Galilee, has a mosaic floor depicting the sacrifice of Isaac. Also in a sixth-century synagogue near the Gaza shore, there are images of animals, and King David appears dressed as a Byzantine emperor, playing the lyre.

What motivated the biblical legislator to prohibit the use of graven images? Most likely, it was the fear of idolatry. If there is any theme that runs through the entire Hebrew Bible, it is the fear that Israelites, and later on, Jews, would worship alien gods represented by concrete images. God, many Israelites believed, is a jealous God, who does not tolerate any competition (see below). However, the prohibition of making concrete images of other gods does not imply that one can make an image of *YHVH*. The dominant teaching of the Bible is that God cannot be portrayed by any shape or form. In a dialogue with Moses, God tells him, "You cannot see My face, for a human being may not see Me and live" (Exod. 33:20). Similarly, in the Book of Deuteronomy, Moses reminds the Israelites that God can be heard but not seen: "You saw no shape [*t'munah*] when the Eternal your God spoke to you" (Deut. 4:15), and therefore, the text continues, "[do] not act wickedly and make for yourselves a sculptured image in any likeness whatever: the form of a man or a woman" (v. 16), for purposes of worship. This Deuteronomic text implies that *YHVH* may indeed have a "shape" but the Israelites did not see it. It is true that in a few cases, certain individuals have, in fact, seen God in person and were not harmed by it. For example, Moses, we are told, saw God face to face (Num. 12:8; Deut. 34:10), and a number of people, including Moses, ascending Mount Sinai, "saw the God of Israel—under whose feet was the likeness of a pavement of sapphire, like the very sky for purity" (Exod. 24:9–11). Similarly, the prophet Isaiah beheld God in the Temple (Isa. 6:1), and Ezekiel saw God in the heavens as "the semblance of a human form" (Ezek. 1:26). However, neither text has a description of the Divine. In Judaism, especially post-biblical Judaism, God is imageless, invisible, and incorporeal; God does not have a physical form and therefore cannot be portrayed in any physical medium. Remarkably, in a world where worshiping gods through an image was so pervasive, as evidenced by the numerous statutes of gods found in archaeological digs in the ancient Near East, the Bible vigorously proclaims that *YHVH* is aniconic. Where and how the idea of imageless worship of *YHVH* emerged is not clear, but soon it became the fundamental teaching of the Bible.

The Second Word in Rabbinic Teachings

Rabbinic custom prohibits the placement of any kind of painting or a sculptured image of a human being in the sanctuary of the synagogue, even though it allows paintings and embroidery of animal figures on the walls or ceiling, as well as pictures of religious and lay leaders in the foyer. In some more liberal synagogues, pictures of famous sages do appear within the sanctuaries, but this is rare. According to many, the fear is that the presence of an image may lead to idolatry. During medieval times, Maimonides ruled that idols and images are prohibited if they represent other gods that are worshiped (*Sefer HaMitzvot*, negative commandments, 1–7). The implication is that if they are not worshiped, they are acceptable. Even today, the question of imagery in modern synagogues and the extent to which it is acceptable in Jewish life continues to be raised in the responsa literature.

Rabbi Solomon B. Freehof, in his responsum on the placement of a portrait bust in the synagogue, concluded that it is not appropriate to put it in the sanctuary but that it would be acceptable in the lobby. However, he added, "If the lobby will be used as a sort of a chapel, the statue should not be put where it will be directly in front of the worshipers."[6] In another responsum, titled "Statuettes in the Synagogue" (1974), he argued that "there is no basic objection to statues, especially in the lobby [of a synagogue] where they do not distract from actual worship."[7]

In 1979, the Central Conference of American Rabbis Responsa Committee discussed the following question: May the floor of a synagogue or entrance hall be decorated with Jewish symbols or with any other kind of decoration employing the figures of people or animals? After reviewing the related rabbinic material on this subject, it ruled that "any kind of decoration in the floor of the synagogues has long since gone beyond the ancient concern for possible idolatrous expression, and our synagogues contain representative figures, cut and decorated stone, metal, and woodwork. Such decorations must, of course, not contain the Divine Name of God. The custom of some modern synagogues of copying the mosaics of floors from ancient Jewish synagogues should be encouraged as another link to our past and to the land of Israel."[8]

"You Shall Not Bow Down to Them or Serve Them"

In addition to manufacturing an object of worship, the Bible prohibits "bowing down to" and "serving" other gods. The Second Word states, *Lo tishtachaveh*,

"You shall not bow down" (Exod. 20:5; Deut. 5:9). "Bowing" is done during a religious service (e.g., Neh. 10:6). According to *Sefer HaChinukh*, this could be either when the hands and feet are spread on the ground or when the face itself is buried in the ground. It further states that "merely bowing down to touch the ground without the intention of worship is not prohibited" (#28). Today, most Jews simply bend their heads slightly, or bow halfway, and do not prostrate themselves all the way to the ground during worship. Perhaps the only exception to this practice is during Yom Kippur's *Avodah* service in the afternoon, when some prayer leaders fall down and touch the ground with their faces.

The Second Word also prohibits "serving" other gods: *lo ta-ovdem* (the way it is pronounced by most Sephardic Jews), "you shall not serve them" (Exod. 20:5; Deut. 5:9). "Serving" refers to offering a sacrifice by bringing an animal to be slaughtered by the priests on the altar or presenting to God a meal offering made of flour as well as a libation. An Israelite is not allowed to worship another divinity by bringing an offering of any kind. Jewish tradition identifies four types of "serving": *zibuach*, ritually offering a sacrifice; *kitur*, burning an object on the altar; *nisukh*, pouring a libation; and *hishtachavayah*, prostration. Today, without a Temple or a priest, "serving" simply means worshiping by means of prayers. A Jew bows down, if ever, only to God and addresses prayers not to any intermediary such as a saint or angel, but only to the Eternal.

The prohibition of worshiping idols is one of the three cardinal "sins" in Rabbinic literature, the other two being murder and illicit sexual relations (BT *Sanhedrin* 74a). These laws, the Rabbis teach, apply not only to Jews but also to all humanity through the universal laws given to Noah. They include six negative commandments and one positive commandment: thus, in addition to idol worship, murder, and illicit sexuality, every human being is prohibited from resorting to blasphemy, stealing, or eating a limb from a living animal, and all are ordered to set up courts of law (BT *Sanhedrin* 56a; *B'reishit Rabbah* 34:8).

The Second Word does not contain a penalty clause, but the Rabbis derived it from a biblical law, which states, "Whoever sacrifices to a god other than the Eternal shall be proscribed" (Exod. 22:19) (*M'khilta, Bachodesh* 6). Here the punishment is total annihilation and the destruction of the criminal's property (see Lev. 27:29). By the Rabbinic period, "proscription" (*cherem*) meant total social ostracism, or excommunication.

An Impassioned God

The Second Word is accompanied by a long motive clause that tries to explain the rationale of the law and God's eventual reaction in case of infraction. Israelites are not to worship other gods or make images of God, for God is *El kana* (Exod. 20:5; Deut. 5:9). This expression is variously translated as "jealous God," "impassioned God," or "zealous God." The verb *kinei* originally meant "to become intensely red" (with anger), that is, jealous with rage. Thus, in Deuteronomy, God complains that the Israelites "incensed Me [*kin'uni*] with no-gods" (32:21). The Psalmist cries out, "How long, O Eternal, will You be angry forever, will Your indignation [*kinatekha*] blaze like fire?" (Ps. 79:5). Intense jealousy between siblings and spouses is also expressed by the same verb: "Rachel came to envy [*t'kanei*] her sister" (Gen. 30:1). When a husband suspects his wife of unfaithfulness, "a fit of jealousy [*ruach kinah*] comes over him and he is wrought up about the wife [*kinei et ishto*] who has defiled herself" (Num. 5: 14). In Proverbs, "The fury [*kinah*] of the husband will be passionate" (Prov. 6:34) against a wife who commits adultery.

In the Decalogue, *YHVH* requires exclusive worship. Israelites are not allowed to worship any god but *YHVH*. If they do resort to idolatry, then, as the second half of the motive clause indicates, they will suffer terrible consequences: The Eternal will "visit [*pokeid*] the guilt of the parents upon the children, upon the third and upon the fourth generations of those who reject Me, but showing kindness to the thousandth generation of those who love Me and keep My mandates" (Exod. 20:5–6; Deut. 5:9–10). The verb *p-k-d* has a wider application and means "to attend to," "to observe," "to seek out," as well as "to punish." Here, the expression "third and fourth generations" should not be taken literally. It simply means a long time. Similarly, "thousands" implies "forever."

The concept of children suffering because of their parents' mistakes is clearly expressed in some of the early biblical texts, including Exod. 34:7 and Num. 14:18, and is reflected in many biblical episodes where punishment is exacted not only from the guilty party but from all those associated with the culprit. Thus, for example, Joshua executes the entire family of Achan because of what Achan had done by stealing consecrated goods (Josh. 7:24–5). Similarly, King David turns over to the Gibeonites a number of King Saul's family members for the crime of King Saul and his household against the said Gibeonites (II Sam. 21:1–9). We have confirmation of this extended punishment in the case of King Hezekiah of Judah (mid-eighth century

BCE), who is told by the prophet Isaiah that his support of the Babylonian king will cause problems not only for him but for his sons as well (II Kings 20:12–19). This belief is also expressed by the generation that witnessed the destruction of the First Temple; they thought this was caused by their own fault: "Our fathers sinned and are no more; / And we must bear their guilt" (Lam. 5:7). Some Rabbinic texts and liturgical passages echo this assumption, too: "On account of our sins we were exiled from our land" (*Musaf* for the *Amidah* during the festivals). However, some Talmudic rabbis found this thinking disturbing and tried to soften its message by saying, "This happens only when children follow their parents' misguided path" (BT *Sanhedrin* 27b; cf. BT *B'rakhot* 7a/b).

There is an element of truth in this biblical teaching. Often, children do pay for their parents' misdeeds: A mother who takes damaging drugs during her pregnancy does hurt her fetus and the health of the child's life later on. When we pollute our world by casting chemicals into the water or throwing toxic vapors into the air, we leave a legacy of destruction to our children. Yet, it is not fair to say, as in the old Hebrew proverb, that in all cases, "Parents eat sour grapes and their children's teeth are blunted" (see Ezek. 18:2–4; Jer. 31:29–30). This is not always true. Not all children suffer because of their parents' mistakes. Individuals do have some free will, and they have the ability to choose between good and bad.

The concept of corporate responsibility was challenged in the biblical period in the eighth or seventh century BCE, and soon it gave way to a new idea of individual moral responsibility. Thus, we find in Deuteronomy, "Parents shall not be put to death for children, nor children be put to death for parents: one shall be put to death for one's own crime" (Deut. 24:16). Similarly, the prophet Ezekiel proclaimed, "The person who sins, he alone shall die" (Ezek. 18:20; cf. Jer. 31:29–30). The new belief must have been operative during the late monarchic period, because the Book of Kings makes an extra effort to state that King Amaziah (eighth century BCE) "put to death the courtiers who had assassinated his father the king [i.e., Joash of Judah]. But he did not put to death the children of the assassins, in accordance with what it is written in the Book of the Teaching of Moses [in Deuteronomy 24]" (II Kings 14:5–6).

Some scholars argue that these two principles existed side by side. The first, namely, the belief that children suffer because of their parents, operates in the natural realm as part of God's providence, whereas the second, namely, individual responsibility, applies to human agency. However, it is most likely that with the emergence of the new concept of individuality in society, the principle was simply changed. This appears to be clearly recognized by Rabbinic sages who stated, "Moses pronounced an adverse sentence on Israel, and it was revoked by Ezekiel" (BT *Makot* 24a).

The idea that God could be "jealous" bothered some of the Rabbinic commentators. For example, the midrash, assuming that an idol is truly powerless, asks, "A hero is jealous of another hero, a rich man is jealous of another rich man, but has the idol any power that one should be jealous of it? Rabbi Gamliel said to him [i.e., the person who asked the question], 'Suppose a man would call his dog by the name of his father.... Against whom would the father be incensed? Against the son or the dog?'" (*M'khilta, Bachodesh* 6). The answer is obviously the son, because he has free will and acted knowingly. Also, some Jewish medieval thinkers were bothered by the notion of God being "jealous," because they could not believe that God functioned with human feelings. Thus, for example, Maimonides argued that when the biblical text refers to God's compassion and mercy, in reality it is referring to "the actions proceeding from God" (*Guide of the Perplexed* 1:54). For, as he believed, God is a simple being, with no extra attributes added to God's being. In reality, he added, "Every attribute that is found in the books of the Deity, may He be exalted, is therefore an attribute of His action and not of His essence" (*Guide* 1:53). However, biblical authors thought otherwise and were not shy to ascribe to God all types of human emotions, including anger and jealousy. Today, many people who believe in a "personal" God accept that God does, in fact, have emotions and feelings, whereas those who prefer a naturalistic view of God as Power or Energy deny the idea that God acts with any kind of human emotion but only through the laws of nature.

"Those Who Love Me and Keep My Commandments"

What does it mean "to love" or "to reject" God?

In the Bible, the concept of "love" derives primarily from the world of ancient diplomacy and international treaties and basically means "to be loyal" to another party. When an overlord tells his vassal, "You shall love me," he really means, "You shall be loyal to me." For example, the Assyrian king Esarhaddon (seventh century BCE) issued a curse on Ramataya, his vassal, in case he did "not love the crown prince... as you do your own lives" (*ANET*, 537, #24). King Rib-Abdi of Byblos (fourteenth century BCE) writes to the Pharaoh, "Behold the city! Half of it loves the sons of Abdi-ashirta, and half of it loves my lord" (El Amarna Letters, 138:71–73). Similarly, the Bible records that Hiram, the king of Tyre, "loved David always" (I Kings 5:15); that is, they were allies. In the same vein, when the lawgiver commands, "You shall love the Eternal, your God," (Deut. 6:5), the text implies that you must be loyal to *YHVH*, the Eternal One, by not worshiping other divinities. The verb "to love" also has an extended meaning in the Bible. One example of romantic love is "Jacob loved [*vaye-ehav*] Rachel" (Gen. 29:18). Caring for another person is also expressed with the word "love," such as "Isaac favored [*vaye-ehav*] Esau, because he [Esau] put game in his mouth, but Rebekah favored [*ohevet*] Jacob" (Gen. 25:28).

In the Second Word, "those who love [*l'ohavai*] Me" (Exod. 20:6; Deut. 5:10) are those Israelites who are loyal to God by keeping God's commandments, and by contrast, "those who reject [*l'son'ai*] Me" (Exod. 20:5; Deut. 5:9) are those who worship other gods and refuse to carry out God's mitzvot. Judaism is deed-oriented and requires not only pure thoughts and good intentions but good actions to benefit others. One of the Rabbis in the midrash maintains that the biblical clause refers to "those who dwell in the Land of Israel and risk their lives for the sake of the commandments" (*M'khilta, Bachodesh* 6). This probably reflects the hard times Jews had under the Romans and later rulers, when they enjoyed limited freedom or no freedom at all to circumcise their sons, study Torah, or celebrate their holidays as prescribed.

Modern Idolatry

As we indicated above, many people think that idolatry and the worship of many gods are matters of the past. It is very rare to find anyone worshiping objects of art made of wood or stones today. Judaism and Islam prohibit the use of paintings or sculptures in their sanctuaries. However, there are some religions that are not monotheistic, and there are those that come close to worshiping what we would consider idols. For example, Hinduism and many animistic religions around the world today are polytheistic and have many gods in their pantheons. The religion of Yoruba, which is popular in many Central American countries like Cuba, features orishas (i.e., large statutes reflecting one of the manifestations of the divine) in their sanctuaries. Each orisha is inspirited by a god. In that respect, the images are holy in themselves. Obviously, this is totally prohibited by Judaism and by other major Western religions today.

Monotheism, as a religious movement, does not always oppose the display of images. Catholicism, for example, is a monotheistic religion, yet it allows religious icons in churches. That was not always the case. Based on the teachings of the Second Word, early Christians prohibited the use of images in churches. However, flourishing in a Greco-Roman world, later Christians ignored the biblical command and adopted the use of statues, carvings, and paintings in their holy spaces, not only of the divine Jesus but also of many saints as well.

In addition to its literal sense of the word, idolatry in a metaphoric sense is highly prevalent in our society. Idolatry can be the excessive devotion to or reverence for some person or thing. More perceptively, the Jewish commentator Nehama Leibowitz defines it as "the transformation of means, even perfectly legitimate ones, into ends in themselves."[9] In this sense, there is plenty of idolatry in our present world. Unlike the popular meaning of the English word "idol," which simply means "a person worth emulating," people in the past (and even in the present) have given ultimate allegiance to, and hence worshiped, power, the state, and money, lifting certain human beings to a level close to divine.

The idea that idolatry in this figurative sense exists in the modern world was recognized by the sages of the past, too. Leibowitz quotes Isaac Arama, a Spanish rabbi of the fifteenth century, who writes, "Under the category of idolatry we must include a form which is particularly virulent today—the devoting of all energies and thoughts to the accumulation of wealth and achievement of worldly success."[10] Similarly, the German Jewish philosopher Franz Rosenzweig (d. 1929) decried the new trend by saying, "Names change, but polytheism continues. Culture, civilization, people, state, nation, race, art, science, economy and class—here you have what is certainly an abbreviated and incomplete list in the pantheon of our contemporary gods."[11]

In his book *The Art of Loving*, the psychoanalyst Erich Fromm discusses the effects of what he calls "idolatrous love." He writes, "If a person has not reached the level where he has a sense of identity, of I-ness, rooted in the productive unfolding of his own powers, he tends to 'idolize' the loved person. He is alienated from his own powers and projects them unto the loved person, who is worshiped as the *summum bonum*, the bearer of all love, all light, all bliss. In this process he deprives himself of all sense of strength, loses himself in the loved one instead of finding himself."[12] He reminds us that self-love is not the same thing as selfishness, for even the Bible reminds us that you must love another as yourself (Lev. 19:18). Idolatrous love is destructive. Zalman

M. Schachter-Shalomi maintains that "real idolatry today is the worship of money, technology, addictions, absolute political systems—even of 'Judaism' and of the personal ego."[13]

To summarize:

> When we state that our perspective and our truth are the only possible ones—this is idolatry.
> When we are consumed by material gain—this is idolatry.
> When we pursue narcissistic goals or claim to be the center of the universe—this is idolatry.
> When we put the country, the party, or our ideology before the needs of other individuals—this is idolatry.
> When we place religious rules and practices above the health and well-being of our neighbors—this is idolatry.
> When we venerate other individuals, as the Chasid does with his Tzaddik, and swear blind loyalty to an individual under any and all conditions—this is idolatry.
> When we confuse ends with means—this is idolatry.

The Second Commandment comes to tell us to steer clear of these examples and to devote our lives to using our will and ability for the benefit of humanity at large.

The detailed study of the Second Word has shown that Jewish teachers, along with other religious thinkers of our time, have urged us, almost from early biblical times until now, to consider as God only that which is of ultimate concern, to worship only that which is placed as the highest level in the list of our priorities, and to do so without any imagery and without any representation. It is not always easy to reach this goal, but it is one that we must continuously strive to achieve every day of our lives.

The Third Word: Misuse of God's Name

The Scope of the Third Word

In the past it was very common to wash the mouths of children with soap as a means of punishment for lying, cursing, talking back, or using God's name in vain. This was a symbolic cleansing of a mouth that had uttered an unacceptable word. It was widely practiced in the United Kingdom, Australia, and even recently in the United States. According to a news report, in August 2011, a woman by the name of Jessica Beagley was convicted (but received probation) for punishing her seven-year-old adopted son from Russia for misbehaving in school by pouring hot sauce down his throat and then giving him a cold shower—all the while videotaping what she was doing so she could be considered for an appearance on a national TV show.[1] Today, washing a child's mouth with soap is considered violent, humiliating, and hardly a deterrent. Besides, swallowing the soap could be harmful to the child's health.

Why would parents believe their children's mouths needed such dramatic actions to become clean again? Were these children breaking the third commandment? This may be only one of the two main interpretations of the Third Word, which could refer either to perjury (namely, swearing falsely) or frivolous use of God's name, including cursing by using God's proper name, *YHVH*. The meaning of the third commandment, as we shall see below, is not clear. In modern times, the Third Word was interpreted broadly and applied to all types of idle discourse. Let us study this development closely.

The Text of the Third Word

The Plaut Torah commentary translates the full text of the commandment as follows: "You shall not swear falsely [*lo tisa et shem . . . lashav*] by the name of the Eternal [*YHVH*] your God; for the Eternal will not clear [*lo y'nakeh*] one who swears falsely by God's name."

The law is formulated in the second person masculine singular, but as in other commandments of the Decalogue, it applies to both men and women, and the Mishnah confirms this understanding (*Mishnah Sh'vuot* 3:11).

The Third Word deals with the misuse of God's name but is worded ambiguously. Therefore, various translations have been offered. The New Revised Standard Version has "You shall not make wrongful use of the Name." The Jerusalem Bible renders it "You shall not utter the Name to misuse it." The Catholic Study Bible has "You shall not take the name of the Lord, your God, in vain." Everett Fox prefers "You are not to take up the name of YHWH your God for emptiness." And there are those who favor "You shall not speak the name of *YHVH* to that which is false," meaning, do not identify a false god with *YHVH*.

Terminology

The problem of translation revolves around the interpretation of two key Hebrew expressions in the text: *lo tisa et shem* and *lashav*. Let us study each separately:

Lo tisa et shem means "do not lift, raise, carry a name," in the sense "do not bring upon your lips" the name of another. For example, "I will have no part of their [i.e., the idolaters] bloody libations; their [i.e., the idols'] names will not pass my lips" (Ps. 16:4). Or, "And to the wicked, God said: 'Who are you to recite My laws, and mouth [*vatisa . . . alei fikha*] the terms of My covenant?'" (Ps. 50:16). In these examples, the uttering of a god's name, either the name of another god or the name of the God of Israel, is prohibited.

On the other hand, "do not lift a name" may be a short form of saying, "do not lift up *your hand* to speak the name," a popular gesture used in swearing, as in the case of God saying, "Lo, I raise My hand to heaven and say: 'As I live forever'" (Deut. 32:40), meaning, "I swear." Similarly, the author of Daniel states, "Then I heard the man dressed in linen, who was above the water of the river, swear by the Ever-Living One as he lifted his right hand and his left to heaven" (Dan. 12:7).God's name is often invoked when a person swears, such as when Joab, King David's general, says, "As God lives" (II Sam. 2:27).

This rendition finds its support in the ancient Near Eastern practice of swearing by the name of the gods to conclude a transaction. In fact, many ancient international treaties were finalized by invoking the divine beings as guarantors of the documents. For example, the treaty between Idrimi and Pilliya (ca. 1500 BCE) ends with "Whoever transgresses this agreement, Shamash and Ishhara, and all the (other) gods will destroy him" (*ANET*, 532); in one of King Esarhaddon's vassal treaties (seventh century BCE), we find at the end, "May Nabu, who holds the tablets of fate of the gods erase your name, and make sure your descendants disappear from the land" (*ANET*, 541). Similarly, biblical books, which follow the literary pattern of the ancient Near Eastern treaty form, conclude with a list of blessings and curses, such as the ones found in Lev. 26:3–38 and Deut. 28:1–68.

In some cases in the *Tanakh*, God is invoked in an oath formulated as a self-curse. A good example is the one that Ruth utters to her mother-in-law Naomi, who wants Ruth to go back to her country and family. Ruth refuses and makes an oath, "Thus and more may the Eternal [*YHVH*] do to me if anything but death parts me from you" (Ruth 1:17). Another example is the curse that King Saul utters against his son Jonathan that almost cost his life: "Thus and more may God [*Elohim*] do [to me]: 'You shall be put to death, Jonathan!'" (I Sam. 14:44).

The question for us is whether, in the Decalogue, the prohibition of "lifting up the name" of God applies to an oath during which God's name is mentioned or simply when such name is uttered during a frivolous conversation. The analysis of the second expression, *lashav*, may shed some light on this matter.

The Hebrew word *lashav* can mean "without power" or "in vain." Examples include "The help of man is worthless [*shav*]" (Ps. 60:13), "Unless the Eternal builds the house, its builders labor in vain [*shav*]" (Ps. 127:1), and "You beautify yourself in vain [*lashav*]" (Jer. 4:30; cf. 2:30). Hence, the third commandment can be interpreted as prohibiting the use of God's name improperly or in a profane setting, and not during uttering an oath. Those who prefer this interpretation argue that if this were not the original meaning of the commandment, there would be no reason to include another commandment on bearing false witness in the Ninth Word, which deals with this very subject. Maybe the original intention of the Third Word was to make sure that no one used God's name in magic or voiced it inappropriately.

However, the expression *shav* can also mean "false," as in "You must not carry false [*shav*] rumors" (Exod. 23:1) or "Reach Your hand down from on high...from the hands of foreigners whose mouths speak lies [*shav*] and whose oaths are false [*shaker*] " (Ps. 144:7–8), where *shav* and *shaker* are used in parallel, meaning the same thing, "false." The parallelism in Psalm 24, "Who may ascend the mountain of the Eternal? . . . He who has clean hands and a pure heart, who has not taken a false oath [*lo nasa lashav*] by My life or sworn deceitfully [*nishba l'mirmah*]" (vv.3–4), clearly indicates that *lashav* can mean "deceitfully" or "false." This idea may finds its confirmation in another law (where the verb *shav* and the noun *sheker* are used together), found in the Book of Leviticus, which states, "You shall not swear [*tishav'u*] falsely [*lashaker*] by My name, profaning the name of your God" (Lev.19:12). Therefore, the original intention of the Third Word, these critics maintain, must have been to prohibit swearing falsely by God's name.

The question remains: Does our Third Word prohibit the frivolous use of God's name (i.e., "use God's name...in vain), or does it say no to swearing falsely in God's name, namely, perjury? The text is not clear and may have been left as such on purpose to cover both possibilities. My impression is that the original intention was to make sure no one uttered the name of God in magic or sorcery to manipulate the Divine into doing things in their favor. In time, this meaning was expanded to cover even the possibility of swearing falsely in God's name, which is the way it is usually interpreted in the Rabbinic tradition.

The Name—Which Name?

In the ancient Near East, the name of anything had to do with the essence of that thing. Nothing exists until it has a name. The object even comes into being by receiving a name. According to the Babylonian Creation story, *Enuma Elish*, the gods "Lahmu and Lahamu were brought forth; by name they were called" (*ANET*, 61). Similarly, in the biblical Creation story, "God called the light Day, and called the darkness Night" (Gen. 1:5). Also, God decides that "whatever the man [*haadam*] called it [each living being], that became the creature's name" (Gen. 2:19). Adam names all the animals and even his wife (Gen. 2:20–23).

During his encounter with God at the Burning Bush at Horeb, Moses asks the Eternal for God's name, arguing, "When I come to the Israelites and say to them, 'The God of your ancestors has sent me to you,' and they ask me, 'What is His name?' what shall I say to them?" (Exod. 3:13). God responds in an elliptical way: "*Ehyeh asher ehyeh*," continuing, "Thus shall you say to the Israelites, *Ehyeh* sent me to you" (Exod. 3:14). The expression *ehyeh asher ehyeh* can be translated as "I am that/who I am" or "I will be who/what I will be." How this expression is related to God's proper name in the Bible, *YHVH*, is not clear, even though *ehyeh* seems to invoke *YHVH*, both meaning something like "existence" or "being."

In the Bible, many people are named after their personality traits. Thus, for instance, the patriarch Jacob, who deceives his brother and father in his lifetime, is first named something akin to "cheater." After his twin brother, Esau, is born, we are told, Jacob "came out holding Esau's heel [*akev*], so they named him Jacob [*Yaakov*]" (Gen. 25:26), a play on the Hebrew word *akev*, which can also mean "to overreach" (Ps. 49:6), "to supplant" (Gen. 27:26), or "to cheat" (Jer. 9:3).[2] Similarly, before David becomes king, he marries Abigail, whose former husband was Nabal (in Hebrew, "foolish" or "wicked"), a rich but uncouth Calebite. The biblical text tells us that when Abigail meets David, he is angry at Nabal for having refused him supplies for his troops. So, she tells him, "Please, my lord, pay no attention to that wretched fellow Nabal. For he is just what his name says: his name means 'boor,' and he is a boor" (I Sam. 25:25).

A change of name in the Bible is often a sign of a change in status. Thus, for instance, Jacob becomes Israel after his fight with the angel (Gen. 32:29), Joseph becomes Zaphenath-paneah after becoming a high official in Pharaoh's court (Gen. 41:45), and Moses changes Hosea's name to Joshua when he sends the spies into Canaan (Num. 13:16). Similarly, Esther's name prior to becoming a queen is Hadassah (Esther 2:7).

In the Bible, *shem*, a name, also means reputation. Thus, for example, the stated goal of the builders of the Tower of Babel is "to make a name for ourselves" (Gen. 11:4). Furthermore, a fine reputation cannot be bought by money; it must be earned: "A good name is better than fragrant oil" says the Book of Ecclesiastes (7:1).

The prophets make clear that God cares for God's name and reputation: "For the sake of My name I control My wrath" (Isa. 48:9); "The House of Israel rebelled against Me in the wilderness.... Then I thought to pour out My fury upon them in the wilderness and to make an end of them; but I acted for the sake of My name, that it might not be profaned in the sight of the nations before whose eyes I had led them out" (Ezek. 20:13–14). On the other hand, when the priests bless the people, God's name becomes a blessing: "Thus they shall link My name with the People of Israel, and I will bless them" (Num. 6:27).

The Third Word prohibits the misuse of God's name. Which name does the text have in mind? As discussed earlier (see "The First Word: God"), God in Judaism is known by many names. Does the commandment wish to prohibit all the names attributed to God, or is it concerned only with one particular one?

It is the opinion of many critics today that the Third Word primarily prohibits the misuse of the proper name of God, namely *YHVH*, which is the only one mentioned in our text. But, in time, the scope of the commandment was enlarged through interpretation to cover other names as well.

In Rabbinic literature we find a tendency to avoid mentioning God's name just in case doing so leads to its desecration. Thus, we often find different ways of invoking God, by using, for example, the expression *HaShem* (the Name) or *Avinu Shebashamayim* (Our Father in Heaven). Even God's proper Name, *YHVH*, was pronounced by the Rabbis as *Adonai* (Master). (See "The First Word: God.")

Cursing and Blaspheming

To curse is to wish or pray for trouble for a person or thing. When one curses God, it is called blasphemy.

There are several verbs in Hebrew that translate as "curse," including *arar*, *kalal*, and *alah*. A person may curse another human being. Yiddish has many colorful curses, such as "May you swallow an umbrella and may it fully open in your belly" and "May you lose all your teeth except one and may that one give you a toothache." In all of these cases, the person who is uttering an imprecation is simply saying, "I don't like you; may something bad happen to you." However, in biblical times, inasmuch as God's word is deed, any invocation of the divinity in a curse would be construed as using God's name in vain; for example, "The Philistine cursed [King] David by his gods" (I Sam. 17:43).[3]

Blaspheming is speaking contemptuously about God and is the extreme form of misusing God's name. Exodus 22:27 states, "You shall not revile [*t'kaleil*] God [*Elohim*]." Leviticus 24:10–16 deals with the case of a half-Israelite, who during a fight with an another individual, pronounces a blasphemous curse against *YHVH* (*vayikov... et hashem vay'kaleil*). The text does not specify what he said, or which name of God he invoked, or why. It simply states that he blasphemed "the name" (*hashem*) (Lev. 24:11). This "name" most likely was the proper name of God, *YHVH*.

The culprit in Leviticus 24 was placed in custody, and the matter was referred to a "decision of the Eternal [*YHVH*]" (Lev. 24:12), mostly likely by means of an oracle or the use of the Urim and Thummim in Aaron's breastplate (see "Torah and Law in Judaism"). The Eternal told Moses to take the blasphemer outside of the camp, for reasons of ritual purity, and asked all the hearers to "lay their hands upon his head" (Lev. 24:14), as a way of transferring the guilt of the listeners (who heard the desecration of *YHVH*'s name) on the culprit, and finally, to let the entire community stone him. This episode leads to the formulation of the following law: "Anyone who blasphemes [*y'kaleil*] God [*Elohav*] shall bear the guilt; and one who also pronounces the name Eternal [*v'nokeiv shem YHVH*] shall be put to death" (Lev. 24:15–16). Here, it appears that the desecration happens only when God's name is pronounced, which implies that if a person invokes evil on God but does not pronounce the name of God, he is not punished by death. Thus, for example, Job's wife, seeing her husband's misery, urges him to "blaspheme God and die" (Job 2:9). Here the Hebrew word for "blaspheme" is *bareikh*, namely "bless," because the author or the scribe of this passage could not bring himself to write that a person would actually "curse" God. Job refuses and accepts his fate. According to Rabbinic law, the blasphemer (*ham'gadeif*) is not culpable unless he pronounces the Tetragrammaton and two witnesses had warned him prior to his transgression (*Mishnah Sanhedrin* 7:5). In the Talmud, Rabbi Meir extends this law even when God's attributes are invoked (BT *Sanhedrin* 56a). The law, therefore, is as follows: the one who uttered the name *YHVH* is stoned; those who have uttered God's attributes are flogged (Maimonides, *Mishneh Torah, Hilkhot Avodat Kokhavim* 2:7).

In Postbiblical Literature

In postbiblical literature, commentators understood the Third Word more widely. Philo of Alexandria argued that the prohibition covered both swearing a false oath as well as using the name frivolously (*On the Decalogue*, 84–91). Similarly, Onkelos, in his Aramaic translation of the Pentateuch, used both "in vain" and "falsely" in parallel. This is also the understanding of Umberto Cassuto, a biblical critic of the twentieth century, who interprets the commandment broadly, not only covering false oaths but also all types of profane use of God's name in magic and sorcery.[4] In general, however, Jewish tradition has tended to interpret our Third Word as prohibiting swearing falsely.

Thus, for instance, the *M'khilta* states that this command deals with what it calls *sh'vuat shav*, "swearing falsely" (*Bachodesh* 7).

Other sages, however, argued that the commandment deals primarily with the vain use of God's name and secondarily with false witnessing. Their argument is this: There are two similar laws regarding this matter, one in Lev. 19:12, which prohibits swearing falsely in God's name, and the other in our Third Word, which prohibits the use of God's name *lashav*. Given the Rabbinic rule that two commandments cannot deal with the same subject, the third commandment, they concluded, has to deal with a prohibition about frivolous oaths or even using profanity during which the name of God is invoked. Thus, for example, the *Sefer HaChinukh* (#30) refers to this commandment as involving one who *nishba l'vatalah*, namely "he swore in vain," that is, to no valid purpose. As an illustration, the author tells us that the law deals with four kinds of oaths: (a) if someone swears about something that everybody knows is not so ("a pillar of marble is made of gold"), (b) if one swears about something that everybody knows that it is so ("wood is wood"), (c) if someone swears to violate a mitzvah that is enjoined upon us, and finally, (d) if someone swears to do something that he has no power to do ("he will not sleep for three days"). In all of these cases the use of God's name is a transgression of our Third Word. Furthermore, the author includes in this prohibition not only oaths but even vows. It is only a side development of this law, he tells us, that it also covers swearing falsely, which he names "an oath of falsehood" (*sh'vuat sheker*).

Other Talmudic rabbis, interpreting the law even more broadly, stated that "whoever says a blessing that is not necessary [*she-enah tz'rikhah*] transgresses the command of "You shall not take the name of the Eternal in vain" (BT *B'rakhot* 33a). In this connection the question was raised: What is a "vain blessing or prayer"? The Talmud records a conversation between a reader and Rabbi Chanina. It appears that this prayer reader praised God by saying, among other things, that God was great, mighty, awesome, majestic, powerful, strong, fearless, and honored. Rabbi Chanina rebuked him, "Have you concluded all the praises of your Master?" The obvious answer is no. Then, Rabbi Chanina gave an example of this unnecessary list of praises: "It is as if an earthly king had a million denarii of gold, and someone praised him as possessing silver ones. Would it not be an insult to him?" (BT *B'rakhot* 33b). The Talmudic lesson seems to be that no human words can fully express the greatness of God, and piling up praises amounts to a vain prayer. In fact, according to *Midrash T'hillim*, "You have no right to add to the order (of prayers and texts drawn) by the sages (regarding praises for God)" (on Psalm 19). Shlomo Ganzfried, in his *Code of Jewish Law* (late nineteenth century), states that "great care should be taken not to utter a benediction in vain, God forbid; nor should one create for oneself an occasion over which to utter an unnecessary benediction. If by inadvertence, we do utter a benediction in vain, or we mention the name of God unnecessarily, we should thereafter say, 'Blessed be the name of God's glorious name forever and ever'" (1:6, #4).

The Mishnah, stating that "to cry over the past is a vain prayer [*t'filat shav*]" (*Mishnah B'rakhot* 9:3), gives us two illustrations. The first one: "If a man's wife is pregnant and he says, 'May [God] grant that my wife have a male child,' this is a vain prayer." Obviously, the reason is because the sex of the child has already been determined, and no amount of prayer, however fervent, will alter the course of nature. The second one: "If he is coming from a journey and he hears cries of distress in the town, and says, 'May [God] grant that this is not in my house,' this is a vain prayer." This prayer is considered vain because the matter is already in progress, and it is too late to change the course of events by any kind of prayer. Besides, it is immoral, because it implies that one is hoping that the distress may be in someone else's house. The rationale behind these teachings is that in the opinion of some sages, "one does not rely on miracles" (BT *P'sachim* 64b).

Ganzfried states that the injunction of Exod. 20:7 applies not only to the name *YHVH* but even to all other names of God, including all the attributes of God. He also says that it is prohibited to mention God's name in vain not only in Hebrew, but in all languages. He adds, "One should not mention His great name unless it is by the way of praise or blessing whenever required, or when one studies the Torah" (*Code of Jewish Law*, 1:6, #3). He would not allow the incorporation of God's name even in a written letter in the form of the French word *adieu* (meaning "to/with God").

The Preservation of God's Name in Print

It is a dominant theme in Jewish tradition that God's name is sacred and should not be destroyed. Thus, it is customary in Jewish life to bury prayer books or religious documents that carry God's name. According to Maimonides, "A scroll of Torah that has become old or unfit for use is placed in an earthen vessel and buried beside a scholar" (*Mishneh Torah, Hilkhot Sefer Torah* 10:3). The practice of preserving religious texts carrying the name of God has led to the creation of a *genizah* (short for *beit genizah*, "hiding/storing place") in some synagogues. The most famous *genizah* is the one found inside the Ezra Synagogue, in Fustat, a suburb of Cairo, Egypt, belonging to the Palestinian Rabbanite Jews. In 1897, Solomon Schechter, professor of Talmudic literature at England's Cambridge University, extracted about 140,000 items from what came to be called the Cairo Genizah and brought them to England for study. Among the manuscripts that Schechter found are the Hebrew text of Ben Sira, fragments of Aquila's Greek translation of the Bible, "The Covenant of Damascus" belonging to those Jews who lived in the Dead Sea area, ancient liturgical texts, legal documents about local Jews, and material regarding the Karaites, a Jewish sect. The study of this material opened up an entirely new field in Jewish life and cast light onto the life of Jews during medieval times. The practice of burying sacred texts continues even now in our communities. A religious service for this purpose—*Seder K'vurat Sh'mot*—is featured in the Rabbinical Assembly's (Conservative) *Rabbi's Manual*.

The Desecration of God's Printed Name

Given the fact that Jewish tradition prohibits the destruction of God's name in print, a number of responsa have dealt with some specific issues. In the Reform Movement, both Rabbis Solomon B. Freehof and Walter Jacob have answered a few queries on this subject.

In 1963, Solomon Freehof discussed the question of spelling the word "God" as "G-d" and whether this abbreviation is considered sacred. He pointed out that "the primary prohibition against erasure (by act or neglect) of the name of God applies to the sacred names in the properly written text of the Torah, and even in the Torah itself, those names of God are not sacred unless the scribe, by a specifically uttered formula, sanctifies them."[5] Moreover, he stated that "the sanctity which the law ascribes to the written name of God applies only to the name as written in the Hebrew language, in the sacred tongue." He then added that according to Rabbinic law there are seven different names of God that have the same sanctity and must be carefully preserved against erasure and neglect. They are *YHVH*, *Adonai*, *El*, *Eloah*, *Elohim*, *Shaddai*, and *Tz'vaot*. "God" is an English word and is not sacred. Therefore, he concluded, "We will continue to spell the name 'God' in full." Regrettably, at present, many people still use the unnecessary abbreviation of "G-D" and even "L—D" as if they were sacred. They are not.

In 1990, Walter Jacob was asked about the appropriate way to deal with Israeli newspapers and magazines that regularly deal with religious issues and often contain the Tetragrammaton in print, as well as what to do with photocopies used in religious schools that have the name of God. In his answer, he pointed out that in the past, "sanctity was limited to texts written by the pious Jews with sacred intent both explicitly stated or in the mind of the writer. A piece written without such intent could be erased."[6] Consequently, newspapers and magazines can be destroyed because no sacred intent was present. However, he adds, "it is a different matter when we are dealing with photocopies of Torah portions or prayer books. The text of these are educational tools that should be treated as sacred, for this too is part of the religious education of our children. They should learn appropriate respect for prayer books, Bibles and other traditional literature. When such loose pages are no longer usable they should not be discarded but either buried or incinerated if that is possible."[7]

In 1991, Walter Jacob answered a question about shredding texts of religious services and other material for children that contain the name of God. He responded by saying, "It would be appropriate to shred such texts especially if the shredding machine were able to grind the material into very narrow strips. That would totally destroy their usefulness and it would be almost akin to incineration. We should only be certain that once the text has been shredded it is not used as packing material, but recycled."[8]

The same year, Walter Jacob discussed the issue of erasing the name of God from a computer screen, and said, "The computer disk intends to make the text available for study and not for any sacred purpose. Furthermore...the recorded form is not Hebrew but binary, and it becomes Hebrew only through a transformation which takes place through the computer program....It is permissible to utilize the text on the computer and to erase it when the user has finished it."[9]

The Penalty

The Third Word does not contain a penalty clause but only a motivating rationale that includes a threat: "for the Eternal will not clear [*y'nakeh*] one who swears falsely / uses God's name in vain" (Exod. 20:7; Deut. 5:11). The reason may be because the misuse of God's name could be done in secret and therefore away from an authority figure who could then impose a penalty.

The Third Word does not have a human victim in mind. Who then is being harmed by the misuse of God's personal name? Primarily it is God, for, when people use God's name *lashav*, either "in vain" or "falsely," they undermine

God's authority and God's reputation. And that affects the covenantal bond between God and the People of Israel. John Durham goes further and argues that this commandment is there to protect not only God but also humanity at large, for "to treat Yahweh's name with disrespect is to treat his gift lightly, to underestimate his power, to scorn his Presence, and to misrepresent to the family of humankind his very nature as 'The One Who Always Is.'"[10]

So, how is the punishment applied? The biblical text says only that the culprit *lo y'nakeh*, "shall not be cleared." Various interpretations have been offered for this expression. Literally it means that God will not leave the deed unpunished (cf. Prov. 6:29)—adds Nahum Sarna, "even though it may go undetected or not actionable in a human court of law."[11] In the Rabbinic period, the severity of the penalty was softened. The *M'khilta* states that God "clears those who repent but does not clear those who do not repent" (*Bachodesh* 6). Later Rabbinic texts decreed that the penalty would be *malkot* (whiplashes). Thus, according to the Mishnah, "If [he uttered the vain oath] wantonly he is liable to whiplashes, and if unwittingly, he is exempt" (*Mishnah Sh'vuot* 3:11).

The Extended Meaning of the Third Word

Like many other commandments in the Bible, and particularly in the Decalogue, the Third Word, too, has been applied to other and much diverse situations in modern times. In his comments on this commandment, C. Matthew McMahon, using a Christian framework for his approach, gives us a list of actions that would constitute the breaking of this particular biblical command:

> We use God's name in vain... when we live hypocritically; when we use it in idle discourse, when we worship with our lips and not with our hearts; when we pray but do not believe; when we teach bad theology; when we make a promise and do not keep it; when we set God's name next to any wicked action; when we use our tongues in a way that dishonors God's name; when we make rash vows; when we grumble and gripe against God, and, finally, when we falsify a promise.[12]

For Nehama Leibowitz, writing within a Jewish context, "not only are graven images and all physical objects of sight prohibited to us as deities, but our mortal desires, too, the 'isms, slogans, ideologies, programmes and manifestos produced by the human mind. If we deify them, we take the Lord's name in vain."[13] For Joseph Telushkin, the importance of this command lies in the fact that "when a person commits an evil act, he discredits himself. But when a religious person commits an evil act in the name of God, he or she discredits God as well. And since God relies on religious people to bring knowledge of Him into the world, He pronounces this sin unpardonable."[14]

In Conclusion

The underlying assumption of the Third Word is that words have power. In the Bible, God commands and the thing comes into being: "And God said, 'Let there be light!'—and there was light" (Gen. 1:3). This idea is echoed by the Psalmist: "By the word of the Eternal the heavens were made" (Ps. 33:6). The author of Job understood the impact of words when he said, "How forceful are honest words" (6:26 [NRSV]). Well-chosen words can heal, but badly thought words can destroy another person. Avtalyon, one of the early sages in the Mishnah, is recorded as having said, "Oh wise men, be careful about your words" (*Pirkei Avot* 1:11). Similarly, there is a popular saying, "Be careful of the words you say; keep them short and sweet; you never know, from day to day, which ones you'll have to eat." Since ancient times, agreements between individuals depended on the reliability of our promises. Today, there are some business transactions, particularly among jewelers, where a word and handshake clinch the deal. We could not live peaceably in a world if we could not rely on each other's verbal utterances. And when this link is broken, our trust in that person is shattered, at times irretrievably.

We often use God's name when we invoke the highest in life and misuse it when we do so deceitfully. In the Bible, the original intention of the Third Word is obscure and perhaps irretrievable. The injunction may have been prompted by the fear that some people would use God's name in magic or sorcery by attempting to control the divinity, or in an oath or a vow that is not sincere, or even by the belief that God's sacred name was so fraught with danger that it would be better not to utter it at all. In modern times, with a wider application of the commandment, the misuse of God's name is being viewed not only as an affront to the highest we know but also to others around us who are affected by our manipulation, misjudgment, and insincere attitude.

The Fourth Word: The Sabbath

The Queen of Days

In the third century, Origen, the church father of Alexandria, reports that Celsus, a Roman Platonist philosopher of the previous generation, had made fun of the Sabbath observance among Jews and Christians, because he could not believe that God, the Master of the universe, could be tired, like a bad workman who stands in need of rest to refresh himself (*Contra Celsum*, 5:66). Jews and early Christians, however, had a very different concept of the Sabbath and considered it the Queen of Days. In this chapter we will analyze in great detail how the fourth commandment was observed in the past and how it is kept today in light of the exigencies of contemporary economic and social conditions, both in Israel and in the Diaspora.

The Text of the Fourth Word

The Fourth Word is one of the longest commandments in the Bible and appears in the Pentateuch in Exod. 20:8–11 and Deut. 5:12–15, though with a dissimilar motive clause in each instance. The translation of the text in Exodus 20 reads as follows:

> Remember [*zakhor*] the Sabbath day and keep it holy; six days you shall labor and do all your work, but the seventh day is a sabbath of the Eternal your God: you shall not do any work [*m'lakhah*]—you, your son or daughter, your male or female slave, or your cattle, or the stranger who is within your settlements—for

in six days the Eternal made heaven and earth and sea (and all that is in them) and then rested on the seventh day; therefore the Eternal blessed the Sabbath day and hallowed it.

The full version in Deuteronomy 5 is this (differences are highlighted in boldface):

> **Observe [*shamor*]** the Sabbath day and keep it holy, **as the Eternal your God has commanded you.** Six days you shall labor and do all your work, but the seventh day is a sabbath of the Eternal your God; you shall not do any work [*m'lakhah*]—you, your son or daughter, your male or female slave, **your ox or your ass,** or any of your cattle, or the stranger who is within your settlements, **so that your male and female slave may rest as you do. Remember that you were a slave in the land of Egypt and the Eternal your God freed you from there with a mighty hand and an outstretched arm; therefore the Eternal your God has commanded you to observe the Sabbath day.**

Both texts begin with an imperative absolute in the second person masculine, but the command binds both men and women. According to Jewish tradition, the two versions were uttered by God simultaneously, something that human beings cannot do (BT *Sh'vuot* 20b). The medieval commentator Ramban explains the difference between "remember" and "observe" by saying that *zakhor* ("remember") is a positive commandment, whereas *shamor* ("observe" in the sense of "do not forget") is a negative commandment (see his commentary on Exod. 20:8). In the Dead Sea Scrolls and in the Nash Papyrus, the two versions of the Decalogue appear conflated (see 4Q Deut. n 5:12–15).

Pseudo-Philo (first century CE), a book attributed to Philo of Alexandria, has a slightly different text, combining various biblical references:

> Keep the sabbath day to sanctify it. Six days do thy work, but the seventh day is the sabbath of the Lord. In it thou shall do no work, thou and all thy laborers, saving that therein ye praise the Lord in the congregation of the elders [cf. Ps. 107:32] and glorify the Mighty One in the seat of the aged. For in six days the Lord made heaven and earth, the sea and all that are in them, and all the world, the wilderness that is not inhabited, and all things that do labor, and all the order of the heaven, and God rested the seventh day. Therefore God sanctified the seventh day, because he rested therein [cf. Gen. 2:3].[1]

Biblical critics, on the other hand, see in these texts the hand of various editors at play, hence the duplication and various rationales.

The Fourth Word of the Decalogue assumes the practice of the Sabbath and does not set it up as something new. It claims that it was the end result of the formation of the world as reflected in the biblical Creation story (Gen. 2:1–3).

Origin of the Sabbath

The Sabbath (*Shabbat* in Hebrew) is one of Judaism's greatest gifts to humanity. People in the ancient Near East had nothing similar to the Jewish concept of a weekly sacred day of rest. As Nahum Sarna points out, "The Sabbath is wholly an Israelite innovation."[2] Other cultures in the past knew of a seven-day week based on the phases of the moon, but the Israelite Sabbath is not connected to the movements of celestial bodies. It stands apart. Furthermore, the origin of the word *Shabbat* is obscure. Various scholarly theories have been advanced to resolve the puzzle, with none being totally satisfactory. Some derive it from the Akkadian *shab/pattum* which corresponded to the fifteenth day of the month as a day of quieting god's heart; others argue that it comes from the Akkadian *sebutum*, meaning "the seventh day"; some claim that Moses learned about the Sabbath from Jethro, his Kenite father-in-law. The historian Josephus ridiculed the opinion of his antagonist, Apion, a Greco-Egyptian grammarian who lived in Rome, who said that after the Exodus from Egypt, "when the Jews traveled a six days' journey, they had buboes in their groin; and that on this account it was that they rested on the seventh day...for that malady of buboes in their groin was named Sabbatosia by the Egyptians" (*Against Apion*, 2:3, Whiston). It is also not clear how the noun *Shabbat* was originally connected to the verb *shavat*, meaning "to rest," or if one was actually derived from the other. At some point, however, they were viewed as related; for example, *v'shav'tah haaretz shabbat l'YHVH*, "the land shall observe a Sabbath of the Eternal" (Lev. 25:2).

In priestly writings, the Sabbath is viewed as "a holy day" (i.e., set aside for God) and the concluding phase of the world's creation (Gen. 2:1–3) as well as a perpetual memorial (*ot*, "sign") of Creation (cf. Exod. 31:13, 31:17; Ezek. 20:12, 20:20).[3] Exodus 16, which deals with the double portion of the manna received from God in the wilderness after the Exodus, refers to the day of rest as *shabbaton:* "Tomorrow is a day of rest [*shabbaton*], a holy

Sabbath [*Shabbat*] of the Lord" (Exod. 16:23). According to Nahum Sarna, the expression *shabbaton* "is an abstract form meaning 'restfulness.'"[4]

We don't know how pervasive Sabbath observance was during early biblical times. It appears that it was not so popular among the Israelites, because a number of prophets express their frustration at their contemporaries' lack of enthusiasm for the holy day of rest. Outside the Book of Genesis, which is considered a late book but containing early material, the earliest reference to the Sabbath is in the Book of Amos (eighth century BCE). The prophet voices his disappointment by stating, in his usual irony, that people cannot wait for the Sabbath to be over in order to engage in regular business: "If only the new moon [*chodesh*] were over, so that we could sell grain; the Sabbath [*v'hashabbat*], so that we could offer wheat for sale" (Amos 8:5). During the exilic period, the prophet known as Second Isaiah urged his people to pay special attention to the Sabbath: "If you refrain from trampling the Sabbath, from pursuing your affairs on My holy day; if you call the Sabbath 'delight,' the Eternal's holy day 'honored'; and if you honor it and go not your ways, nor look to your affairs, nor strike bargains—then you can seek the favor of the Eternal" (Isa. 58:13–14). Upon their return from Babylonia, Nehemiah, the governor of Judea, berated the nobles of Judah, "What evil thing is this that you are doing, profaning the Sabbath day!" (Neh. 13:17).

In spite of this criticism, Sabbath observance remained constant among Jews for many centuries, from the biblical to the modern times, as an element of their personal and communal identity. It was Ahad Ha'am (Asher Ginzberg) (1856–1927), the Russian Jewish thinker and author, who once reputedly said, "More than Jews kept the Sabbath, it was the Sabbath that preserved the People of Israel."

What Is "Work"?

The Fourth Word does not define the meaning of *m'lakhah*, "work," and its interpretation and scope have remained a major problem for centuries for all the commentators as well as those who observed the Sabbath. In the Bible, this word, coming from a presumed root *m-l-k*, means not only "work" but also the result of work. Legal biblical texts outside of the Decalogue record only two specific prohibited actions on the seventh day that constitute "work": lighting a fire, and plowing and reaping. In Exod. 35:3 we read, "You shall kindle no fire throughout your settlements on the Sabbath day." Before electricity and the invention of matches, making a fire in order to prepare food required labor. In their attempt to ease the restrictions of this law, Talmudic rabbis allowed the use of a fire lit before the Sabbath as long as it is not refueled during the sacred day. The Karaites, however, rejected this interpretation and spent the Sabbath in darkness. Plowing and reaping were also prohibited on the Sabbath, because they involved work: "Six days you shall work, but on the seventh day you shall cease from labor; you shall cease from labor even at plowing time and harvest time" (Exod. 34:21). As noted above, in the eighth century BCE, the prophet Amos includes trading as one of the Sabbath prohibitions (Amos 8:5). Among the other prohibitions, Jeremiah mentions "carrying burdens" (*masa*) on Shabbat (Jer. 17:21), and Isaiah seems to include ordinary work (Isa. 58:13).

Some narratives give us a few examples of what "work" could mean during biblical times. The first one is the case of the wood gatherer:

> Once, when the Israelites were in the wilderness, they came upon a man gathering wood on the Sabbath day. Those who found him as he was gathering wood brought him before Moses, Aaron, and the whole community. He was placed in custody, for it had not been specified what should be done to him. Then the Eternal said to Moses, "The man shall be put to death: the whole community shall pelt him with stones outside the camp." So the whole community took him outside the camp and stoned him to death—as the Eternal had commanded Moses. (*Num. 15:32–35*)

Even though the text does not specify it, it appears that the purpose of gathering wood here was to make a fire, which was forbidden on the Sabbath (Exod. 35:3). Because this action was not specifically prohibited by God, Moses did not know what to do and must have turned to God for an answer. How he obtained God's command on this subject is not stated.

The other example comes from Nehemiah, who states, "I saw men in Judah treading winepresses on the Sabbath, and others bringing heaps of grain and loading them onto asses, also wine, grapes, figs, and all sorts of goods, and bringing them into Jerusalem on the Sabbath. I admonished them there and then for selling provisions" (Neh. 13:15). Obviously by his time, these specific agricultural activities were also considered "work" and therefore prohibited.

The prohibition of gathering manna on Shabbat provides another example. Even though no specific prohibition is listed in the law, Moses commands the Israelites not to pick up the manna on Shabbat: "Six days you shall gather it [the manna]; on the seventh day, the Sabbath, there will be none" (Exod. 16:26). Collecting manna required labor.

The exact meaning of "work" remained fluid even in postbiblical times, with some people observing it more strictly than others. Among the later ones, a group of Jews, perhaps identified with the Essenes at Qumran, created a very rigid Sabbath discipline for themselves, as outlined in the text attributed to them, the Damascus Document:

> On the day of the Sabbath, no one should say a useless or stupid word. He is not to lend anything to his fellow. He is not to discuss riches or gain. He is not to speak about matters of work or of the task to be carried out on the following day.... He is not to walk more than a thousand cubits outside the city. No one is to eat on the Sabbath except what has been prepared; and from what is lost in the field, he should not eat.... He is not to send a foreigner to do what he wishes on the Sabbath day. No one is to wear dirty clothes.... No one should fast voluntarily.... No one should remove anything from the house to outside, or from outside to the house.... No one should help an animal give birth on the Sabbath day."[5]

The *Book of Jubilees*, a pseudepigraphal text, also contains a rigid interpretation of the Sabbath: "Any man who desecrates this day [the Sabbath], who lies with a woman, who says anything about work on it... or who on it draws water that he had not prepared for himself on the sixth day, or who lifts any load to bring it outside his tend or his house is to die" (50:8).

The biblical rules and regulations about the Sabbath rest covered only a few aspects of daily life. The Rabbis created a more comprehensive system about what was allowed and what was prohibited on the seventh day (see below).

The Penalty

The Fourth Word does not specify the punishment to be inflicted on anyone who disregards the command to observe the Sabbath. Neither does the Sabbath law in Exod. 34:21 nor the one in Lev. 23:3. The punishment is derived from other biblical sources, such as Exod. 31:14, which states that "one who profanes it [the Sabbath] shall be put to death" (cf. Exod. 31:15), and Exod. 35:2, "Whoever does any work on it shall be put to death." How is this penalty to be carried out? The answer comes from the example of the wood gatherer mentioned above: whoever breaks the Sabbath law is stoned to death by the whole community (Num. 15:35). It is interesting to note that the death penalty in Exod. 31:14 is accompanied by a second punishment, namely *kareit*. The nature of this type of punishment is debated among scholars. Some, like John Durham, understand it as "exclusion from the community";[6] others, like Moshe Greenberg, argue that it is "punishment by God."[7] According to the *M'khilta*, "To be cut off merely means to cease to exist [*hafsakat hanefesh*]" (*Shabbata* 1).

In many parts of the world today, not keeping the seventh day as a day of rest is punishable by law as part of the so-called "blue laws,"[8] which attempt to enforce religious standards on society. For example, in many countries where the majority of the population is Christian (e.g., Chile and Norway), the sale of alcohol is prohibited on Sunday, the Christian Sabbath (see below). In the United States, most of the blue laws have been repealed by the courts, even though in many parts of the country it is still prohibited to sell liquor on Sundays. Because Jewish courts have no power to enforce rabbinic law, Jews are not punished today for breaking the Sabbath. Yet, I would not put this to the test at Meah Shearim in Jerusalem, where some of the extremely Orthodox Jews live, who have been known to stone cars that move through their streets on the Sabbath. For most Jews today, the lack of Sabbath observance among those who take the day of rest seriously only creates a guilty feeling. How to keep the Sabbath properly continues to be a quandary for most Jews (see below).

The Rationale

The Sabbath commandment comes accompanied by two very different rationales. The one in Exodus highlights God's role in Creation: having created the universe in six days, God "rested" on the seventh day. The reasoning is *imitatio dei*, that is, just as God rested on the seventh day, so should you. However, the law also has a social component, as reflected in the same motive clause. Not only is an Israelite expected to rest, but so are his family, slaves, the resident aliens (*gerim*) living in his community, and even his animals. Thus, on the Sabbath, Creation returns to its original harmony. This rationale reflects the thinking of the priestly writers.

The command in Deuteronomy, on the other hand, is motivated by a historical reason: you must rest on the Sabbath because God redeemed the Israelites from Egypt and "freed you from there with a mighty hand and an outstretched arm" (Deut. 5:15). This historical reference reflects the style and thinking of the editor(s) of the Book of Deuteronomy, who attached it to other laws as well, like the law on releasing someone from debt slavery (15:15) or observing the Festival of Sukkot (16:12). However, unlike Exodus 20, the motive clause in Deuteronomy does not explain the origin of the Sabbath and is altogether unclear as to why the people should observe it with so many restrictions. Besides, it is not made clear how the Exodus could be related to the Sabbath. This question has elicited various interpretations. Some commentators argue that the motive clause attached to the Sabbath law in Deuteronomy makes the point that the seventh day of the week must be observed as a day of rest because God wants to remind the Israelites that they themselves were slaves in Egypt, and consequently, they, who understand the rigors of slavery, must remember with gratitude this past event and treat their own servants with kindness on the seventh day of rest. Others maintain it is God's kindness toward the Israelite slaves in Egypt as well as God's authority over them, not their own remembrance of slavery, that compels the Israelites to be kind to their servants by means of imitation of God's deeds. We do not know which of the two represents the original thinking of the legislator.

There is no need to view the rationales attached to Exodus and Deuteronomy in opposition to one another, for as Jeffrey Tigay points out, both motivations can be considered complementary: "Exodus explains the origin of the Sabbath, while Deuteronomy explains its aim and offers a motive for observing it."[9]

In Rabbinic Literature

Though the extent of Shabbat observance during early biblical times is not known, by the Rabbinic period it had already become an established institution. The Rabbis placed a high priority on the Sabbath and infused it with high values. In addition to considering the Sabbath a day of rest (*m'nuchah*), a day of sanctification (*k'dushah*), and a day of joy (*oneg*), the sages highlighted the fact that it was a "sign" of the covenant with God (cf. Exod. 31:17), a reminder of our liberation from Egypt and our commitment to freedom (*zeikher litziat Mitzrayim*), and a day of peace (*Shabbat shalom*). The Sabbath was special gift to Israel (BT *Shabbat* 10b). On this day, a Jew is spiritually transformed. The Talmud states that "on the eve of the Sabbath, God gives a person an extra soul [*n'shamah y'teirah*] (BT *Beitzah* 16a). Sabbath observance equals all the other mitzvot: "If you succeed in keeping the Sabbath,

I [God] shall account it to you as if you had kept all the commandments of the Torah" (*Sh'mot Rabbah* 25:12). The Rabbinic sages also decreed that the Sabbath should be welcomed at sundown on Friday night with candle lighting, a blessing over the wine (*Kiddush*), and a blessing over the bread (popularly called *HaMotzi*) and that it should be dismissed on Saturday night with the ceremony of *Havdalah* (meaning "separation"), with light, spices, and wine. This is still the practice today.

Regarding the institution of the Sabbath, the Rabbis had to deal with three major issues. One was philosophical: how can it be said that God, the Omnipotent, became so tired and needed to rest? Their answer is as follows:

> God allowed it to be written about Him that He created His world in six days, and rested, as it were, on the seventh. Now by the method of *kal vachomer* you must reason: If God, for whom there is no weariness, allowed it to be written that He created the world in six days and rested on the seventh, how much the more so should humans [who are prone to weariness]...must rest on the seventh day. (*M'khilta, Bachodesh 7*).

The second issue dealt with human nature: Can a human being's work ever be finished? The *M'khilta* asks, "Is it possible for a human being to do all his work in six days? It simply means, rest on the Sabbath *as if* all your work were done. Another interpretation: Rest even from the thought of labor" (*Bachodesh 7*).

The third issue was to create a more comprehensive system of dos and don'ts so that Jews would know how to behave properly on the seventh day. The Rabbis, who inherited the instructions regarding the Sabbath day from the Bible, developed a list of thirty-nine prohibited actions, which they considered as "work." They derived this list from the instructions regarding the building of the Tabernacle in the wilderness and reflect an agricultural social setting (see Exodus. 35). Here are the thirty-nine categories of prohibited actions (*avot m'lakhot*):

> Sowing; plowing; reaping; binding sheaves; threshing; winnowing; selecting; grinding; sifting; kneading; baking; shearing wool; washing wool; beating wool; dyeing wool; spinning; weaving; making two loops; weaving two threads; separating two threads; tying; untying; sewing two stitches; tearing; trapping; slaughtering; flaying; salting meat; curing hide; scraping hide; cutting hide up; writing two letters; erasing two letters; building; tearing a building down;

extinguishing a fire; kindling a fire; hitting with a hammer; taking an object from the private domain to the public, or transporting an object in the public domain. (*Mishnah Shabbat* 7:2)

In subsequent times, the practical issues of daily life led the ancient Rabbis to go beyond this list, and they developed countless rules and regulations about Sabbath observance that reflected the realities of community life and the political and social conditions of their times. Their discussions are recorded in many pages set aside for this purpose in the Talmud, codes, and responsa literature. At times, they advocated strict observance of the law. On other occasions, they gave in to the needs of their communities and became more tolerant. Thus, for example, one rabbi taught, "One may visit theaters and circuses on the Sabbath for the purpose of attending to communal needs" (BT *Shabbat* 150a), presumably to talk to civil authorities. Others taught that "one may make arrangements on the Sabbath for the betrothal of young women and for the religious instruction of a child, even for teaching of a trade" (ibid.). The rationale for both was that one is not allowed to engage in personal business on the Sabbath, but "for the affairs of heaven" (namely for the community's religious issues), these ostensibly prohibited activities are permitted (ibid.). Unlike other sectarian Jews (see above), the Rabbis allowed and even encouraged sexual relations on Shabbat between husbands and wives as part of the *oneg* (joy) of Shabbat and permitted traveling on foot during Shabbat up to two thousand cubits in any direction (*Mishnah Rosh HaShanah* 2:5). They also insisted that to save a life (*pikuach nefesh*), every Sabbath law could be ignored and offered examples such as rescuing a child from the sea, breaking apart a wall that has collapsed on a child, breaking down a door about to close on an infant, and extinguishing a fire (BT *Yoma* 84b). Thus, Rabbi Shimon ben Menasya says, "[It is written:] 'And the children of Israel will observe Shabbat.' The Torah is saying that you may desecrate one Shabbat for a person so that he will be able to observe many Shabbatot" (ibid.; cf. Mark 2:27). In more recent times, the rule of breaking the Sabbath for *pikuach nefesh* has been extended to include contemporary needs, such as calling up an ambulance to help a person who needs medical care, or even to anticipate a threat to a person's life as in the case of machines in an intensive care unit that could break and cause the death of a patient.[10] In these and other similar cases, one is not only permitted but is obligated to break the Sabbath rule (see *Shulchan Arukh, Orach Chayim* 328:2). In creating these rules and regulations about Sabbath observance, the sages tried to connect them with biblical laws, because they believed them to have originated at Mount Sinai, although even they had to acknowledge that these numerous Rabbinic injunctions stood "like mountains hanging by a hair" (*Mishnah Chagigah* 1:8), namely, with little support from the biblical text.

In more recent times, the effort to respond to new emerging situations has led rabbis to come up with newer rules, some stricter than others. For example, in light of the biblical law that prohibits the use of fire on Shabbat, some contemporary rabbis, who identify "fire" with "electricity," prohibit turning on and off all electric devices on the Sabbath. Others, especially more liberal rabbis, arguing that turning on a light is akin to tying a temporary knot, which is allowed by Rabbinic law, permit using electricity on Shabbat. However, even some liberal rabbis prohibit shaving, doing the laundry, or cooking on the Sabbath. And many of them would agree that "a person's gainful occupation is classified as work and should not be engaged in on Shabbat."[11]

From Saturday to Sunday

Shabbat has been observed by Jews for millennia from sundown on Friday until sundown on Saturday, but most Christians celebrate the Sabbath not on Saturday but on Sunday. According to the *Catechism of the Catholic Church*, "The sabbath, which represented the completion of the first creation, has been replaced by Sunday which recalls the new creation inaugurated by the Resurrection of Christ."[12] How did this change take place, and when?

In his critical article on this subject, Samuele Bacchiocchi argues that the change from Saturday to Sunday occurred after Bar Kokhba's rebellion against the Romans in 135 CE and originated not in Jerusalem, but in Rome.[13] The early Christians followed the Jewish pattern of observing the Sabbath on the seventh day, Saturday. Even when Christians gathered for prayers on Sunday, the day Jesus was allegedly resurrected, the Sabbath remained a holy day for them. In fact, the Nazarenes, a Jewish-Christian group in Judea, kept this practice until the fourth century. When Bar Kokhba's rebellion failed, the Jerusalem church lost its prestige in favor of the Roman church. Slowly a theology of separation developed, and the Sabbath began to be viewed as a day of darkness, a day of sorrow for Jesus's death. Sunday was chosen by Christians in Rome to replace Saturday because "sun worship" took place on Sunday among the adherents of Mithraism, the official religion of Rome. Sunday was finally legalized as the Christian holy day when the emperor Constantine issued a decree in 321 CE asking that townspeople set aside Sunday as "the venerable day of the sun."

As Christianity moved west, the early settlers in America included both Sunday observers, like the Puritans who landed in Plymouth, Massachusetts, in 1620, as well as Sabbath keepers like the Seventh Day Baptists who established their first church in Newport, Rhode Island, in 1671. However, when the Puritans mentioned the word "Sabbath," they meant Sunday, and they passed strict rules (e.g., the so-called Blue Laws of Connecticut in the 1650s) enforcing the observance of the "Sabbath" from sunset on Saturday to sunset of Sunday. Today, even though some Protestants (like the Seventh Day Adventists) keep the Sabbath on Saturday, most Christians around the world observe the "Sabbath" on Sunday. The *Catechism of the Catholic Church* gives broad guidelines on how to keep this special day:

> On Sundays and other holy days of obligation, the faithful are to refrain from engaging in work or activities that hinder the worship owed to God, the joy proper to the Lord's Day, the performance of the works of mercy, and the appropriate relaxation of mind and body. Family needs or important social service can legitimately excuse from the obligation of Sunday rest. The faithful should see to it that legitimate excuses do not lead to habits prejudicial to religion, family life, and health.[14]

When Reform Judaism was first established in Europe in the early nineteenth century, the question of Sabbath observance was extensively discussed by liberal rabbis, because they realized that the Sabbath was in conflict with civic life. Whereas some, like Rabbi Samuel Adler, argued that the Sabbath needed to be protected, others, like Rabbi Samuel Holdheim, maintained that it could be transferred to Sunday, using not the Sabbath liturgy but the daily service in the prayer book. Many observant Jewish immigrants who arrived in North America in large numbers in the late 1800s and early 1900s felt the pressure to work on the Sabbath in order to support their families, and felt guilty doing so. Other Jews adopted the local custom and began to rest on Sunday like the rest of the population, until this practice progressively lost its attractiveness and Sabbath services were slowly restored.[15]

Sabbath in Modern Times

The observance of the Sabbath continues to be problematic in modern times, because what was once considered "work" is no longer viewed as "labor" today. Besides, living in a non-Jewish milieu where Sabbath is often an ordinary working day or a day set aside for shopping, going for medical care, or even playing sports, it is becoming more and more difficult to observe the Sabbath as the early Rabbis ordained or as some of the Orthodox rabbis of our time demand. So, many Jews ignore all the Sabbath requirements, and many others, who do care for the Sabbath, are compelled to resort to a new definition of "work," by finding loopholes in the law in order to carry on certain activities without a sense of guilt. The responsa literature has played a great role in today's Sabbath observance by clarifying what is appropriate on the Sabbath and what is not.

Almost everyone agrees that the Sabbath day ought to be set aside as a special day dedicated to the enhancement of the spirit, but how to achieve this goal remains controversial. The main issue today is how to define "work" in the twenty-first century. Abraham Chill (1912–2004), an Orthodox rabbi, defines "work" as follows: "The biblical concept of *m'lakhah* applies to work involving the production, creation, or transformation of an object. One may spend the entire Sabbath opening and closing books until one drops with exhaustion and yet not violate the Sabbath. On the other hand, the mere striking of a match, just once, is a desecration of the Sabbath because it involves creation."[16] Among the more liberal thinkers, Erich Fromm, a Jewish psychoanalyst as well as a teacher of Judaism, argues that today "work is any interference by man, be it constructive or destructive, with the physical world. Rest is a state of peace between man and nature.... The Sabbath is the day of complete harmony between man and nature."[17] *Gates of the Seasons*, a Reform Jewish publication, states, that "certain activities which some do to earn a living, others do for relaxation or to express their creativity. Clearly, though, one should avoid one's normal occupation or profession on Shabbat whenever possible and engage only in those types of activities which enhance the *oneg* (joy), *m'nuchah* (rest), and *k'dushah* (holiness) of the day."[18]

However, how to accomplish this goal is far from clear. Some liberal Jews take upon themselves certain restrictions on the Sabbath, for example, not doing the laundry, not doing housecleaning, or not going shopping. Others take a different approach and prefer to do special activities, such as attending a cultural program, driving to see family and friends, or taking a hike in the park or the woods.

Since the creation of the State of Israel in 1948, the Sabbath there is considered a day of rest; government offices and schools are closed, and buses do not run. But many Israelis, too, feel the tension between Sabbath observance and secular life and try to accommodate both. For example, on Shabbat, while some flock to synagogues and meticulously observe the day, many others live a normal secular life: they use the phone, watch TV, drive, go to the beaches, attend soccer games, eat at (nonkosher) restaurants or bars; airlines (except for El-Al) fly in and out of the country, and the airports function as always. Sunday, on the other hand, is a regular workday.

Jews are not the only ones who are trying to keep the Sabbath properly. Some observant Christians, too, like the Seventh-Day Adventists, find ways to observe it in their own fashion, and others, who observe it on Sunday, restrict their daily routine. Here is an interesting example: Chick-fil-A, a restaurant chain in the United States, carries on its web page the following statement: "Our founder, Truett Cathy, made the decision to close on Sundays in 1946 when he opened his first restaurant in Hapeville, Georgia. He has often shared that his decision was as much practical as spiritual. He believes that all franchised Chick-fil-A Operators and their Restaurant employees should have an opportunity to rest, spend time with family and friends, and worship if they choose to do so. That's why all Chick-fil-A Restaurants are closed on Sundays. It's part of our recipe for success." Similarly, when I was the president of the Needham (Massachusetts) Clergy Association in years past, we, both Jewish and non-Jewish clergy, did our best to pressure coaches and athletic leaders not to schedule games on Saturday and Sunday mornings, which would inevitably conflict with religious services in synagogues and churches. We were, however, not always successful.

From the Responsa Literature

Many observant Jews who need to know about the proper behavior on the Sabbath often send their questions to prominent rabbis in order to get practical answers. Consequently, numerous responsa have been issued to clarify what "work" could mean today. Some are more liberal than others.

Monique Susskind and Diana Villa, both Conservative rabbis, deal with a variety of ordinary Sabbath questions on the web page of the Schechter

Institutes' "Ask the Rabbi" section. Responding to whether driving on Shabbat with a non-Jewish driver is permissible (September 2010), they write, "A Jew should not ride on a bus driven by a Jew. To ride on a bus driven by a non-Jew is OK if the non-Jew does not drive the bus specifically for the Jew. In other words, if the driver drives knowingly for a Jew, it is a transgression for the Jew to ride in this car or bus. For example, you cannot take a cab on Shabbat, even if the driver is not Jewish, because he would drive specially for you."[19]

About the permissibility to use musical instruments on Shabbat (October 2009), they comment, "Jewish Law permits a Jew to ask a non-Jew to do work that falls under the category of rabbinical prohibitions, for the sake of fulfilling a *mitzvah* [a commandment] (*Shulchan Arukh, Orach Chayim* 307:5). For example, one can ask a non-Jew to play an instrument on Shabbat for the sake of rejoicing with the bride and groom (see *Shulchan Arukh*, ibid. 338:2). In the case of playing music in the synagogue on Shabbat, one could claim that it is allowed to ask a non-Jew to play, for the sake of enhancing the Shabbat prayers."[20]

To the question of whether a person may speak on the phone during Shabbat, they answer, "The fact that a non-Jew lifts the receiver (and will put it down) does not allow the Jew to speak on Shabbat, unless there is an emergency. In an emergency, one is allowed to ask the help of a non-Jew. If it is a matter of life and death, then a Jew can use the phone on Shabbat. Lastly, in my humble view, the spirit of the Shabbat is not well respected if one watches television (with or without a timer) or one speaks on the phone like they would on every other day in the week. Shabbat should be a day of rest, and of well being, cut off a little from the rush of the world. A day of introspection, dedicated to G-d, family and friends."[21]

Most Reform Rabbis do not object to driving on the Sabbath, watching TV, or using the telephone. They, too, have dealt with questions involving Sabbath observance from their theological perspective. Here are a few examples taken from Reform Jewish responsa.

To the question if whether men may light the Sabbath candles (1960), Rabbi Solomon B. Freehof responds, "Both men and women are enjoined to make sure that the lights are kindled. The primary duty rests upon the woman. Nevertheless, travelers and students are expected to light the lights in their lodging places. The law, then, is that both sexes share in the obligation to be sure the lights are lit. The woman should light them, but if she is ill the man may do so; or, if the man is away from home he must light them where he lodges."[22]

Another question deals with the issue of a wedding taking place on Saturday before dark (1963). Freehof answers, "On the rare occasion in which, due to an error with daylight saving time, it is not quite dark when the hour set for the marriage comes, it would be wise to delay as long as is possible. Then, if it is not absolutely dark when we officiate, it is not too great a crime."[23]

As to sports and games during the Sabbath (1952), another Reform responder, Israel Bettan, writes, "In an age like ours, when we have come to view sports and games of all sorts as proper forms of relaxation on rest days, to hark back to the puritanic rigors of the rabbinic Sabbath is to call in question the relevancy of religion to modern life."[24]

Regarding blowing the shofar on Shabbat (1923), Jacob Lauterbach responds, "The Babylonian Gemara (*Rosh HaShanah* 29b) declares that blowing of the shofar is an art but not work, and, hence, by biblical law, is permitted on Saturday, but that Rabbinical law prohibits it on Saturday lest it might happen that the one who is to perform the ceremony would wish to go to an expert in order to practice, which act (that is the carrying of it) is prohibited on the Sabbath)." Hence, he concludes, "There is no reason why the shofar should not be blown on a Rosh HaShanah which falls on a Saturday in congregations where only one day of Rosh HaShanah is observed."[25]

Is fundraising on Shabbat acceptable (1990)? To this question, Walter Jacob answers, "There is ample time during the week for business discussions of all kinds. The necessity of holding such a meeting [of temple leaders] on Shabbat either before or after services has been eliminated. It would be permissible to conduct such meetings during emergencies, but this should not become a regular habit of the congregational officers."[26]

Sabbath as a Day of Sanctification

Observing the Sabbath in our time requires a personal commitment. It is much easier to observe in the State of Israel, where it is the official day of rest. There, beginning with Friday afternoon, the whole country seems to slow down into a quiet mood, until it returns to normal life on Saturday night. In the Diaspora, living in a non-Jewish environment, which does not ascribe to the seventh day of the week a sense of sanctity, a committed Jew must set aside the Sabbath because of a personal decision, working against the trend of modern life. That is not easy.

Jewish thinkers have advanced views to highlight the special values of the Sabbath for us. Abraham J. Heschel spoke of the Sabbath as a day when we celebrate time rather than space: "Six days a week we live under the tyranny of things of space; on the Sabbath we try to become attuned to holiness in time. It is a day on which we are called upon to share what is eternal in time, to turn from the results of creation to the mystery of creation; from the world of creation to the creation of the world."[27] Lawrence A. Hoffman maintains that "Shabbat rest is the end, not the means.... Instead of the Shabbat existing so that Israel, who sanctifies God's name, can rest, the Sabbath provides rest itself (along with peace, joy, and comfort) so that God's name is hallowed. Sanctification has replaced rest as the goal of Shabbat."[28] In an undated note in my files titled "A Decalogue of Decency for Our Age," a text adapted from Maurice N. Eisendrath (1902–1973), the former president of the Union of American Hebrew Congregations (today called Union for Reform Judaism). The anonymous writer says this about the Sabbath: *"Remember the Sabbath Day to Keep it Holy*—in order that through decent leisure, men may feel again their dignity as children of God, that they may no longer feel, as many do today, to be mere machines and tools, motes of dust on a vast conveyer belt, slots in an IBM calculator."

In Conclusion

Given the fact that "work" today means something very different than in the past, a modern Jew needs to turn the Sabbath into a special day, a "sacred day," a day unlike any other during the week, by consciously stepping back in order to gain a new perspective on his or her life. Writes Mordecai Kaplan, "The Sabbath represents those moments when we pause in our brush-work to renew our vision."[29] If the ultimate purpose of the Sabbath is to help us become more human and engaged in the issues of the spirit, then each individual Jew who is looking for purpose and meaning in his or her life must decide, from among the numerous rabbinic rules, which activities on the Sabbath enhance this role and which ones stand in the way. This will make the Sabbath observance more personal and authentic. And Jews who feel the same way will tend to gravitate toward one another, thus establishing a community that shares values and activities. As Jews, we are committed to the idea of the Sabbath and, therefore, must create newer structures that will enable us to pursue peace among one another, develop personal growth through study and meditation, and enhance the sense of joy and contentment as human beings who are grateful for being among God's creations.

The Fifth Word: Honoring Parents

Depending on Each Other

Children love their parents because they provide food, shelter, and protection. During the first years of their lives, babies depend on their parents for everything they need. But slowly, children learn how to become self-sufficient and progressively assert their individuality and independence. They learn how to feed and dress themselves and how to spend time alone or with their friends. As they become older, they mature and begin to move away. In the path of life, we gain, we lose, and we grow. As Judith Viorst points out, "These losses are a part of life—universal, unavoidable, inexorable. And these losses are necessary because we grow by losing and leaving and letting go."[1] But the bond between the generations usually continues to remain strong, even if, at times, it suffers some tension because of different emotional, social, and economic needs that emerge as parents and children grow older.

The Fifth Word deals with the vital relationship between the generations, including the responsibilities, both financial and moral, of the young regarding the old and the limit of their mutual obligations. In our time, these matters have become more complicated for a number of reasons. Today we define "family" much wider than a traditional model of a husband and wife with their own children. Presently a "family" includes stepparents, adoptive children, gay and lesbian partners, and so on. Given medical advances, people are now living much longer than before, and the responsibility of being a caregiver devolves not only on the children toward their elderly parents but often vis-à-vis their own offspring. The greater geographical distances that at times separate children from parents make it at times more difficult to carry out the intent of the Fifth Word. Consequently, the application of the mitzvah of "honoring the parents" has a wider focus and brings along new social and moral problems with which children of all ages need to grapple.

Let us start with the analysis of the wording of the commandment as it appears in the Bible, try to understand how it was interpreted through the centuries, and finally, look at how it can be implemented today.

The Text of the Fifth Word

The fifth commandment, one of the two positive ones in the Decalogue, is a bridge between what the Rabbis called commandments "between humanity and God" (*bein adam LaMakom*) and those "between one human being and another" (*bein adam lachaveiro*).

The translation of the Fifth Word in Exodus reads as follows:

Honor [*kabeid*] your father and your mother, that you may long endure on the land that the Eternal your God is assigning to you." (*Exod. 20:12*)

The parallel text in Deuteronomy is slightly different:

Honor your father and your mother, **as the Eternal your God has commanded you,** that you may long endure, **and that you may fare well,** in the land that the Eternal your God is assigning to you." (*Deut. 5:16*)

The boldface phrases represent two small additions to the text in Exodus. It is interesting to note that in the Septuagint, these extra phrases appear both in Exodus and in Deuteronomy. The Fifth Word contains a motivating clause in the form of a hope for a long life to encourage compliance. In context, the reference to "the land that the Eternal your God is assigning you" is the Land of Israel.

In postbiblical times, there are clear references to our Fifth Word in the writings of the Jewish historian Josephus (first century CE; *Ant.* III, 5:5) and Philo of Alexandria (first century CE; *Decalogue*, 106–7), but the longest paraphrase appears in Pseudo-Philo, a Jewish chronicle attributed to Philo, which was composed around the second century CE and preserved in Latin: "You shall love [*dilige*] your father and mother and fear them: and then shall your light shine, and I will command the heaven and it shall give you rain, and the earth shall hasten her fruit and your days shall be many, and you shall dwell in your land, and shall not be childless, for your seed shall not fail, and those who dwell in it" (9:9). It is noteworthy that Pseudo-Philo appears to widen the meaning of the commandment by asking that children not only "honor" their parents but also "love" them (see below for discussion).[2] In the Apocrypha, Ben Sira (second century BCE) equates the honor due a parent with the honor due to God: "Whoever glorifies his father will have long life, and whoever obeys the Lord will refresh his mother; he will serve his parents as his masters" (3:7 [RSV]; see below, *M'khilta, Bachodesh* 8; cf. BT *Kiddushin* 31b).

Kabeid, "You Shall Honor"—Who Is "You"?

Even though *kabeid* ("you shall honor") is in the imperative, second person masculine singular and could, therefore, imply that the obligation to honor a parent is placed only on sons, it is assumed that like other commandments in the Decalogue, women too are bound by this law, just as they are not to murder or commit adultery. The Rabbis are quick to specify that "all obligations of a son toward his father enjoined in the Torah are incumbent on both men and women" (*Mishnah Kiddushin* 1:7; *M'khilta, Bachodesh* 8). This means that both men and women are commanded to carry out this non-time-bound mitzvah of (in Rabbinic language) *kibud av va-eim*, honoring the father and mother.

Who is likely to be addressed in this Fifth Word? A young child or an adult? Some would argue that the commandment to honor the parents is incumbent upon everyone, young and old. However, it would make more sense if this command were to be addressed primarily to an older person who is taking care of an aging parent. As James F. Keenan rightfully points out, "The best way young children can honor parents is by being obedient. But for the remaining forty or fifty years, we as adults need to honor our parent."[3] Martin Noth (1902–1968), a biblical scholar, states that this commandment "does not apply to children who stand under the *patria potestas* [Latin for "power of the father," namely, the power that a father exercises within the family] but to adults who themselves exert the *patria potestas* and are to show due honor to their aging parents."[4] John I. Durham also points out that in this commandment "the focus is upon those who are responsible and 'in charge,'"[5] namely, an adult person. This idea finds additional support in the documents of adoption of children that were discovered in ancient Nuzi, the Hurrian capital at Kirkuk, modern Iraq (fifteenth to fourteenth century BCE), where the main purpose of adoption was to provide support for parents during old age. Respect for elderly parents is highlighted in Proverbs: "Listen to your father who begot you; do not disdain your mother when she is old" (23:22). Similarly, in *The Instructions of Ben Sira*, the master teaches, "O son, help your father in his old age, and do not grieve him as long as he lives" (3:12).

The Context of the Law

In the biblical world, respect for parents was highly valued. According to the Book of Proverbs, "A wise son brings joy to his father; a dull son is his mother's sorrow" (10:1). The prophet Malachi states as a matter of course, "A son should honor his father" (Mal. 1:6). Honoring parents was part of the biblical ethos that expected deference toward one's elders, parents or not. Thus, Leviticus ordains, "You shall rise before the aged and show deference to the old [*zakein*]" (Lev. 19:32). Even though one Talmudic source states that here *zakein* means one who has acquired wisdom (BT *Kiddushin* 32b), another sage taught that any old person deserves this honor (ibid., 33a), and the law is according to the latter. In ancient Egypt, the respect due parents extended even beyond the grave, and dead relatives were often worshiped.

Parents and elders have life experience. Even if they are not knowledgeable individuals, they have learned how to handle difficult situations in their daily life by experience. They have acquired practical wisdom through interaction with others. Therefore the older generation is a source of information and, consequently, an object of reverence. It is in the context of this respect due the elderly that the commandment of honoring the parents must be viewed and understood. Cornelis Houtman highlights this nuance better when he translates our commandment as "Treat your father and mother with respect."[6]

Why should parents be honored or respected? Because they brought us into the world, for which we must express gratitude. In Rabbinic literature, parents are considered as co-partners with God in the miraculous birth of a child: "Three parties are involved in the creation of a human being: God, the father, and the mother" (BT *Kiddushin* 31b). Thus, respect for a parent is equated with the reverence due God: "When a person honors his father and mother, the Holy One says, 'I account it to them as though I were dwelling among them, and they were honoring Me'" (ibid.; cf. *M'khilta, Bachodesh* 8). Parents are representatives of God.

As people get old, their energy declines, and they become more and more dependent on others. This creates for them existential frustration and fear. They start to worry, "Who will take care of me now?" The Psalmist voices this concern when he movingly turns to God and states, "Do not cast me off in old age; when my strength fails, do not forsake me!" (Ps. 71:9). In the majority of cases, children take good care of their parents, but even in ancient times some children lacked respect for their parents and are condemned for this unseemly behavior. One of the worst cases of being an evil son is provided by the Aramaic "Story of Ahikar," a counselor of an Assyrian king. Ahikar adopts his nephew, Danin, but instead of showing gratitude for this generous action, Danin frames his uncle by issuing fraudulent letters and causing him untold problems.[7] In the Bible, too, we find a few examples of mistreatment of parents. For example, Noah's son, Ham, fails to show reverence for his father when he tells his brothers about the nakedness of their father (Gen. 9:22). Jacob misleads his father, Isaac, in order to obtain a blessing due his brother, Esau (Gen. 27:19). Reuben, Jacob's son, sleeps with his father's concubine, and his father finds out (Gen. 35:22; cf. 49:4). Both Absalom (II Samuel 15) and Adonijah (I Kings 1:5ff.) rebel against their father, David, during David's lifetime. The prophet Isaiah assumes as a given that children respect their parents but finds troublesome that some may rebel against them (Isa. 1:2). The prophet Micah says that social disintegration occurs when "son spurns father, daughter rises up against mother" (Mic. 7:6). Hence, the death penalty is imposed upon those who insult their parents (Exod. 21:17). This also explains the need to formulate a commandment, our fifth, urging children to show *kavod* (respect) to their parents, especially when they are old and cannot fend for themselves.

"Your Father and Your Mother"—Who Are They?

It is noteworthy that in the Bible, in spite of its patriarchal background, the obligation to honor a parent is applied not only to the father but also to the mother: "Honor your father and your mother" (Exod. 20:12; Deut. 5:16). Though in ancient times fathers were usually held in higher esteem, the Bible clearly states that mothers are to be honored equally: "You shall each revere [*tira-u*] your mother and your father" (Lev. 19:3), where mother is even placed first. The word "revere" (from the Hebrew root *y-r-'*) here literally means "to stand in awe of."

In Rabbinic literature, the father seems to be given precedence over the mother. Thus, we read in the Talmud: "A widow's son asked Rabbi Eliezer: 'If my father had ordered, 'Give me a drink of water,' and my mother did likewise, which takes precedence? [Rabbi Eliezer answered,] 'Leave your mother's honor and fulfill the honor of your father'" (BT Kiddushin 31a). The *M'khilta* puts forward another suggestion about the precedence given a father: "A man honors his mother more than his father because she sways him with persuasive words. Therefore in the commandment to honor, He [i.e., God] mentions the father before the mother" (*Bachodesh* 8). But not in the Decalogue. Mother and father are placed in the same category.

In Rabbinic literature, the responsibility of honoring a parent is extended to cover not only the biological father or mother, but also the stepparents and in-laws (*Shulchan Arukh, Yoreh Dei-ah* 240:21, 240:24). This honor is further extended beyond the grave: When mentioning their name within twelve months after their departure, one says, "I am an atonement in his [or her] place." After this period, one says, "May his [or her] memory be a blessing in the life of the world-to-come" (see BT *Kiddushin* 31b).

The Fifth Word seems to have in mind only biological parents, who gave birth to a child and nourished him or her throughout the years. What about adoptive parents? The custom of adopting children was prevalent in the ancient Near East, which had even devised special formulas to be used in such legal documents (such as in Nuzi; see above). It is surprising that the Bible does not contain any adoption document. However, it does include language reflective of the adoption practice, such as "You are my son, I have fathered you this day" (Ps. 2:7) and "Mordecai adopted [lit. "took"] her [Esther] as his own daughter" (Esther 2:7).

Are adopted children obligated to honor their adoptive parents according to Jewish law? The case is not at all clear. There is no law, biblical or Rabbinic, that obligates an adopted child to honor his or her adoptive parents. Yet, many commentators, citing the Talmud, "Whoever raises an orphaned boy or girl in his home is viewed by the Torah as if he himself had brought the child into the world" (BT *M'gillah* 13a), and extending the meaning of the Fifth Word in our time, argue that adopted children should view "their adoptive parents as their natural parents and treat them in precisely the same way as biological children treat their parents."[8]

The Concept of "Honoring"

In the Bible, the verb *kabeid*, "to honor," literally means to "give weight," "to give importance," "to reward and make rich." The word *kaveid*, which derives from the same root, *k-b-d*, means "heavy," like a burden (cf. Ps. 38:5). *Kaveid* also means "liver," considered to be one of heaviest of the viscera, and the seat of emotions in the Bible. *Kavod*, from the same root, means "abundance," "honor," or "glory," including God's glory (i.e., God's weightiness). Thus, about the prophet Samuel the text says *ish nikhbad*, "the man is highly esteemed" (I Sam. 9:6). Balak, the king of Moab, tells the pagan prophet Balaam that if he helps him out against the Israelites, *kaveid akhabedkha*, "I will reward you richly" (Num. 22:17). The prophet Malachi reminds his listeners that "a son should honor [*y'khabeid*] his father" (Mal. 1:6). God's name is *nikhbad v'nora*, "honored and awesome" (Deut. 28:58). When Moses ascends Mount Sinai, the Bible tells us, "The Presence [*k'vod*, lit. "glory," "heaviness"] of the Eternal abode on Mount Sinai" (Exod. 24:16).

In the past, expectations of and laws regarding respect for parents and those in position of authority appear to have been much stricter. In Roman law, a father had absolute power over his children, including their property and person, and demanded total obedience. In the ancient Near Eastern patriarchal societies, the father was an authoritarian figure in his household, whose words were often definite and final.

The Bible does not give us many examples of how a child is expected to honor a parent. In the Book of Genesis, Shem and Japheth, two brothers, reportedly take a coat and, out of respect for their father Noah, walk backwards to cover the nakedness of their father who has gotten drunk (9:23). Joseph leaves Egypt on a short trip to give his father, Jacob, a proper burial in the Cave of Makhpelah (Gen. 50:13). The Book of Proverbs states that a child is expected to pay attention to the parents' advice: "Heed the discipline of your father, and do not forsake the instruction of your mother" (1:8). It also warns against "the eye that mocks a father and disdains the homage due a mother" (30:17). Ben Sira tells us that one must honor parents with word and deed (3:8), to show forbearance if they lack knowledge (3:13), and not to forsake or anger them (3:16). Thus, it is not enough to show respect by saying the right word. Loving deeds are also necessary.

In the Rabbinic literature, the ancient Sages provide us with a number of examples of honoring the parents, though they may appear to us as highly exaggerated. Here are two stories about a non-Jew who greatly honored his father and mother during the Roman period:

> Go forth and see what a certain heathen, Dama son Nethinah, did in Ashkelon. The Sages once desired merchandise from him, in which there was six hundred thousand [gold denarii] profit, but the key was lying under his father, and so he did not trouble him. (*BT* Kiddushin *31a*)

> He [Dama] was once wearing a gold embroidered silken cord and sitting among Roman nobles, when his mother came, tore it off from him, struck him on the head, and spat in his face, yet he did not shame her. (*Ibid*).

Here is a story about Rabbi Tarfon: "When his mother needed to go to bed, he [Tarfon] would bend down to let her ascend [the bed]" (BT *Kiddushin* 31b). And one about Rabbi Yosef: "When he [Yosef] heard his mother's footsteps, he would say, 'I will arise before the approaching *Shekhinah* [Divine Presence]'" (*ibid*).

Noting that the Bible mentions both "honoring" (*kibud*) and "revering" or "standing in awe" (*yira*) before a parent, the Rabbis give us some specific directions as to how this commandment should be carried out. Thus, according to the Babylonian Talmud, "*mora* [reverence/respect] means that a son should not stand or sit in his father's place; he should not contradict his [the father's] words, and [when his father argues with another person] he [the son] should not take it upon himself to tip the scales against him. *Kavod* [honor], on the other hand, means that a son should provide his father with food and drink, with clothes and garments, and should assist him as he enters and leaves a room" (BT *Kiddushin* 31b).

Some commentators take these Rabbinic teachings literally, while others widen their meaning. The *Shulchan Arukh* suggests that "not sitting in his place" would include not taking the regular seat the father uses in the synagogue or at home and not becoming part of his social circle; "not contradicting the father [or the mother]" would imply that the son or daughter must be respectful of the parent in case he or she has a disagreement with someone else on a specific topic (*Shulchan Arukh, Yoreh Dei-ah* 240:1). According to Rashi, if a parent has a disagreement with another person, the child must not side with the opponent (see his comment on *Kiddushin* 31b). Similarly, children should not rush to judgment of their parents but, on the contrary, be tolerant of them: "Jewish children should be taught to feel: 'Have my parents had the opportunities in life that they have given me?'"[9]

According to biblical and Rabbinic teachings, children are obligated to feed and clothe their parents and emotionally support them with good cheer. We have a good example of this in the Rabbinic literature. According to Rabbi Avimi, "One may give one's father pheasants as food, yet drives himself away from the world, whereas another child may make him grind in a mill and still brings him to the world to come" (BT *Kiddushin* 31a–b). In other words, according to Jewish law, children who provide their parents with delicious food but do so with ill grace incur divine punishment. Parents need to be shown deference because of their status. In practical terms, that would mean watching our language when we talk to them. For example, don't address them, "Hey, you," or, worse, curse them. We must be respectful in our dealings with our mothers and fathers and treat them graciously, even patiently. In general, caring for the parents requires great sensitivity and tact. As Richard E. Address reminds us, the Jewish tradition cautions us not "to take away their sense of self-respect, almost infantilizing them, making them feel totally dependent on us."[10]

Today adult children very often feel responsible to care not only for their parents but also for other family members, such as a spouse, a sibling, an in-law, a child, even a friend. Address calls our generation a "club sandwich generation,"[11] because many of us look after our parents as well as our own children at the same time. Often, because of distances, the responsibility of taking care of another person necessarily falls upon a good friend or a compassionate individual who happens to be close by. When my parents were alive in Philadelphia, with my brother at his daily work and me in Boston, our family depended on the goodwill of my sister-in-law who lived nearby for taking care of our parents' daily needs. Similarly, when my Argentinian mother-in-law moved to the Greater Boston area, my wife took care of her until her last moment, while my brother-in-law in Buenos Aires could only visit her once in a while but called her up regularly, and luckily was present when she breathed her last.

Honor and Love

As noted above, in the Fifth Word, the Bible expects a child to "honor" (*kabeid*) his or her parents, not necessarily to "love" or "obey" them. This implies that children do not necessarily have to "love" or even "like" their parents as long as they "honor" them. Often, however, the two go together. What is the difference between "love" and "honor"?

It is difficult to define "love" in a comprehensive manner, because it is such a complex idea. Throughout history, poets and writers have attempted to describe different aspects of it without fully covering the whole scope. To say that love is an intense feeling of deep affection for another person is only partially true. Love must not only be felt in the heart but must also be demonstrated in concrete acts. Thus, Erich Fromm defines love as "the active concern for the life and the growth of that which we love."[12] Furthermore, love is experienced differently by children and adults, by people of different cultures, and by modern human beings are opposed to people in ancient times.

The Bible is clear: you must honor your parents. As Maimonides points out in one of his letters to Obadiah, the proselyte, "it is possible for a person to honor, hold in awe and obey one whom one does not love."[13] So, what are we to do? Leonard Fine put it succinctly: "We honor our parents because it is they who gave us life. If they are lovable, we may love them. But whether or not they are lovable, we must honor them."[14]

Limits of Respect and Responsibility

Even though Jewish law expects children to honor their parents, it does set some limits. What if a parent asks his or her child to break the law? What is the obligation of a child toward an abusing parent? These are real but difficult issues to confront and resolve. Jewish law, however, does provide some guidelines.

The relationship between parents and children is deemed reciprocal in all societies. Parents are expected to care for their children, and children, in return, express their appreciation by showing them respect. Each side must go to great lengths to fulfill their role in this area, but there are limits as well. According to the Talmud, just as children must feed and clothe their parents, it is the father's duty to circumcise his son, teach him Torah, marry him off, and teach him a craft. Some say, even to teach him how to swim (BT *Kiddushin* 29a). Furthermore, according to Jewish law, a father cannot become a heavy burden on his children (*Shulchan Arukh, Yoreh Dei-ah* 240:19).

In Jewish tradition, every Jew is expected to carry out the mitzvah of "honoring parents." What if a personal mitzvah is in conflict with the mitzvah of honoring the parent? In this circumstance, we need to look at the details of the case. In the opinion of Eleazar son of Mathia, "If my father orders me, 'Give me a drink of water,' while I have another mitzvah to perform, I disregard my father's honor and perform the precept, since both my father and I are bound to fulfill the mitzvot." Opposing this position, Rabbi Issi son of Y'hudah states, "If the mitzvah can be performed by others, it should be performed by others." The halakhah is according to Rabbi Issi. (See BT *Kiddushin* 32a; cf. *Shulchan Arukh, Yoreh Dei-ah* 240:12).

Children are required to honor their parents but not to obey them when there is a good reason to do so. Thus, for example, according to Rabbinic law, if a father orders his son to break a Torah law, the son should ignore his demand (*Shulchan Arukh, Yoreh Dei-ah* 240:15). Also, if a man has chosen to marry a particular woman, and the parents object to this marriage, the adult child is not obligated to follow his parents' wishes (*Shulchan Arukh, Yoreh Dei-ah* 240:25). Similarly, if a person wants to make aliyah to Israel and the parents object, the person can disregard the parents' opinion and carry out the mitzvah of aliyah.[15]

Even though a child must sustain his parents with food and clothing (see above), the question is raised by the Rabbis: Who pays for these expenses? Rabbi Y'hudah opines that the son pays. Rabbi Nachman, however, states that it must be paid out of the parents' resources, and later rabbis agree with him (BT *Kiddushin* 32a). Obviously, if the father is too poor to afford to spend this kind of money, the child is obligated to support him.

According to Jewish tradition, even though the responsibility of caring for a parent devolves upon the children, in cases where this is not possible, either because of distance or lack of expertise, it is possible to turn to others for help. In case of a medical need, for example, it would be permissible to turn to specialized venues, such as nursing homes or in-home nursing care, whether part-time or full-time. Presently, the expenses for these services are usually paid by governmental programs (e.g., Medicaid) or personal savings of the parents. If these are lacking, appropriate funds could be requested from children or even close relatives.

The Fifth Word in the Contemporary Scene: Specific Cases

In modern times, often because of the wider definition of "family," a number of contemporary issues are getting special attention.

Who Is a Parent Today?

In the past, "father" and "mother" primarily referred to biological parents. In our time, the meaning of these terms has been extended beyond the blood connection, and more and more, even with many legal and cultural barriers still in place, society appears to accept this reality, as demonstrated by *Modern Family*, a popular TV program that features a gay couple becoming legal parents of a child. Furthermore, given the possibilities of in vitro fertilization, surrogacy, or cloning, it is not always easy to determine today what is a "father" or a "mother" in legal terms. Some mothers are "birthing mothers" (i.e., they provide the egg), yet others are "social mothers" (i.e., what was called in the past "adoptive mothers"). The same applies to "sperm fathers," who only provide the sperm for another woman, whether married or not. Are these entitled to parental honor? In the spirit of Jewish law, one can forcefully argue that all adoptive parents, straight or gay, deserve to be honored by their children. However, it is unlikely that an uninterested sperm donor (e.g., a college student who does it for the money) or a surrogate mother (e.g., an outsider who bears a child for another person for a variety of reasons, including economic) would or should receive any honor. Yet, I would argue that if the sperm donor or the surrogate mother is close to the legal parents (such as a close friend or relative), the children who know the reality of their birth should be morally expected to show some deference for their biological parent.

Sexual or Emotional Abuse

There is no doubt that in the past, parental sexual and emotional abuse did take place, but today we are more sensitive about this issue and ready to defend the children against their abusive parents. In a recent article, Michael Chernick, professor of Talmud at the Hebrew Union College–Jewish Institute of Religion, stated that "in cases where a child has experienced real physical or sexual abuse at the hands of the parent, the abusing parent is regarded by the tradition as a *rasha*, a wicked individual who has violated the Torah's commandments (*Tosafot*, BT *Kiddushin* 32a; s.v. Rabbi Judah)," and "the child is free from all responsibility to the parent."[16]

Years ago, during my tenure as a congregational rabbi I dealt with a dramatic situation of sexual abuse. A woman once came to tell me that her father was severely ill but that she could not care for him. Surprised, I reminded her of the Torah's law to honor one's father and mother. "You don't understand, Rabbi," she retorted. "I was sexually abused by my father and cannot stand him. Am I still obligated to care for him?" I told her that in my opinion (which is at variance with Rabbi Chernick's position), the obligation to care for the parent still stands but that if she could not fulfill this duty personally, she needed to pay someone else to do it.

Intergenerational Strife

What should happen when parents and children have severe disagreements and the tension between them is so high that they cannot stand to be together? In the past, most children would have swallowed their pride and done the parents' bidding. Not today. The CCAR was recently asked whether it was appropriate to hold a wedding without the attendance of the groom's parents with whom both the groom and the bride have had disagreements over the ceremony. In his response (May 1990), Walter Jacob pointed out that in the past, parents were able to exercise some control over their children and that they sought to guide them through whatever means were available, but that ultimately in matters of matrimony the decision rested with the couple. Given the disagreements between the two generations, however, it was indeed appropriate to hold the ceremony without the presence of the groom's parents.[17]

The CCAR's Responsa Committee has supported a child even when there is no abuse but simply lack of contact between the generations. In April 1988, the CCAR Responsa Committee was the recipient of the following *sh'eilah* (question): A bat mitzvah candidate is the offspring of a divorced couple. The father has sole custody of the child. He has remarried and the daughter lives with him and his new wife. The daughter's natural mother has absolutely no contact with her and the daughter feels estranged from her natural mother. The natural mother, however, insists that she has a right to share in her daughter's forthcoming bat mitzvah. This potential participation sorely troubles the child, who perceives her mother in negative terms and accuses her of child beating. May the mother be excluded from the bat mitzvah? Does the mother possess natural, inherent rights to participate? Walter Jacob resolved the problem in this manner:

> Here, the child seems to have been subjected to unusually bad treatment by her mother. This apparently led the court to give sole custody to the father without visitation rights. This judgment by a neutral outside party combined with the feelings of hostility of the child toward her mother indicates that it would be *inappropriate* for the mother to participate unless some reconciliation has taken place. The natural mother may, of course, attend the service and should be encouraged to do so although a stipulation of good behavior with appropriate safeguards may be set for her attendance.[18]

Abandonment

In the past, many parents lived with their children when they became old and needed regular help. This was made easier by the fact that most people lived in the same neighborhood for many years, and children rarely moved out very far. In my own family, too, I remember my great-grandmother living with us until the day of her death. Things have changed in our time. Most children when they grow up move away, often far from their childhood home. Elderly parents, therefore, either are left alone or move to retirement communities. Contact between parents and children becomes more sporadic and, in many cases, rare. Judy B. Shanks was asked the following question: "My two siblings have left the daily care of our elderly, widowed father to me because we live in the same city. I love Dad dearly, but I'm always pulled in so many directions by him, by my own children, and by the demands of my career. My siblings each visit Dad once a year and use the opportunity to criticize the decisions I've made for him. Dad treats them like royalty when they visit and forgets I exist until they leave. Help! I can't go on." In her responsum, Rabbi Shanks states that the mitzvah to honor one's parents does not have geographical limits and that the questioner should encourage and even ask her siblings to make more frequent visits and for these visits to coincide at times with the questioner's vacations, during which the siblings would assume regular caretaking responsibilities.[19]

In my rabbinic career, I have had to counsel and help many elderly people who had been either ignored or even abandoned by their adult children. So, the question comes up as to whether the community has an obligation to take care of these older people. The community's role in forcing children who do not take care of their parents was raised in one of the CCAR responsa. In June 1982, Walter Jacob, after reviewing all the Rabbinic texts on this subject, argued that "the community may go to considerable length to force children to support their parents." The responsum also added, "If the community does not succeed in obtaining such support, as the enforcing powers of modern community are limited, then the community itself is obligated to support the parents."[20]

"That You May Long Endure"

The second half of the Fifth Word contains the rationale for the mitzvah of "honoring the parent" in the form of a promise: "that you may long endure on the land [namely, the Land of Israel] that the Eternal your God is assigning to you" (Exod. 20:12).

Many biblical laws are accompanied by motivational clauses indicating the reason for observing them.[21] In some cases the clause attempts to explain the intent of the law, such as "You shall not wrong nor oppress a stranger, for you were strangers in the land of Egypt" (Exod. 22:20). In other cases, the law is followed by a phrase indicating that heeding the command will result in well-being. In the Fifth Word, we do not have an explanatory note but a promise that if children honor their parents they will be rewarded; it is expected that this hope and divine promise would encourage the young to put the law into practice.

The medieval commentary *Sefer HaChinukh* spells out the rationale for the Fifth Word in these words: "It is for a person to realize that his father and mother are the cause of his being in the world; hence in truth it is proper for him to give them every honor and every benefit that he can, since they brought him into the world and then, too, labored through many troubles over him in his early years."[22]

What did the biblical lawgiver mean by the promise "that you may endure"? The text seems to imply that honoring the parents will bring happiness and blessings to the children, but was this meant literally? The *M'khilta* takes it as such and comments, "If you honor them [the parents], the result will be that your days will be long, and if not, the result will be that your days will be short" (*Bachodesh* 8; see also Rashi ad loc). Nachmanides goes even further and claims that the person will live to old age in this world and his days will also be long in the world-to-come. Similarly, Talmudic teachers think that both additions to the text in Exodus really refer to "the world that is entirely long" and to "the world that is entirely good," namely, the world-to-come (BT *Kiddushin* 39b).

The promise recorded in the Fifth Word is problematic for many people today. We realize that not all children who honor their parents have a long life, and plenty of people who mistreat their parents live to old age with little sense of guilt. Maybe the promise needs to be taken much more broadly, meaning that children need to acknowledge that they owe their existence to their parents, for which they must be grateful, and do their part for future generations. Similarly, taking the phrase more figuratively and more in consonance with our times, Nahum Sarna states, "Respect for parents is deemed to be vital for the preservation of the social fabric; dishonoring parents imperils the well-being of society."[23] It is also possible, and perhaps more likely, that the "you" (in "you may endure") does not refer to the individual child who honors his or her parent, but to the People of Israel. As David N. Freedman points out, "This is a national promise to Israel that they will enjoy a long existence on Israelite soil, without being harassed or exiled by foreign enemies, as long as they adhere to this commandment."[24]

The Deuteronomic Additions

How do we account for the fact that the text in Deuteronomy contains two additional statements, namely, "as the Eternal your God has commanded you" and "and that you may fare well" (Deut. 5:16)? Jacob ben Asher, the author of *Baal HaTurim* (fourteenth century) noted this difference and, by counting all the additional letters, remarked that the seventeen more letters found in Deuteronomy have the same numerical value as the word *tov* (good). And, why is there a reference to "good" (*yitav*) in the second version of the Decalogue (Deut. 5:16) but not in the first (Exod. 20:12)? The Talmud answers: it is because the first tablets were destined to be broken (BT *Bava Batra* 55a). The Sephardic Torah anthology *Mei-am Lo-eiz* (eighteenth century) prefers a more theological answer: Noting that the addition "as the Eternal your God has commanded you" is difficult to understand since God had already given all the commandments before, the commentator adds that this extra phase really means that honoring parents must be done not because it is ethically correct but primarily because it is God's will. Thus, carrying out the divine command will result in additional benefits. Modern biblical scholars say that the addition "as the Eternal your God has commanded you" implies that the editor of Deuteronomy, who lived long after the formation of the Exodus text, is stating that he is quoting an earlier text found in the Book of Exodus. And the addition "that you may fare well" is characteristic Deuteronomy language (see Deut. 4:40, 5:26, 12:25, 22:7).

In Conclusion

Respect for parents is among the primary human duties of every individual. It is good for the stability of the family and the well-being of society. Unless there are severe hardships, the duty remains valid until the parent dies. However, I agree with Rabbi Chernick, who states, "It is not the appropriate role of children to become 'parents' to their parents, unless no choice remains."[25] In ancient times, parents could impose their will, at times even in an autocratic way. Nowadays this respect, though popularly acknowledged as the right thing to do, must be earned through words and deeds. "The greatest achievement open to parents," says Rabbi Joseph H. Hertz, "is to be ever fully worthy of their children's reverence and trust and love."[26] Ultimately, family members must treat each other with care, concern, love, and loyalty.

The Sixth Word: Homicide

The Scope of the Commandment

The Sixth Word is the first in the remaining second half of the Ten Commandments, which deal with the relationship between individuals, what the ancient Rabbis called *bein adam lachaveiro* (between one human being and another). Also, along with the two following commandments, it has the shortest formulation, without any motivating clause attached to it. It prohibits the act of homicide, which regrettably happens all the time.

Hardly a day goes by without learning that someone in our global community has died a violent death. The newspapers report willful killings in our cities and around the world on a regular basis. The TV and other media display videos or still pictures about wars or regional conflicts in faraway places where, at times, hundreds of people lose their lives. World literature is full of novels, works of art, and musical pieces that deal with stories of homicide. Murder mysteries are a staple of movies and television. Slaying, we admit, has always been a reality in human history. Soon after the earth was formed, the Bible tells us, it did not take too long before the first murder happened, when Cain slew his brother Abel (Gen. 4:8).

However, most civilized people, both past and present, have realized that it is wrong to take another person's life willfully, based on a variety of reasons ranging from self-preservation to respect for human life, and quote the Ten Commandments to justify their position. In popular parlance, this prohibition is expressed as "You shall not kill" and rendered as such by a variety of

Bible translations, such as the Jerusalem Bible (1968), the New American Bible (1970), and the Catholic Study Bible (1990).

The expression "You shall not kill" is much more general than "You shall not murder." "Murder" is usually understood as "the unlawful killing of a human being with malice aforethought,"[1] although in the United States, the precise definition of "murder" varies from state to state.

The question we are confronting here is whether, in the original Hebrew, the Sixth Word of the Decalogue means "You shall not kill," a very broad commandment, or, in a more specific way, "You shall not murder." The difference between the two is most significant, for if the sixth commandment means "You shall not kill," it would imply that any and all kinds of killing, even self-defense, are prohibited. If this were the case, one could also argue that all wars, even defensive ones, are immoral. How do we understand abortion in the context of this commandment? If the law means "You shall not kill," we need to ask ourselves whether the state has the right to impose the death penalty on criminals. And what about euthanasia? Is it justifiable under any condition? Do we take the principle of "an eye for an eye" literally?

The answer to these critical questions lies in the proper understanding of the original Hebrew text, which reads, *Lo tirtzach*. And, as we shall see, the answer is not so clear.

The Meaning of *Lo Tirtzach*

The Hebrew Bible uses different verbs to describe the act of slaying of another human being, such as *ratzach*, *harag*, *meit*, *hakeh*, *shafakh dam*, and *katal*. It recognizes that some killings are carried out with intent and premeditation (i.e., murder), whereas others are committed by accident (i.e., manslaughter). The penalty for each case is different.

The Sixth Word forbids the action designated by the verb *ratzach*. This verb, which occurs a little over forty times in the Bible, some in its verbal form, others in its noun form, is never used in relation to killing during war or slaying an animal, but solely in cases of homicide. The inference of this commandment is made clear in the Aramaic translation of Onkelos (second century CE), which specifically states, "Do not kill [*tiklot*] a person."

The Hebrew verb *ratzach* does not seem to have a clear cognate in any of the ancient Near Eastern languages that could help us with its meaning.[2] So, we are left only with our biblical data in order to understand the scope of this verb, most of which depends on personal interpretation. The question for us is this: What is the range of meaning assigned to the verb *ratzach* in the Hebrew Bible? Unfortunately, the evidence is not conclusive. The eighth-century prophet Hosea seems to quote our Decalogue but uses the verb *ratzach* by itself, without any qualification that would be helpful in determining its meaning: "[False] swearing, dishonesty, and killing/murder (*ratzoach*) and theft and adultery are rife" (Hos. 4:2; cf., similarly, Jer. 7:9). Similarly, in Prov. 22:13, a lazy person is afraid that a lion would kill him: "I shall be killed [*eiratzei-ach*] if I step outside."

At times, the verbal root *ratzach* is found in the biblical text in parallel to *harag*, implying they mean the same thing, "homicide." But is it "murder"? For example, "They kill [*yaharogu*] the widow and the stranger; they slay [*y'ratzeichu*] the fatherless" (Ps. 94:6). The context is not clear for us to decide whether *ratzach* here means "murder" or not. It could easily mean "kill." In one case *ratzach* parallels *katal*: "The murderer [*rotzei-ach*] arises in the evening [*laor*] to kill [*yiktol*] the poor and the needy, and at night he acts the thief" (Job 24:14). Here, it is not so clear if the act is premeditated or not.

On occasion, *ratzach* is used to refer to unintentional killing. Therefore, the purpose cannot be "murder." For instance, in the case of a killer who escapes to the city of refuge (see below), the text reads, "Now this is the case of the manslayer [*harotzei-ach*] who may flee there and live: one who has killed [*yakeh*] another unwittingly, without having been an enemy in the past" (Deut. 19:4; cf. Josh. 20:3).

We stand on more solid ground regarding the meaning of "murder" in a passage from the prophet Hosea, who states, "The gang of priests is like the ambuscade of bandits who murder [*y'ratz'chu*] on the road to Shechem" (Hos. 6:9). Here *ratzach* refers to a preplanned act, because it is clarified by the clause *ki zimah asu*, "for they encouraged depravity."

In Numbers 35, which deals with the cities of refuge, the verb *ratzach* is used in connection with accidental as well as premeditated slaying of another human being. Verse 11 clearly refers to unintentional killing: "You shall provide yourselves with places to serve you as cities of refuge to which a manslayer [*rotzei-ach*] who has killed a person unintentionally [*bishgagah*] may flee." However in verse 30, "murder" better fits the context: "If anyone kills [*makeih*] a person, the murderer may be executed [*yirtzach et harotzei-ach*] only on the evidence of witnesses,"[3] because the act of the *rotzei-ach*, the murderer (most likely the blood-avenger), is premeditated. Similarly, in Deut. 22:26, which deals with the rape of a woman in the countryside, we are told that the victim goes free, because "this case is like that of one person attacking and murdering [*ur'tzacho*] another."

We have a clearer example in the Bible where *ratzach* refers to an act of premeditated homicide. The prophet Elijah confronts King Ahab of the Northern Kingdom of Israel (ninth century BCE) upon hearing that Ahab's wife Jezebel had orchestrated the death of his neighbor Naboth, in order to take over Naboth's piece of land, which he had refused to sell to the king. As Ahab is on his way to take over Naboth's land, God says to Elijah, "Say to him, 'Thus said the Eternal: Would you murder [*haratzachta*] and take possession?'" (I Kings 21:19). Here it is clear that Queen Jezebel, with the assumed knowledge and approval of King Ahab (see *M'tuzdat David*, ad loc), had planned the act, and Ahab is now ready to derive benefit from it. This is a clear case of murder. Similarly, the verb *ratzach* is used in the case of a Levite who, in the Book of Judges (19–20), willfully murders his concubine. She is called in the text *ha-ishah hanirtzachah*, "the murdered woman" (Judg. 20:4).

Given the fact that *ratzach* could be used either for premeditated or accidental killings, the problem of how best to translate the Sixth Word becomes a matter of personal preference. I would vote for the restrictive meaning "Do not murder," because under certain conditions, the Bible does approve of spilling of blood, such as during war (e.g., Deut. 20:10–18), for legal executions (e.g., Exod. 21:14), and even in cases of self-defense (e.g., Exod. 22:1; cf. BT *Sanhedrin* 72a: "If someone is coming to kill you, rise and kill him first"). Based on this understanding, the Sixth Word has been rendered as "You shall not murder" by many Bible translations, such as the New Jewish Publication Society (1999), the New Revised Standard Version (1989), the New English Bible (1972), and the New King James Version (1982).[4]

If the real intention of the Torah is to prohibit murder, then the Sixth Word cannot be used to justify either pacifism (which the Bible rejects) or the abolition of the death penalty (which the Bible accepts as punishment for certain crimes).

The Penalty for Homicide

In the ancient Near East, capital punishment was imposed on the manslayer. In the Sumerian Laws of Ur-Nammu (ca. twenty-first century BCE), we read, "If a man commits a homicide, they shall kill that man" (#1). However, it is not clear whether this law deals with murder or accidental killing. In later law collections, we find that, at times, the penalty depends on the status of the person who was killed. Thus, for instance, according to the Laws of Hammurabi (LH; eighteenth century BCE), which were written in Akkadian, if a free man kills another freeman's daughter, "they shall put his daughter to death" (LH 210). But, if he kills a female slave, he only pays twenty shekels (LH 214). Similarly, in the Middle Assyrian Laws (MAL; eleventh century BCE), the manslayer is left at the mercy of the head of the victim's household. If he chooses, he can put him to death, or he may reach a financial accommodation with the family of the victim (see MAL 10). The Torah, on the other hand, prohibits such monetary compensation in cases of homicide, even though in earlier times it may have accepted it as valid (see I Kings 20:38–43). The Book of Numbers, reflecting later custom, makes it clear that monetary compensation cannot be accepted in capital cases: "You may not accept a ransom for the life of a murderer [*rotzei-ach*] who is guilty of a capital crime; he must be put to death" (Num. 35:31).

The Sixth Word does not tell us what is to be done to a person who breaks the commandment of *lo tirtzach*. The penalty clause is missing. In the rest of the Hebrew Bible, however, the punishment for spilling blood is clearly stated: it is death ("One who fatally strikes another person [*makeih ish vameit*] shall be put to death" [Exod. 21:12; cf. Lev. 24:17; Deut. 19:11–12]). Even a beast that took the life of a human being was put to sleep (Gen. 9:5).

In ancient times, it was the "blood-avenger" (or "blood-redeemer," *go-eil hadam*), a member of the victim's immediate family, such as the father or the brother, who was primarily charged with the responsibility of punishing the killer upon encounter (Num. 35:19). Later on, the culprit was turned over to the blood-avenger for execution only after the courts had convicted him (Deut. 19:12).

The Rationale for the Death Penalty

The Hebrew Bible seems to exact the highest penalty in cases of homicide, whether the victim is male or female. It is uncompromising. It does not allow for discretion. What is the rationale for this harsh judgment? According to the Book of Genesis, this is based on the idea that human life is sacred, and anyone who dares to put an end to God's given life is expected to pay dearly. Murder is a sin against God:

The shedder of human blood,
That person's blood shall be shed by [another] human [baadam];

For human beings were made
In the image of God. (Gen. 9:6)[5]

In this chiastic statement, the word *baadam*, "by [another] human," is ambiguous, for it could mean either "in compensation for a human being" or "through the instrumentality of other human beings," namely, through the legal courts. Furthermore, the expression "the image [*tzelem*] of God" is unclear. Based on an Akkadian word, *tzalmu*, meaning "image" or "statue," it is possible to argue that the intention was to state that human beings have a "kingly image" like God, or as Nahum Sarna puts it, "each person bears the stamp of royalty."[6] In Rabbinic tradition, the expression "image of God" refers to the intangible qualities attributed to God, such as compassion, creativity, and morality, thus making all human beings as the representatives of God in the world. Radak, a medieval rabbinic commentator writes, "Man is the highest of God's creation; he is created in His image and enjoys the gift of intelligence" (ad loc).

Ancient Near Eastern law does not provide us with a rationale for any kind of penalty in cases of homicide. The Bible is different. As one commentator notes, "The idea that human beings are created in the image of God (Gen. 1:26–27) requires a higher degree of respect for human life."[7] Life comes ultimately from God. Just as God gives life, only God can take it away (cf. Job. 1:21). If the penalty for murder appears to be excessive, ending in the death of both the victim and the culprit, it is because the perpetrator has committed an unauthorized act that infringes upon God's prerogative to generate life. The evil act becomes an affront to God's authority and majesty, and the offender needs to pay for it in kind.

Unintentional Killing

At times, taking the life of another human being is done with advance planning (i.e., murder), but it can also happen tragically as a result of an unfortunate accident, such as when a child suddenly jumps in front of a car without paying attention to the traffic. What should be the penalty for the driver in this case? In our present legal system, the culprit may go free, because the driver is not at fault. In the past, perpetrators of unintentional homicides were given an opportunity to escape to a shelter.

The privilege of asylum in a sanctuary has a long history in the Western world. It was granted both in ancient Egypt and in Greece. Christian churches have been used as sanctuaries as far back as the fourth century (see Theodician Code of 392 CE). During the Vietnam War (ca. 1955–1975), many antiwar activists took refuge in churches and in a few synagogues (also in some libraries) in order to escape being sent to Vietnam to fight an unpopular war. The modern concept of sanctuary was probably inspired by the Hebrew Bible, which discusses the role of the "cities of refuge" for unintentional slayers.

According to the Bible, six "cities of refuge" (*arei miklat*) were built on both sides of the Jordan River, where the killer waited for a trial before the elders of the community (e.g., Exod. 21:12–13; Num. 35 9–15; Deut. 4:41–43; Josh. 20:2–9). In addition to these cities, the Bible also speaks of "Levitical cities" (Joshua 21 and I Chronicles 6), and it is not clear whether they are one and the same. There is disagreement among biblical scholars about the historical verifiability of the Levitical cities. Some argue that the Levites administered these sites. Others, however, maintain that these Levitical cities were simply a utopian construct, whereas the cities of refuge may have existed in reality.

The Book of Joshua states that the unintentional killer could remain in the city of refuge until he stood trial before the assembly and/or (it is not clear which) the death of the High Priest who is in office at the time of the killing (Josh. 20:6). He could then return to his home.[8] Within Israel proper, too, the altar at the Temple of God provided such an asylum (I Kings 1:50–53, 2:28–34). However, if the act of homicide was committed with a prior plan, the Torah states, "You shall take that person from My very altar to be put to death" (Exod. 21:14). We have a case in the Book of Kings that illustrates this point. Adonijah, the brother of Solomon, wanted to become king after David. When the group supporting Solomon heard about the preparations for the takeover, they convinced King David to declare his son Solomon as his successor. Upon hearing this news, Adonijah escaped and went right away to the Tent of Meeting and grasped the horns of the altar, thinking that this act would save him from death. Solomon had someone tell Adonijah that he would not be harmed "if he behaves worthily . . . ; but if he is caught in any offense, he shall die" (I Kings 1:52). Adonijah agreed and was sent home safely. At times, however, even holding the horns of the altar was not a guarantee of survival. Once, King Solomon ignored the sanctuary rule and had Joab, a general under David and a supporter of Adonijah, killed for the crime of murder he had committed against two army commanders, even though he was clinging to the horns of the altar (I Kings 2:28–34).

People Who Got Away with Murder

The Bible is adamant about imposing capital punishment in cases of homicide. However, it also records some events where the culprit simply got away free. The first is the case of Cain and Abel, sons of Adam and Eve. According to the story in the Book of Genesis (Gen. 4:1–12), Cain, a farmer, brings a sacrifice to God, but his offering is rejected. Abel, his brother, a keeper of sheep, too, brings a sacrifice, and his offering is accepted by God. This leads Cain to kill (*harag*) his sibling. As the result of that act, he is banished from before God and becomes a ceaseless wanderer on earth, but he is not put to death.

This episode is a remnant of what must have been a much longer mythical text. What we have in the Bible is just a skeleton. The purpose of the narrative is not clear: Is it to contrast the role of the farmer versus the semi-nomad, or to teach that success and failure cannot always rationally be explained, or can it be that the narrator wants to tell us about the terrible consequences of jealousy and aggression? We don't know. Furthermore, it is not stated why God accepts Abel's offering while rejecting Cain's. There is a hint in the text that Cain offered an ordinary product "from the fruit of the soil" (Gen. 4:3),[9] whereas Abel brought in "the choicest of the firstlings" (Gen. 4:4). Also, the text itself has a lacuna: "Cain said to his brother Abel . . . and when they were in the field, Cain set upon his brother Abel and killed him" (Gen. 4: 8). We are not told what Cain says to his brother. A few ancient versions, including the Aramaic and Greek versions, insert, "Come, let us go out into the field." And, what is most pertinent to our subject here, it is unclear whether this is a premeditated killing, or (the verb *ratzach* is not used here) a homicide that just happens on the spur of the moment. Rashi argues that it is premeditated: "He picked up a fight with him in order to find cause to kill him" (see ad loc). Similarly, a contemporary biblical scholar, Claus Westermann, opines that this is a "deliberate and premeditated" act that would make it a murder.[10] Others, however, like the medieval Sforno, feel that it is "without a prior fight" and therefore an ordinary killing. Nahum Sarna explains the deed by saying, "Cain's depression gives way to an irrational act of aggression."[11]

What about the punishment? Cain is banished from before God, becomes a wanderer, and gets a protective sign from God but is not put to death. The text seems to imply that Cain's expulsion is as bad as death: "My punishment is too heavy to bear! Seeing as now You have expelled me from the face of the soil . . ." (Gen. 4:13–14), says Cain to God. Some Rabbis argue that the death penalty is not imposed on Cain because death has not been experienced yet

(*B'reishit Rabbah* 22:12) and there is no law against it. Cain, who kept striking Abel, did not know from which part of Abel's body would his soul go out until he reached his neck (*Tanchuma, B'reishit* 9). Others conjecture that Cain has become an example to penitents (*B'reishit Rabbah* 22:12). A contemporary author imagines that Cain lives in a kind of "mobile city of refuge."[12]

The second example of a killer escaping the death penalty is King David, who, after committing adultery with Bathsheba has her husband, Uriah, killed (II Sam. 12; see details in "The Seventh Word: Adultery"). However, contrary to biblical law that demands the death penalty for an adulterer (see Lev. 20:10; Deut. 22:22), he escapes punishment, because King David readily admits his guilt and repents: "David said to Nathan, 'I stand guilty before the Eternal!' And Nathan replied to David, 'The Eternal has remitted [*he-evir*; literally, "transferred"] your sin; you shall not die. However, since you have spurned [the enemies] of the Eternal by this deed, the child about to be born to you shall die" (II Sam. 12:13–14).

The Rabbis are bothered by this decree (see, for example, Radak, ad loc) and attempt to mollify it by coming up with various justifications. First, they state that when King David calls for Bathsheba, she is already divorced, because, following the custom of the time, Uriah has already given her a bill of divorce, just in case he does not return back safely from war.[13] Furthermore, they point to the twenty years that King David spends in penitence, during which the holy spirit is taken away from him (*Yalkut*, II Samuel, 165). Even though no one, not even the king, is above the law (see Deut. 17:14–20), it is clear that in this case King David gets away with murder.

Another example of a killer going scot-free is King Ahab (see page 116), who has Naboth murdered and, in fact, reigns for twenty-two years (I Kings 16:29). In what appears to be a later addition to the text (I Kings 21:27–29), King Ahab, we are told, repents. God tells the prophet Elijah, "Have you seen how Ahab has humbled himself before Me? Because he has humbled himself before Me, I will not bring the disaster[14] in his lifetime; I will bring the disaster upon his house in his son's time" (I Kings 21:29). King Ahab is killed in battle and buried in Samaria (I Kings 22:34–37).

Crimes and Methods of Punishment

The Hebrew Bible not only tells us that the penalty for murder is death, but it also provides a basic procedure for it. Though the precise details escape us, a broader guideline can be gleaned from it.

In the Bible, the death penalty is imposed in cases of homicide (Exod. 21:12; Lev. 24:17), idolatry (Lev. 20:2), adultery (Deut. 22:22), rape of a betrothed woman (Deut. 22:25), desecration of the Sabbath day (Num. 15:32–36), blaspheming God (Lev. 24:15–16; cf. v. 23), and having carnal relations with a beast (Lev. 20:15). Here, it is important to note that in order to avoid an unfair punishment, biblical law requires at least two witnesses: "The testimony of a single witness against a person shall not suffice for a sentence of death" (Num. 35:30). In fact, according to Deuteronomy, "a person shall be put to death only on the testimony of two or more [lit. "three"] witnesses" (Deut. 17:6; cf. 19:15–16).

In biblical times the two basic methods for executing criminals were stoning and burning. Stoning was the standard form (e.g., Lev. 24:23) and was to be carried out by the "whole community" and "outside the camp" (e.g., Lev. 24:14–16). Burning was prescribed only for two offenses: marrying both a woman and her mother (Lev. 20:14) and for a priest's daughter who degrades herself by becoming a harlot (Lev. 21:9). Regrettably, stoning is still practiced in some parts of the world, such as Afghanistan, Somalia, and Sudan. During the Middle Ages, burning at the stake was the standard punishment in England and Spain for heresy and witchcraft. It was the favorite method of punishment by the Inquisition, called "auto-da-fé" (an act of faith). Judicial burning remained in England all the way through the eighteenth century in cases of murder.

In addition to these two methods, there are biblical references for death by sword (Exod. 32:27; Deut. 13:16), shooting with arrows (Exod. 19:13), and beheading (II Kings 6:31–32). Hanging was done in order to expose the body of the criminal after his execution as a public warning to the community at large. According to the Torah, however, the corpse was not to be left on the stake overnight, it being an affront to God, and the body needed to be buried the same day (Deut. 21:22–23). Judicial hanging is still the standard form of putting a murderer to death in many countries, including Japan, Singapore, Malaysia, South Korea, India, Pakistan, Bangladesh, several African countries, including Botswana and Zimbabwe, and some Middle Eastern countries.[15]

One of the remarkable aspects of biblical law is that capital punishment is never applied in cases of damage to property. It was different in other ancient Near Eastern countries. Here is an example from the Laws of Hammurabi: "If a man has committed robbery and is caught, that man shall be put to death" (LH 18). In comparison, according to the Bible, the owner of a house is justified in killing a thief only if it happens during a night entry and solely in self-defense, but not during broad daylight when, presumably, he could call for help (Exod. 22:1–2).

"An Eye for an Eye"

To what extent do you punish a person who has slain another or caused bodily damage? What are the limits? What is fair? Ancient societies struggled with these ideas for a long time and came up with various solutions. Retaliation is one of them.

According to the Bible, retaliation is required for bodily injuries sustained by the victim, what many biblical commentators refer to by the Latin expression *lex talionis* (talion law). A clear expression of this principle is found in the Book of Deuteronomy with reference to false witnesses: "You shall do to the one [the false witness] as the one schemed to do to the other...life for life, eye for eye, tooth for tooth, hand for hand, foot for foot" (Deut. 19:19–21; cf. Exod. 21:23–25; Lev. 24:19–20). Apparently, this is what happens to King Adoni-bezek, who, after the death of Joshua, is defeated by the tribe of Judah. According to the biblical text, they cut off his thumbs and big toes. The king declares, "Seventy kings, with thumbs and big toes cut off, used to pick scraps under my table; as I have done, so God has requited me" (Judg. 1:7).

It is interesting to note, however, that the Bible requires talion only for the guilty party, not his relatives. It was different in other legal systems of the ancient Near East. For example, according to the Hittite Laws, "If anyone pushes a man into a fire so that he dies, he will give his son" (no. 44; *ANET*, 1941). Similarly, vicarious punishment was applied in ancient Babylonia (see page 117, LH 210; *ANET*, 175). Furthermore, whereas the Laws of Hammurabi required retaliation only among the free members of society, the Bible applies talion to everyone: "You shall have one standard for stranger and citizens alike" (Lev. 24:22).

In the past, some scholars have claimed that *lex talionis* was primitive and represented the old desert law. From the study of many ancient Near Eastern law collections (for example, cf. the older Laws of Eshnunna 42–47 and the newer Laws of Hammurabi 195–205), we now know that compensation preceded talion and that this principle was most likely introduced by Hammurabi, perhaps reflecting his own Amorite cultural traditions. The principle behind the law was probably to establish a balance between the crime and punishment in the hope that the punishment would fit the crime. In the Bible, talion law not only was an expression of equality between the parties, but it also came to curb unrestricted retaliation and personal vengeance.

Homicide in Rabbinic Literature

The Talmud tells us that capital punishment was abolished forty years before the destruction of the Second Temple in 70 CE (BT *Sanhedrin* 41a). Yet, we know that on rare occasions it was imposed on criminals, even after this period, whenever the Jewish community had the power to do so, such as in Muslim Spain.[16]

Postbiblical sages inherited the sixth commandment from the Hebrew Scriptures and, realizing that they did not have the authority to impose the death penalty, progressively broadened its moral scope and used the biblical laws on this subject as educational tools. For example, reiterating their biblical belief in the sanctity of human life, they point out that at the beginning of Creation only one person, namely Adam, was formed by God, to teach us that whoever destroys a single life thereby destroys all of humanity and, conversely, anyone who saves an individual, it is as if he had saved an entire world (*Mishnah Sanhedrin* 4:5). Furthermore, they remark that the Ten Commandments are arranged in such a way that those injunctions that face each other on the tablets are placed there to teach us a special lesson (see "Text and Context"). For example, "I the Eternal am your God" stands opposite "You shall not murder." This means, "If a person sheds blood, it is accounted to him as though he had diminished the divine image" (*M'khilta, Bachodesh* 70–75).

Two basic principles seem to have guided the ancient Rabbis as they evaluated the imposition of the death penalty in the Bible. First, given the biblical command to "love your neighbor as yourself" (Lev. 19:18), they ordained that a Jew is expected to love him by giving him the most humane death possible. Second, they taught that Jews are commanded not to mutilate or destroy the body of the criminal (see BT *Sanhedrin* 52a).

Regarding talion law, the Rabbis argued that this law should not be taken literally. An "eye for eye" really means monetary compensation: "Just as in the case of striking an animal, compensation is to be paid, so also in the case of striking a man, compensation is to be paid" (BT *Bava Kama* 83b; cf. *Mishnah Bava Kama* 8:1; see also *M'khilta* on Exod. 21: 24). Thus, the Sages reinstated the practice that was prevalent before the period of Hammurabi.

In dealing with some of the harshest biblical laws that require the death penalty, the Sages, who believed in the divine source of the text, kept the wording but added so many procedural impediments that they made the law practically inoperable. For example, regarding the "stubborn and rebellious son" who deserves to be put to death for his bad behavior (Deut. 21:18–21), the Rabbis not only added other demands to make the law almost inapplicable, but clearly stated that this case "never happened and it will never happen," and that the law was given purely "so that you may study it and receive reward" (BT *Sanhedrin* 71a)—in other words, for scholarly and educational purposes. Also, horrified by the consequences of capital punishment, they taught, "A Sanhedrin that carries out the death penalty once in seven years is designated 'destructive.' Rabbi Elazar ben Azaryah commented, 'Once in seventy years.' Rabbi Tarfon and Rabbi Akiva said, 'Had we been members of the Sanhedrin, no one would ever receive the death penalty'" (*Mishnah Makot* 1:10). Yet, this teaching, though mentioned in the name of prominent sages of their time, was not universally approved. A minority opinion, cited in the name of Rabban Shimon ben Gamliel, has it, "(Without the death penalty, the sages) would also have multiplied the number of those who shed blood in Israel" (ibid.).

In the Middle Ages, some rabbis broadened the scope of the Sixth Word and pointed out, as, for example, Ibn Ezra did, that it applies not only to cases of physical violence but also to "the poison of the tongue," namely, tale bearing and false testimony, for they too destroy another human being. In particular, Rabbi Yaakov Culi (1689–1732), the author of *Me'am Loez*, written in Ladino, states that under the category of murder, Jewish law prohibits damaging another's reputation, encroaching upon another person's territory by taking away his livelihood and depriving him of his daily bread, and even humiliating him in public.[17]

Capital Punishment in the Western World

Even though many countries around the world still impose the death penalty, other Western democracies have already abolished it for a variety of moral reasons (see below). In North America, neither Mexico nor Canada has capital punishment. Currently in the United States, a number of states still impose the death penalty in cases, such as homicide, treason, drug trafficking, and crimes against humanity committed by mentally competent adults; the method of execution varies from lethal injection to hanging.

By the late 1970s, thirty-four states in the Union permitted the death penalty. However, in 1972, the Supreme Court of the United States, in the famous *Furman v. Georgia* case, declared that the imposition as well as the carrying out of the death penalty was cruel and unusual punishment, in violation of the Eighth Amendment to the Constitution. Yet, the Supreme Court left open the possibility that capital punishment could be considered constitutional if it were imposed for certain crimes and applied uniformly.

After this important decision, many state legislatures have passed death penalty laws designed to satisfy the requirements of the Supreme Court. In 1976, the U.S. Supreme Court, in a series of cases headed by *Gregg v. Georgia*, reversed itself and upheld more and more death penalty statutes. In 1987, in the last major challenge, the U.S. Supreme Court upheld the constitutionality of the death penalty by a 5–4 vote. However, there is a growing trend in our country today to restrict the imposition of the death penalty by means of temporary moratoria, presidential pardons, prosecutorial discretion, and better use of DNA technology to make sure that no one is convicted under questionable circumstances.

Capital Punishment in the State of Israel

After the modern State of Israel was established in 1948, during the very first trial, the two chief rabbis of Israel sent a message to the minister of justice reminding him that the imposition of capital punishment was not in the spirit of Jewish law. In 1954, when the penal code was revised, the death penalty was reserved only for treason during war and crimes of genocide. The method of execution was hanging for civilians and shooting for soldiers.

Until now no one has been put to death in the State of Israel except Adolf Eichmann, the Nazi monster who was captured and brought to Israel from Argentina in 1960. During the trial of this notorious criminal, there were some in Israel, including the philosopher Martin Buber, who appealed for mercy, but the public outrage against Eichmann was too high, and he was executed by hanging in June 1962.

The Death Penalty—Deterrent or Not?

The debate to whether to support or reject the death penalty arouses high emotions among people, for it deals with the basic instincts of justice and retribution in society and the value of human life. Therefore, the arguments tend to be subjective or one-sided.

What are the arguments in favor? Most people who support the death penalty believe that capital punishment is a definite deterrent. It scares away prospective murderers from committing a crime. It shows concern for the victim. It expresses the outrage of society. It is less taxing on the financial resources of the community. It prevents a murderer from committing another crime. It imposes the retribution that society needs.

On the other hand, those who oppose capital punishment, as I do, argue that the death penalty is not a deterrent for hard-core criminals. If it were, executions should be aired on TV, but they are not, because they are too gruesome to watch. Furthermore, the death penalty creates a climate of violence in society. To state that capital punishment is cheaper than incarceration is distasteful, for it places a monetary value on human life. The death penalty cannot undo the crime, not does it benefit the victim. It is barbaric, and the state should not be part of it. Also, it is inflicted disproportionately on minorities who cannot afford good legal advice. It is final and irreversible. Judicial mistakes do take place, and there is no way for the state to bring back the wrongly accused for another trial.

Modern Jewish Positions on the Death Penalty

Though some individual Jews and a few Orthodox Jewish groups support capital punishment based on the biblical mandate, the majority of Jewish organizations in the United States today, along with many non-Jewish groups, have voiced their abhorrence of the state-imposed death penalty.

As early as 1959, the Union of American Hebrew Congregations (now called Union for Reform Judaism [URJ]), the umbrella organization of the Reform Movement in America, had argued, "The resort to or continuation of capital punishment, either by a state or by the national government, is no longer justifiable."[19] It has further stated, "The practice of capital punishment serves no practical purpose.... Capital punishment is not effective as a deterrent to crime. Moreover, we believe that this practice debases our entire penal system and brutalizes the human spirit." {Idem}.

The Central Conference of American Rabbis (CCAR), the rabbinic body of the Reform Movement, urged the abolition of the death penalty in 1958 and reaffirmed its position in 1960 (CCAR, 90th Annual Convention, Phoenix, AZ). In 1979, the CCAR went on record as opposing all forms of capital punishment on the basis that "both in concept and in practice, Jewish tradition found capital punishment repugnant, despite biblical sanction for it.... No evidence has been marshaled to indicate with any persuasiveness that capital punishment serves as a deterrent to crime." (idem). The position of the Conservative Movement was already set in 1960 when the Rabbinical

Assembly's Committee on Jewish Law and Standards approved a responsum by Rabbi Ben Zion Bokser stating, "We regard all forms of capital punishment as barbaric and obsolete."[20]

In the same vein, the Reconstructionist Rabbinical Association in 2003 went on record "opposing the death penalty under all circumstances, opposing the adoption of death penalty laws, and urging their abolition in states that already have adopted them."[21]

Medical Deaths

So far, we have analyzed cases of homicide when one person takes the life of another, either with premeditation or by accident. Yet, we are all familiar with highly controversial situations in our time, mostly medical in nature, when people try to take their own lives or turn to professionals to help them die or end a pregnancy. I refer, of course, to euthanasia, suicide, and abortion. The sixth commandment has long been part of the discourse around all three issues. Let's study each by itself with some detail.

Euthanasia

Euthanasia (also called "mercy killing"), whether voluntary or involuntary, is the act of killing an individual who is hopelessly sick and is usually practiced with the aid of a medical professional. It has a long history in human life. In our time, Dr. Jack Kevorkian (1928–2011), an American pathologist from Pontiac, Michigan, admitted taking part in more than eighty assisted suicides over the years, thus forcing the issue to be discussed again on a grand scale.

In principle, Jewish tradition, characterized by its "this-worldly" attitude, disapproves of assisted suicide, on the basis that God gave life and only God can take it away; however, it makes a distinction between hastening death (active euthanasia) and acts that hasten the peaceful end to life (passive euthanasia), disapproving of the first but accepting the second. Already Rabbi Moses Isserles (1520–1572) of Poland permitted the removal of "anything causing a hindrance to the departure of the soul."[22] In his 1969 responsum, "Allowing a Terminal Patient to Die," Solomon B. Freehof, a prominent Reform rabbi, wrote, "If the patient is a hopelessly dying patient, the physician has no duty to keep him alive a little longer," but in the spirit of Jewish tradition, he opposed any attempt to hasten his death.[21] Most Reform rabbis today agree that "heroic measures to keep a person alive through artificial systems of life support are not required."[23] Admittedly, the line between active and passive euthanasia is a very thin one and requires a compassionate judgment on the part of the physician and the family, perhaps consulting with trusted clergy, all working together for the benefit of the dying.

One of the critical issues in this debate is how to determine the exact time of death. In the past, lack of breathing and absence of heartbeat were used as criteria; today, many accept brain death. In fact, in a responsum issued by the CCAR in 1980, Reform rabbis said that "when circulation and respiration only continue through mechanical means...then the suffering of the patient and his/her family may be permitted to cease, as no 'natural independent life' functions have been sustained."[25]

Suicide and Martyrdom

Suicide is the act of taking one's own life voluntarily or by accident. The Hebrew Bible records a few cases of suicide: Abimelech (Judg. 9:52–55), Samson (Judg. 16:30), King Saul (I Sam. 31:4), King David's counselor Ahithophel (II Sam. 17:23), and King Zimri (I Kings 16:18–19). Cases of suicide must have been so rare in ancient Israel, or unreported, that neither the Bible nor the Talmud has a law against it. Such a law appears for the first time in a post-Talmudic text, *S'machot* (chap. 2), where we are told that anyone who commits suicide cannot receive burial rites. However, the tendency in Rabbinic texts is to provide the survivors with multiple justifications so that they would refrain from declaring the deceased a suicide. Only a person who willfully killed himself was deemed as such, and that was very difficult to prove.

In Jewish tradition, the Sages derive the prohibition against suicide from the biblical statement in Gen. 9:5, "For your own life-blood, I will require a reckoning" (see BT *Bava Kama* 91b). Yaakov Culi, in his *Mei-am Lo-eiz*, states, "Committing suicide is considered an act of murder."[24] Yet, for Maimonides suicide is not a punishable act: "(The person who attempts it) deserves to die by an act of God, but is not executed by the court (in cases when it fails)" (*Mishneh Torah, Hilkhot Rotzei-ach Ush'mirat Nefesh* 2:2).

According to Jewish law, "A minor who committed suicide is considered like one who had taken his life accidentally. If an adult committed suicide, and it is evident that the act was prompted either through madness, or through fear of torture, as was the case with King Saul, who feared the wanton treatment of the Philistines, he should likewise be treated as though he had died a natural death."²⁶ In such cases, regular mourning services are conducted, and even a eulogy is provided in order to bring consolation to the mourners.

Jewish tradition recognizes the category of martyrdom, which is giving up one's life rather than rejecting the teachings of Torah and/or overlooking an ethical mandate (it is difficult to make a distinction between the two in Judaism), and, in a restrictive way, even refers to it as *kiddush HaShem* (the sanctification of [God's] name), but attempts to limit its application. According to the Talmud, a person is not obligated to choose death instead of breaking the law, save in the cases of idolatry (*avodat kokhavim*), incest (*gilui arayot*), and murder (*sh'fikhut damim*) (see BT *Sanhedrin* 74a).

Traditional Jewish texts contain many stories of individual Jews preferring death instead of abjuring their religion. In the Bible, Shadrach, Meshach, and Abed-nego are thrown into a fiery furnace for refusing to worship an image of gold, but they miraculously survive (Daniel 3). In postbiblical times, Eleazar, an old scribe, was ordered to eat swine's flesh by the Greek Syrians but refused and was put to death because of it (II Macc. 6:18–31); similarly, seven brothers with their unnamed mother (later identified as Hannah) met the same challenge and died the death of martyrs (II Macc. 7). In the second century CE, Rabbi Akiva was tortured by the Romans for teaching Torah, and he, too, preferred to die a martyr (BT *B'rakhot* 61b). During medieval times, countless people chose death over forced conversion, and in modern times, the victims of the Holocaust are often called *k'doshim* (holy ones) because they died simply for being Jewish.

One of the most dramatic stories about Jewish martyrdom comes to us from the writings of the Jewish historian Josephus (first century CE), who tells us about what happened at Masada, a mountainous fort by the Dead Sea. According to him (some scholars have raised serious questions about the reliability of this episode), in the year 73 CE, three years after the destruction of the Second Temple by the Romans, Flavius Silva, the commander of its Tenth Legion, attacked Masada and conquered it, only to find out that all 960 of the inhabitants (save a few women and children) had killed themselves, choosing death over slavery (*Wars*, 7:8–9). In 1956, Moshe Dayan, chief of staff of the Israel Defense Forces, established the custom of swearing in new soldiers at the top of Masada, the ceremony including the slogan "Masada shall not fall again." Recently, this ceremony has been moved to different venues, including the Western Wall in Jerusalem.

Contemporary halakhic scholars have proposed nuanced positions on the subject of martyrdom. The celebrated rabbi Abraham Israel Kook of

Israel (1865–1935), the first Ashkenazi chief rabbi of the British Mandate for Palestine, considered it only an emergency measure, and the majority of rabbinic authorities today view it as meritorious but not obligatory. This thinking was based on the tension that exists between the Mishnaic text that interprets the biblical command to "love the Eternal your God . . . with all your soul" (Deut. 6:5) as "even if God takes your soul" and, on the other hand, the biblical law that demands, "You shall keep My laws and My rules, by the pursuit of which human beings shall live" (Lev. 18:5), understood by many rabbis as meaning you shall live and not die, implying that death is not required in the pursuit of keeping the Torah.[27]

Abortion

No ethical issue is more hotly debated in our time than the voluntary expulsion of a fetus. It has created uproars in many communities and has led to many ugly political debates. On various occasions, it has even caused the death of physicians and other health professionals who performed abortions.

Most Christians argue that life begins at conception and only God can take away this life. Though some permit abortions in cases of incest or rape, the Catholic Church is on record saying that no reason whatsoever (such as the health of the mother, abnormality of the baby, or mental retardation) "can ever confer the right to dispose of another's life, even when that life is only beginning."[28] On the other hand, Jewish teachers allow and even prescribe abortion when the life of the mother or her health, both mental[28] and physical, is in danger. According to the *Gates of Mitzvah*, "Abortion may be medically indicated in cases where genetic disease or malformation of the fetus is probable."[29] Thus, in Judaism, abortion is not murder.

Jewish law is more concerned about the mother than the fetus. According to the Mishnah, "If a woman in labor has (a life-threatening difficulty), one dismembers the embryo within her, removing it limb by limb, for her life takes precedence over its [the fetus's] life. But once its greater part [and here the *Tosefta*, *Y'vamot* 9, clarifies, "its head"] has emerged, it may not be harmed, for we do not set aside one life for another" (*Mishnah Ohalot* 7:6). The Rabbis refer to the fetus causing health problems as a *rodeif*, a "pursuer," seeking to kill the mother. So, as Maimonides says, the abortion may be performed either with drugs or by surgery (*Mishneh Torah, Hilkhot Rotzei-ach Ush'mirat Nefesh* 1:9).

In 1985, the CCAR Responsa Committee pointed out that during the first forty days, the fetus is considered "mere fluid." From forty days to twenty-seven weeks, the fetus possesses some status as "potential life," and abortion is still permitted. After this period, some rabbis permit abortions if there is a serious danger to the health of the mother or the child. The responsum, however, adds," We do not encourage abortion, nor favor it for trivial reasons, or sanction it 'on demand."[29]

In Conclusion

A survey of Jewish texts dealing with homicide shows that throughout the centuries Jewish teachers have consistently viewed human life as sacred and therefore inviolate. Except for a few limited cases, such as justifiable wars, self-defense, or the imposition of the death penalty, the sages held that just as God gives life, only God can take it away. The Sixth Word, which, in our analysis, prohibits taking the life of another willfully, reminds us of our responsibility to treat each other as created in the "image of God" and, therefore, to consider life as holy. Even in cases of self-defense or war, the death of any human being diminishes every one of us and becomes necessary only as the ultimate resort for self-preservation.

The Seventh Word: Adultery

Marital Infidelity—Then and Now

In 1631, Robert Barker and Martin Lucas, royal printers in London, reprinted copies of the King James Bible, but in the Seventh Word of the Decalogue in Exodus they omitted the word "not" so that the commandment read, "Thou shalt commit adultery." A year later, when the mistake was discovered, the printers were heavily fined and their license revoked. Most copies of the Bible were immediately burned, but a few survived. This special Bible is usually called "The Wicked Bible" or "The Sinners' Bible." I wonder how many people actually found justification in this version for their sexual misconduct.

The act of adultery, usually defined as voluntary sexual intercourse between a married person, male or female, and someone other than his or her lawful spouse, deeply affects not only those who are involved in it but also other members of the family, because it upsets the family trust, harmony, and balance, and where children are born of such a union, it creates problems of inheritance and often sibling infighting. Even though marital sexual infidelity has occurred since ancient times, the way societies have dealt with it has changed over the centuries, depending on people's religious outlook and social values.

In the past, adultery was universally considered a public crime. Currently, many states in the Arab world and Iran still impose the death penalty on adulterers, and in other countries, such as Portugal, Greece, and Mexico, marital infidelity is punishable by a jail sentence. In the United States, the punishment for adultery varies between states, some treating it as a private matter between consenting adults, others imposing a small penalty. For example, in the Commonwealth of Massachusetts, adultery is punishable by imprisonment in the state prison for not more than three years or in jail for not more than two years or by a fine of not more than five hundred dollars (MGL, c.272s), even though hardly anyone is prosecuted for this crime these days.

A casual reading of daily papers shows that issues related to marital infidelity are much more complicated in our time. In the past, there was less toleration for adultery, and the penalties were harsh. Given the complexity of family structures today, the ties that bind husband and wife are more strongly tested than ever before, and the issues discussed more openly as well as frankly in the media. Our society today is more open, and often more tolerant about questions of adultery. This chapter will attempt to analyze the question of adultery as viewed in the Jewish texts of the past and how it is considered in the present time, with all of its complexities.

The Text of the Seventh Word

The commandment about adultery, appearing in the second half of the Decalogue, is the second in the list of three consecutive biblical prohibitions that are formulated succinctly and without a motivating clause. It simply reads, *Lo tinaf*, that is, "You shall not commit adultery" (Exod. 20:13; Deut. 5:17). A similar but longer version, using a different verb ("to place your layer of semen") appears in the Book of Leviticus, "Do not have carnal relations with your neighbor's wife and defile yourself with her" (Lev. 18:20). Many scholars find the rationale for this prohibition embedded in the Israelites' patriarchal structure, which was concerned with questions of paternity and inheritance. A similar view was expressed in medieval times by *Sefer HaChinukh*: God wished that "a human being should always know whose it is [i.e., who is the father?]" (*Yitro*, #35).

Adultery in the Ancient Near East

In ancient Mesopotamia, the ideal family was, for the most part, monogamous, but men were allowed to take concubines, often slave girls. A concubine did not have the rank of a wife, and though bound to her master in a new capacity, she did not automatically gain her freedom. Indeed, even a free woman hardly qualified for the term: she belonged to either her father or her husband, or she was protected by a close family member. When married, she entered the household of her husband and was expected to live in total fidelity to him. Consequently, adultery was a crime committed only by married women. Thus, for example, according to the Laws of Ur-Nammu (twenty-first century BCE, Sumer), "If the wife of a young man, on her own initiative, approaches a man and initiates sexual relations with him, they shall kill that woman; that male shall be released" (#7).[1] Similarly, in the Laws of Eshnunna (eighteenth century BCE), "When she [i.e., a housewife] is caught with another man, she shall not get away alive" (#28; *ANET*, 162). In the Middle Assyrian Laws (eleventh century BCE) we find this law: "If the wife of a man should go out of her own house, and go to another man where he resides, and should he fornicate with her knowing that she is the wife of a man, they shall kill the man and the wife" (#13).[2]

The punishment for adultery in the ancient Near East, at times, depended on the will of the husband or someone in authority. Thus, for instance, in the Code of Hammurabi (eighteenth century BCE), "If a man's wife should be seized lying with another male, they shall bind them and cast them into the water [i.e., for a river ordeal]. If the wife's master allows his wife to live, then the king shall allow his subject [i.e., the lover] to live" (#129)[3] (cf. Middle Assyrian Laws 15 and 16; *ANET*, 181).

In the Roman Empire, during the reign of Augustus (first century BCE), under Lex Julia, adultery was punished only when it took place with another man's wife, and the culprits were banished to a deserted island and suffered the partial confiscation of their property as well as loss of the dowry.

Things changed under Islam later on in the seventh century. Considering adultery as an "abomination and an evil way" (Qur'an, "The Children of Israel," 17:32), it applied the punishment depending on the status of the lovers. If the fornicators were unmarried, the Qur'an required only flogging ("one hundred stripes") ("The Light," 24:2). But if a married woman engaged in lewdness, the penalty was death by stoning, provided there were four witnesses to the act ("Women," 4:15).

Adultery in Ancient Judaism

Though monogamy was the norm in biblical times, there was no objection if a man married another woman or took on a concubine. Thus, for example, Abraham married Sarah, Hagar, and Keturah; Jacob had two wives, Rachel and Leah; Esau had three wives (Gen. 36:2–3). Moses married Zipporah and a "Cushite" woman whose name is not recorded (Num. 12:1). The prophet

Samuel's father had two wives, Hannah and Peninnah (I Sam. 1:2). Kings could afford even more wives and concubines. King David had at least seven wives and many concubines (I Chron. 3:1–9), and Solomon is reputed to have had seven hundred wives and three hundred concubines (I Kings 11:3). King Rehoboam, Solomon's son, had eighteen wives and sixty concubines (II Chron. 11:21). Deuteronomy clearly allows for a man to be married to two wives simultaneously (21:15–17). At times, concubines were given to the husband by the ranking wife. Thus, for example, Rachel, who was barren, offered her husband, Jacob, her own maid Bilhah as a concubine in order to have children through her (Gen. 30:4). Jacob's other wife, Leah, did the same when she offered her maid, Zilpah, to her husband as a concubine (Gen. 30:9).[4] These multiple marriages were not done necessarily for lust but mostly for economic reasons, for "in a society that is overwhelmingly seminomadic and agricultural, the maintenance of several wives would supply an abundant work force to tend flocks and work fields."[5]

Married women were expected to be faithful to their husbands, and husbands needed to learn how to appreciate their wives. The biblical wisdom literature advises, "Find joy in the wife of your youth" (Prov. 5:18), and teaches that "he who commits adultery [*no-eif ishah*] is devoid of sense" (Prov. 6:32). Proverbs warns that an unfaithful married woman "will snare a person of honor" (Prov. 6:26). The adulteress lacks conscience: "She eats, wipes her mouth, and says, 'I have done no wrong'" (Prov. 30:20). According to Job, the adulterer [*no-eif*] thinks he can get away with his crime, for like a murderer he watches for twilight in the darkness of night, "thinking, 'No one will glimpse me then'" (Job 24:15). In his defense, Job claims total fidelity to his wife and invokes curses upon himself "if my heart was ravished by the wife of my neighbor" (Job 31:9). Yet, in spite of these teachings and the stern command of the Seventh Word of the Decalogue, "You shall not commit adultery," marital infidelity was known in biblical times, too.

The Bible, like other ancient Near Eastern traditions, views adultery (in Hebrew, *naaf*) as sexual intercourse only between a man and a married woman. A married man who had an affair with an unmarried woman was not considered an adulterer, because, as noted above, in biblical times, he could marry as many women as he could afford and take on various concubines, all at the same time. Unlike modern times, in biblical custom a woman who is engaged to be married had to display fidelity to her fiancée, just as a married woman. If she slept with another man during the period of her engagement, she was considered adulterous.

The permission of marrying more than one wife continued into the Rabbinic period. According to a Talmudic teaching, "a man may marry any number of women, provided he can support them" (BT *Y'vamot* 65a). This teaching was reaffirmed in medieval times by Maimonides, who ruled that a man may marry "as many as a hundred women . . . as long as he can provide each one of them their required needs of food, clothing, and conjugal relations" (*Mishneh Torah, Hilkhot Ishut* 14:3). The Talmud, however, limits the number of wives to four (BT *Y'vamot* 44a). In time, the practice of polygamy was frowned upon by many rabbis, with one Talmudic teacher even arguing that a wife could divorce her husband if he took on a second wife (BT *Y'vamot* 65a). Monogamy finally became the accepted practice after a *takanah* (ordinance), ascribed to Rabbeinu Gershom ben Y'hudah (tenth to eleventh century, Germany), was issued for Ashkenazic Jews for a period of five hundred years. Even though many Sephardic Jews did not accept this ordinance as valid, eventually they too followed the Ashkenazic custom and accepted monogamy as a life pattern. When the modern State of Israel was established in 1948, some Sephardic Jews, coming from a number of Arab countries, brought in their second wives. Israel accommodated them but decreed that henceforth polygamy would be prohibited.

The Punishment for Adultery

Like many other commandments in the Decalogue, the injunction "You shall not commit adultery" does not provide us with a rationale for this injunction, nor does it indicate its punishment. To find the specific penalty, we need to turn to other biblical texts. And there we find that the penalty for adultery between a man and a married woman is severe and uncompromising—it is death: "If a man commits adultery with a married woman [*v'ish asher yinaf et eishet ish*], committing adultery with another man's wife, the adulterer and the adulteress shall be put to death" (Lev. 20:10; cf. 18:20). Here the question of consent is not discussed. The law assumes that both parties have engaged in sexual dalliance willingly. The woman is a *noefet* (an "adulteress," a consenting participant); she did not become one by force (see Ibn Ezra, ad loc). The man is a *no-eif* (an adulterer) and, having committed this crime with a married woman, suffers the same penalty.

The Book of Deuteronomy appears to limit the scope of adultery by stating that in order to be punished, participants must be discovered *in flagrante delicto*: *Ki yimatzei ish*, "If a man is found lying with another man's wife . . ." (Deut. 22:22). On the other hand, reflecting an earlier norm found in the Hittite Law collections (fourteenth century BCE, #197; *ANET*, 196), Deuteronomy applies the law not only to women who are already married, but also to a woman who is engaged to be married, although it makes a critical distinction between consensual and nonconsensual sex. When a betrothed young woman (*naarah v'tulah m'orasah l'ish*; namely, one who is engaged to be married for whom a bride-price called *mohar* was paid by her father) is sexually assaulted within the city limits (*bair*, "in town"), the adulterers receive the capital punishment, on the assumption that the betrothed woman could have asked for help and did not; that means she was complicit in the act (Deut. 22:23–24). However, if the act occurred in the countryside (*basadeh*, lit. "in an open field"), namely, outside of the city limits, the law assumes that she was raped, and she escapes the death penalty (Deut. 22:25–27). The male attacker, however, is put to death. The text makes his crime analogous to murder: "this case is like that of one person attacking and murdering another" (Deut. 22:26), for which the penalty is death.

In the ancient Near East, the imposition of capital punishment depended on the status of the married woman. If she were a free woman, the penalty was higher; if she were a slave, the penalty was lower. Thus according to the Laws of Ur-Nammu, "If a man acts in violation of the rights of another and deflowers the virgin slave woman of a man, he shall weigh and deliver 5 shekels of silver" (#8).[6] Similarly, in the Bible, if a man had sexual relations with a slave woman who had been designated for another man or was not yet free, the adulterers were not put to death, but "there shall be an indemnity [*bikoret*]" (Lev. 19:20), namely, the paramour needed to pay a sum of money and bring a sacrifice to the Temple, because the sexual encounter had devalued the slave woman, and the owner expected compensation for this damage.

In the Bible, the usual method of carrying out the death penalty was stoning by the public (e.g., Deut. 22:24). Burning is mentioned in Gen. 38:24, and stripping (perhaps before execution?) in Hos. 2:5, 2:12, and Ezek. 16:37, 16:39. According to Rashi, the death penalty for adultery was executed by means of strangulation (see his comment on Lev. 20:10).

Who actually carried out the death penalty? In the ancient Near East, it was often the immediate family that inflicted the punishment. The Hittite Laws state, "If the husband finds them [i.e., the adulterers], he may kill them" (#197; *ANET*, 196). Similarly, the Middle Assyrian Laws indicate that "if the woman's husband puts his wife to death, he shall also put the adulterer to death" (#15; *ANET*, 181). On the other hand, in the biblical period, at least from the seventh century BCE on, all penalties seem to have been administered by "the elders of the town at the gate" (e.g., Deut. 22:18).

Even though biblical law requires the death penalty for adultery, no biblical text states that it was ever carried out. Tamar's sexual intercourse with Judah should be considered as adulterous because Shelah, Judah's youngest son, was already promised to her (Gen. 38:11). But Judah and Tamar escape the death penalty, even though Judah states that she deserves to be burned to death (Gen. 38:24). King David and Bathsheba (see "The Sixth Word: Homicide") have illicit sexual relations and have a child. In this case, too, the adulterers escape the death penalty because of David's repentance (II Sam. 12:13–14). However, even though David fasts and shows contrition, the child dies because of David's sin (II Sam. 12:18). The Bible does not state that Bathsheba gave her consent to this liaison. The text simply states, "David sent messengers to fetch her; she came to him and he lay with her" (II Sam. 11:4). Perhaps she had no choice in the matter; it was almost impossible to say no to a king. In the Rabbinic period, Rabbi Elazar ben Tzadok, a second-generation *Tanna* (ca. 80–120 CE), reports that once the daughter of a priest committed adultery and was burned to death (*Mishnah Sanhedrin* 7:2). This verdict was wrong, adds the Talmud, because the court was made up of Sadducees who did not know the law (BT *Sanhedrin* 72a).

After the death penalty was eliminated from the jurisdiction of the Jewish courts in the first century CE, adulterers were only flogged and compelled to divorce their wives. The adulteress also lost the property rights written in her marriage document, the *ketubah*. She was also prohibited from marrying her lover. During the geonic times (sixth to eleventh century), it was customary to cut off the adulterers' hair as a sign of shame.[7] Interestingly, according to the Talmud, the death penalty was not imposed on a Jewish man who had committed adultery with a gentile married woman (BT *Sanhedrin* 52b).

Attempted Adultery

The Bible includes three cases of attempted adultery: King Abimelech and Sarah (Gen. 20:4), King Abimelech and Rebekah (Gen. 26:10), and Joseph and Pontifar's wife's (Genesis 39). In the first two stories, a man attempts to pass off his wife as his sister, fearing that because of her beauty, she would be taken away from him, and he would be killed. This assumption demonstrates the lower status of a woman in the early biblical times and how easily she could be discarded in cases of imminent danger.

Before we examine these three cases, however, a note about the relationship between the Pharaoh and Sarah in Gen. 12:10–20 is in order, as their case is ambiguous. According to the narrative, Abraham (here called Abram) goes down to Egypt because of a famine. He is afraid, however, that his beautiful wife Sarah would be captured by the Egyptians and he would be killed. Therefore, he tells Sarah to pass herself as his sister, thus ensuring that he would not be hurt.[8] However, when the family arrives in Egypt, "the woman [i.e., Sarah] was taken into Pharaoh's palace" (Gen. 12:15). There is no explicit reference to a sexual relation between the Pharaoh and Sarah, which would make this liaison an adulterous one, but the context implies that it was so, for, as the text goes on to say, "And because of her, it went well with Abram" (Gen. 12:16). However, it is also possible that the gifts Abram received were in compensation for the loss of his sister. The text is not clear.

Postbiblical commentators were bothered by the image of the matriarch's alleged adulterous relations or her rape at the hand of the Pharaoh, so they attempted to come up with different scenarios defending her integrity. Thus, for example, the historian Josephus claims that "God put a stop to his [i.e., Pharaoh's] inclinations, by sending upon him a distemper" (*Ant.* I, 8:1). Some sages maintain that every time the Pharaoh tried to approach Sarah, an angel armed with a stick beat him.[9] Others argue that Sarah was divorced when she arrived in Egypt, thus eliminating the stigma of adultery (*Likutei Torah*, Genesis, 94). The Book of Jubilees (13:11–13) stresses that Sarah was taken from Abram "by force," thus converting the sexual act into a rape in an open field, which does not carry the death penalty for the woman (see page 138 discussion on Deut. 22:25–27). However, these attempts at whitewashing the adulterous relationship are hardly convincing.

In the story of King Abimelech and Sarah (Genesis 20), Abraham passes his wife Sarah as his stepsister, being afraid that he would be killed because of her. So Abimelech has Sarah brought to him but does not have sexual relations with her, because God appears to Abimelech in a dream, telling him, under the threat of death, not to approach the married Sarah. The king restores Sarah to Abraham and gives him gifts. Because of Abraham's intercession with God, Abimelech is even rewarded with children of his own.

The case of Rebekah and King Abimelech (Gen. 26:7–11) is slightly different. Here, unlike Sarah, Rebekah is never taken away, and no adultery takes place. Isaac, we are told, is afraid that because of Rebekah's beauty, she would be captured and he killed, so he passes her as his sister. But when the king sees Isaac "fondling" (*metzacheik*; Gen. 26:8) his wife, he complains to Isaac that what he did was foolish, because "one of the people nearly lay with your wife; you would have brought [suffering] upon us for our guilt!" (Gen. 26:10).

In the story of Joseph, a married woman attempts to seduce a young man working for her husband (Gen. 39:7–20). Potiphar's wife, whose name is not recorded, tries to seduce Joseph by asking him to lie with her, but he refuses. One day, when the two are alone in the house, she takes hold of his garments and forces herself on him. Joseph leaves his garments in her hands and gets away. Potiphar's wife then accuses Joseph of attempting to commit adultery, and he is put in jail, a surprisingly mild penalty.

In addition to these biblical passages dealing with attempted adultery, there is a similar story in the Apocrypha regarding Susanna, the wife of Joakim. She is accused of adultery by two elders and is condemned to death by the assembly, even without cross-examination or her own testimony. However, the accusation is proved wrong, and she is declared innocent.

Suspicion of Adultery

Biblical law is clear that the death penalty applies when the facts of adultery are proved. What happens if there is just a suspicion of marital infidelity? How does the legal system deal with this matter? The Bible covers this issue in two different places.

According to the Book of Deuteronomy, if a husband brings forth an accusation of premarital infidelity, claiming that his new bride was not a virgin when he married her, the wife's parents can produce before the elders of the town a bloody cloth as evidence of her virginity. The husband is then flogged and fined, because his accusation was false (Deut. 22:13–19). However, if the charges prove to be true, then the wife is brought before the entrance of her father's house and stoned to death by the "residents of her town" (Deut. 22:20–21).

There are a number of difficulties with this law, because it disregards the necessity to bring forth two witnesses to verify the crime and overlooks the fact that the parents can easily fake the bride's evidence of her virginity. Furthermore, as Jeffrey Tigay points out, "the law treats the girl's premarital sex as a capital crime, although verses 23:24 and Ex. 22:15–16 indicate that such misconduct calls for execution only if she is engaged."[10] To solve this legal problem, Jewish tradition assumes that the law applies solely when the new bride committed the act of infidelity while she was engaged to be married, and therefore bound by the laws of marriage (*Sifrei* 235–37; BT *K'tubot* 11b, 46a).

Another problematic case is the *sotah*, the suspected adulteress, whose husband has a fit of jealousy (Num. 5:11–31). Here there are no witnesses against the wife, only the husband's suspicion that she had carnal relations with another man during the marriage. In order to find out the truth, the husband resorts to a ritual ordeal. According to the Laws of Hammurabi, a suspicious husband could bring his wife to the river ordeal to determine her guilt by asking the river to act as divine judge (#132; *ANET*, 171). In the biblical case, the husband brings his wife to a priest, who gives her a liquid consisting of water and some earth from the floor of the sanctuary, combined with some ink taken from a document containing priestly curses; the priest then makes her drink the mixed potion. If she can tolerate it, she is considered innocent; otherwise her "belly shall distend and her thighs shall sag; and the woman shall become a curse among her people" (Num. 5:27). The text does not tell us why the husband was filled with jealousy. Maybe the wife is pregnant and he is not sure about the identity of the father. Furthermore, the practical effects of drinking the "water of bitterness" are not clear. Perhaps, the ritual causes a miscarriage or infertility. The wife, however, escapes the death penalty. In the opinion of a biblical scholar, the reason for this is because in biblical law, "the unapprehended adultery remains punishable only by God."[11] The Mishnah tells us that this ordeal was suspended during the Second Temple period, because of the increase of cases of suspected adulteries (*Mishnah Sotah* 9:11). Maybe it was also thought by this time that the water ordeal was not effective and reliable.

The Severity of Punishment

In the ancient Near East, adultery was considered a public crime as well as a religious sin. The Bible calls it "a great sin" (Gen. 20:9) and a "great evil" (Gen. 39:9). It is referred to as a "great crime" in Egyptian literature (*ANET*, 24). In Babylonian literature, the adulterer is viewed as one who had committed a "grievous sin" against the god Ninurta."[12] Yet, in extra-biblical literature of the region, the offense is against the husband, who, if he wishes, could commute the sentence. Thus, for example, according to the Middle Assyrian Laws, "if he [the husband] lets his wife go free, they shall let the man go free (too)" (#A15; *ANET*, 181).

It is otherwise in the Bible. According to Moshe Greenberg, the offense is "not merely a wrong against the husband, it is a sin against God,"[13] and, therefore, absolute and immutable. Thus, for instance, King Abimelech refuses to approach Sarah sexually after he discovers that she is Abraham's wife. "God said to him [Abimelech], 'I do indeed know that you did this with a pure heart, and it is I who held you back from sinning against Me'" (Gen. 20:6). Note that the sin is against God, not against Abraham. Similarly, Joseph turns down the advances of Potiphar's wife on the basis that committing adultery would be a "sin against God" (Gen. 39:9; see also II Sam. 12:13; Ps. 51:1–6). On the other hand, in the biblical wisdom literature, it appears as if the offense is committed against the husband: "The fury of the husband will be passionate; he will show no pity on his day of vengeance" (Prov. 6:34). But, as Jeffrey Tigay argues, "Whether passages from the wisdom literature, with its strong international literary ties, reflect actual practice in Israel is a moot question."[14] The mere fact that the law against adultery is included in the Ten Commandments implies that, at some point in time, the offense prohibited by the Torah was considered an offense against God and therefore punished severely.

The Extended Meaning of Adultery

In the Bible, *YHVH* demands exclusive loyalty: "You must not worship any other god, because the Eternal, whose name is Impassioned, is an impassioned God" (Exod. 34:14). Sacrifices are to be offered only to *YHVH*: "Whoever sacrifices to a god other than the Eternal shall be proscribed" (Exod. 22:19). Worship of another god is called "whoring" (e.g., Deut. 31:16; Jer. 3:1). In prophetic literature, adultery is used metaphorically for religious apostasy. God, the husband (e.g., Ezek. 16:8; Isa. 54:5), accuses Israel, the bride, of worshiping other gods rather than being loyal to the God of Israel. Thus, for example, Jeremiah, speaking in God's name states, "The land was defiled by her [i.e., Israel's] casual immorality, as she committed adultery with stone and wood" (Jer. 3:9). Similarly, Ezekiel says, "They have committed adultery, and blood is on their hands; truly they have committed adultery with their fetishes, and have even offered to them as food the children they bore to Me" (Ezek. 23:37).

In the New Testament, when a man divorces his wife and marries another, he commits adultery against his wife (Mark 10:11). Even "looking on a woman to lust" is considered adultery (Matt. 5:28). Here one is reminded of what President Jimmy Carter acknowledged in his famous interview with *Playboy* magazine in November 1976: "I've looked on a lot of women with lust. I've committed adultery in my heart many times." This position reflects a Rabbinic text stated in the name of Reish Lakish (third century CE), "Lest you think, only he who sins with his body is an adulterer, he who sins with his eyes is also an adulterer" (*Vayikra Rabbah* 23:12). Most of the Rabbis, however, do not accept this interpretation.

For some medieval Jewish commentators, such as Joseph Bekhor Shor (twelfth century, France), all illicit sex is considered adultery; an adulterer is one who has relations with any of those on the forbidden list (Lev. 18:6–20; 20:10–21).[15] Similarly, Rabbi Yaacov Culi includes in this law all kinds of sexual crimes, such as incest, homosexual sodomy, and bestiality, as well as adultery with a woman who is betrothed but not yet fully married.[16] In our time, the meaning of the Seventh Word was extended by some to include "the prohibition of immoral speech, immodest conduct or association with persons who scoff at the sacredness of purity."[17]

Adultery and Divorce

In most Western countries today, adultery is considered grounds for divorce. According to New York Penal Law 255.17, adultery is even considered a class B misdemeanor and defined as follows: "A person is guilty of adultery when he engages in sexual intercourse with another person at a time when he has a living spouse or the other person has a living spouse." According to a recent Associate Press survey, 17 percent of divorces in the United States are caused by marital infidelity. In some states, except for those with no-fault divorce, proof of adultery is required to terminate a marriage.

The Bible accepts the reality of divorce under certain circumstances, even though the prophet Malachi claims that God "detests divorce [*shalach*, lit. "sending away"]" (Mal. 2:16). Abraham dismisses his wife, Hagar, at Sarah's request (Gen. 21:9–14). The Book of Deuteronomy rules on the case of remarriage after divorce (Deut. 24:1–4). During the days of Ezra and Nehemiah, Jewish men were told to dismiss their non-Jewish wives who led the Jews to abandon their faith (Ezra 10:1–4). However, the text does not state that this decree was ever put into practice. The Torah places some restrictions on the husband who wished to terminate his marriage: he could not divorce his wife if he falsely accused her of infidelity (Deut. 22:13–19) or if he sexually assaulted her before marriage (Deut. 22:28–29).

It is not known how prevalent divorce was in Rabbinic times. Family life was cherished. The sages taught that "he who has no wife lives without good, or help, or joy, or blessing, or atonement" (*B'reishit Rabbah* 17:2). Jewish tradition does not view divorce as a sin, even though it considers it a sad event. The Talmud states that when couples divorce, "even the altar cries tears because of it" (BT *Gittin* 90b).

Though the Rabbis accepted divorce, they attempted to restrict the husband's right to act without just cause. They decreed that not only a husband can initiate divorce proceedings; the wife, too, may sue her husband under certain conditions, such as apostasy, his refusal to cohabit, his loathsome disease, or his smelly profession. [i] However, given the clear wording of the biblical law in Deut. 24: 1-4 ("If he writes a bill of divorce..."), the Sages were forced to admit that the court can only coerce the husband to divorce his wife but cannot obligate him.

The Bible does not give us a clear reason for the dissolution of marriage while both parties are alive. It simply states that if a wife fails to please her husband "because he finds something obnoxious about her [*ervat davar*, lit. "the nakedness of the thing"]," he can divorce her by giving her a "bill of divorcement" (Deut. 24:1). This lack of clarity gave rise to two interpretations in the first century CE. According to the school of Shammai, this meant adultery (putting the stress on the word *ervah*, lit. "nakedness"), whereas, according to the school of Hillel, this meant "for any reason whatsoever" (stressing the word, *davar*, "thing"), including, as they stated, "even if she spoils a dish for him" (*Mishnah Gittin* 9:10). Though the interpretation of the school of Hillel won out, the Rabbis created a number of legal instruments to defend the rights of the wife, including a marriage document, the *ketubah*, which included the details of financial benefits to the divorcee.

According to Rabbinic teachings, divorce takes effect when the husband transmits the divorce document (called a *get*) to his former wife or her agent. In medieval times, Rabbeinu Gershom ben Y'hudah (tenth to eleventh century, Germany) decreed that a wife could not be divorced against her will and forbade the husband from marrying a new wife before divorcing the first one. Today, the Orthodox and Conservative Movements require a *get* for purposes of divorce. When a couple marries before a Conservative rabbi, the *ketubah* they sign includes a clause (the so-called Lieberman clause) stating that should the marriage be dissolved, they will appear before the Joint Bet Din of the Conservative Movement and abide by its decision. Reform Judaism, which has maintained total gender equality before the law, does not require a religious divorce and accepts the decree of any civil court for the purpose of remarriage. Increasingly, however, some Reform Jewish couples are beginning to use a liberal *get* that is egalitarian in nature. The Reform *Rabbi's Manual* (CCAR, 1988) includes a religious service called "Ritual of Release" as well as a text titled "Document of Separation."

Presently, the State of Israel, which is dominated by the Orthodox establishment regarding matters of personal status, insists on the husband's exclusive right to divorce his wife, creating a terrible problem for a woman described as *agunah* (lit. "anchored"), whose marriage ended without obtaining a proper *get*, either because of the husband's reluctance to ask the *beit din* to issue one or his disappearance for a number of years. An *agunah* cannot remarry until this problem is resolved. This creates an inequality in the divorce laws. Many halakhic authorities have solved the problem of the "missing" husband by creating a complex procedure enabling the wife to remarry. In Israel today, the attorney general is given the authority to put the refusing husband in prison until he asks the *beit din* to issue a *get*. In some Orthodox circles, the idea was advanced to include a prenuptial clause in the *ketubah* to deal with this question. However, there is still no consensus among the leading Orthodox leaders today as to how to put an end to this unfortunate situation. Reform Judaism has eliminated the problem of the *agunah* by admitting the validity of the civil divorce. A Jewish woman married under Orthodox auspices and then divorced by civil law would have no problem in getting remarried to another person by a Reform rabbi. However, as Mark Washofsky argues, if "a man who was divorced in the civil courts but who refuses to issue a *get* to his wife [who wishes to remain Orthodox] comes to us and asks us for remarriage, . . . we say, 'no,'"[19] based on the reason that the man wishes to use Reform services to secure a remarriage while denying that option to his wife.

Contemporary Perspectives on Adultery

Even though in biblical times adultery was a crime committed only by a married woman, contemporary societies like ours widen its scope by including a sexual act committed by a married individual, male or female, with another person, whether married or not, whereas consensual sexual encounters between single people are viewed as a private matter and not punishable by law. This reality creates new concerns that must be addressed with a new understanding.

In February 2001, the CCAR Ad Hoc Committee on Human Sexuality published a document called "Marital Sexual Infidelity," on the basis that this "is a growing phenomenon that threatens the very fabric of society."[20] It accepted as valid the distinctions made by Rabbi Daniel Schiff between various kinds of marital infidelity that require different legal and moral responses.

Rabbi Schiff argued that that there are five different types of adultery in our culture: (a) *technical*, when a couple is separated before divorce and one of the partners engages in sexual liaisons with another individual; (b) *circumstantial*, when one of the partners is so impaired (such as with a spouse suffering from Alzheimer's disease) that he or she is incapable of feeling being betrayed; (c) *unknowing*, when a married person pretends to be single; (d) *consenting*, when both partners in a marriage agree to engage in sexual affairs with outsiders; (e) *classic*, when the adulterous relations is carried out in secret from the marriage partner. The ad hoc committee's report places the last two, classic and consenting, among the category of "sinful" and "prohibited," but remarkably, it asks that we deal with greater compassion and lenience with deceived partners involved in circumstantial, technical, and unknowing adulteries. It also affirms the necessity of professional counseling for everyone involved and the employment of religious values in therapy sessions, such as penitence and reprobation, retrospectively and whenever appropriate, in order to try to repair the damage caused by these acts of sexual infidelity.

In our time, for a variety of reasons, including the openness of our society, the more frequent encounters between the sexes at work and in social contexts, and—some would add—lower religious sensitivities, there seems to be a more tolerant approach to cases of adultery. Many prominent people like politicians and movie stars have engaged in sexual encounters in recent years without strong negative consequences to their careers, even though the same acts would have been denounced strongly in previous times. President Bill Clinton's intimate relationship with Monica Lewinsky in 1998 almost derailed his presidency (he was impeached by Congress but was later acquitted of all charges), but his marriage remained intact, and he completed his term of office. When François Mitterrand, the president of France, died in 1996, both his wife and his long-term mistress attended the funeral and stood next to one another before his grave, and society tolerated this view. The media often reports on celebrity couplings outside of marriage, but these events do not seem to affect their marketability. Furthermore, matters considered taboo in the past are now being discussed openly, even though the issues are controversial. What if a spouse is put in jail for life? What happens when a spouse is severely ill and destined to be confined to bed for the rest of his or her life? And what about mental health issues that leave the healthy spouse in limbo? Is adultery acceptable in these cases?

In our time, nowhere is marital fidelity more severely tested than when the severe ill health of a spouse leads the healthy husband or wife to relationships outside of marriage. This issue was sensitively featured in 2012, in one of TV's most popular TV shows, *Grey's Anatomy*, where Adele, Dr. Webber's wife, is suffering from Alzheimer's disease, and the husband is tempted to seek companionship elsewhere.[21] The televangelist Pat Robertson created a fire storm in September, 2011 when he suggested in his TV program, *700 Club*, that Alzheimer's is grounds for divorce and remarriage: "I hate Alzheimer's. I know it sounds cruel, but if he's going to do something, he should divorce her and start all over again, but make sure she has custodial care and somebody looking after her." His remarks may have been too frank and even insensitive, but they struck a chord among many people. Though some individuals denounced him vociferously, others, realizing the complexity of the marital ties at a time when one of the spouses is in limbo and the other in need of companionship, came forward with more nuanced positions. Among them, Rabbi Richard F. Address explored the possible responses within Jewish law to this dilemma and supported the view that perhaps a ritual ought to be created, like those proposed for the wife who is considered as *agunah* (see page 146), that would enable the healthy spouse to establish a relationship with another person, while at the same time binding him- or herself to caring for the ill spouse for the rest of their lives.[22] This would be, Address argues, like reviving and readapting to our times the status of the biblical "concubine" (*pilegesh*).[23]

Though most adulteries end in divorce, in some real-life situations, marital infidelity can even save one's life, and rabbinic authorities have given their approval under very strict conditions. Such a case occurred during the period of the Holocaust. Rabbi Ephraim Oshry, an Orthodox rabbi who survived the ghetto of Kovno, was confronted with such a terrible dilemma. Here is the question and his answer:

Question: Immediately after our liberation from the ghetto, a horrifying problem was brought to my attention. It applied not only to the woman who posed it to me but to a large sisterhood of Jewish women who had suffered abominably during the Holocaust years.

A young woman from a respected family in Kovno came to me with tears gushing down her cheeks. She, like many of her unfortunate sisters, had been captured by the accursed Germans and forced into prostitution. The evildoers had not only made free use of her pure body, but had also tattooed the words "prostitute for Hitler's soldiers" on her.

After the liberation she was reunited with her husband who had also survived. Their children had been killed by the Germans, and they hoped to establish a new family on the basis of Jewish sanctity and purity. But when her husband saw the words on her body he was extremely upset, and decided they must clarify first whether he was allowed to live with her according to Halacha, for if she had even once willingly slept with a German she might be forbidden to her husband.

Response: I ruled that this unfortunate woman and all her sisterhood who were so shamed might return to their husbands and live with them as man and wife. The only exception would be when the husband is a Cohen in which case, even though she had been raped, he would be forbidden to live with her.[24] But where the husband is not a Cohen there is absolutely no reason to forbid the woman to her husband.

God forbid that we speak evil of these kosher Jewish women. On the contrary, it is a mitzvah to publicize the great reward that they will receive from Him Who hears the entreaties of the suffering. He will certainly cure their broken hearts, heal them emotionally, and grant them His blessings. We must prevent any additional suffering by these women, as was the case with a number of them, whose husbands divorced them. Woe unto us that this should have happened in our times!

I ruled that there was no need for her to try to have the tattoo obliterated. On the contrary, let her and her sisters preserve their tattoos and regard them not as signs of shame, but as signs of honor, pride, and courage—proof of what they suffered for the sanctification of God. The inscription the murderers used to defile and shame these pure Jewish women is an honor for them and for our people.[25]

In Conclusion

According to biblical teaching, one man and one woman were created at the beginning of time with the hope that that they will become "one flesh" (Gen. 2:24). In Jewish tradition, marriage is encouraged and promoted: "It is not good for man to be alone; I will make a fitting helper for him" (Gen. 2:18).

"We are commanded," writes Rabbi Peter S. Knobel, "to control our sexual appetite, channel our desires into appropriate relations, and preserve the family as the locus of safe human intimacy."[26] Adultery shatters the family unity and the trust within the family. In the words of the Book of Proverbs, "Only one who would destroy himself does such a thing" (Prov. 6:32). It affects not only those who are involved, but also the extended family, and primarily the children. Family discord does not need to end in adultery; if the couple cannot possibly live together, they can get professional help, attempt a trial separation, or, in the worst case, file for divorce, but committing adultery is a breach of trust that cannot always be repaired, if ever. Rabbi Rachel S. Mikva" [goes so far as to suggest, "The 'public' has no right to know [about an adultery], but friends who do know have a right and a responsibility to remind their wayward acquaintances of the vow they took. However, in our time, sensitivity requires that, under very limited conditions, as discussed above, we do not rush to judgment before knowing all the facts and show compassion and understanding when marital infidelity is the only way out to save a life or to provide an outlet for human need and existence.

The Eighth Word: Stealing

What Is Stealing?

Most countries around the world have laws that defend the right of ownership, on the assumption that each person is entitled to the fruits of his or her labor and that another individual does not have the right to expropriate it without the owner's knowledge and approval. In the Commonwealth of Massachusetts, theft is considered a crime and defined as "taking of almost anything of value without the consent of the owner, with the intent to permanently deprive him or her of the value of the property taken" (18 USC, #668). For this misappropriation the culprit can be fined, or imprisoned not more than ten years, or both. If the value of the property taken is low (e.g., less than $500), it is called "petty theft." If the amount is larger, it is "grand theft." The general category of "theft" includes robbery (by force), burglary (entering unlawfully), and embezzlement (stealing from an employer).

It was different in biblical and Rabbinic times. Even though various acts of misappropriation were included in the broad category of "theft," it was often punished only by compensation. Property and life were considered incommensurable. The return of the property was more important to the biblical legislator than the punishment of the thief. In this chapter we shall analyze the question of what stealing meant in various classic Jewish texts as well as the ethical implications of the eighth commandment in our days.

The Text of the Eighth Word

The Eighth Word, the third of the short injunctions in the second half of the Decalogue, simply reads, "You shall not steal" (*lo tignov*); it is short and laconic. It does not tell us the scope of the commandment, nor does it give us the specific reason for observing it. Yet, a critical reading of many biblical texts shows that taking away property was viewed not only as an assault on the right to ownership but also an attack on people's dignity. There is a hint of this thinking in a biblical law that states that if one takes away his neighbor's garment in pledge, he must return it to him before sunset, for "it is his only clothing; the sole covering for his skin. In what else shall he sleep?" (Exod. 22:26). Property is an extension of one's self, and needs to be protected by law. For ancient Jewish legislators, stealing, viewed as a broad category of misappropriation, included all kinds of deceptive behaviors that deprived the owners of their legal property rights. The Aramaic translation of the Pentateuch attributed to Yonatan ben Uziel has a longer midrashic rendition of the eighth commandment: "Sons of Israel, My people, You shall not be thieves, nor companions nor associates of thieves: there shall not be seen in the congregations of Israel a people of thieves; that your sons may not arise after you to teach one another to have companionship with thieves: for on account of the guilt of theft famine comes upon the world."

In the Hebrew Bible, the basic verb for "stealing" is *ganav*. A thief is called a *gannav*. A related verb *gazal* refers to stealing by force or intimidation, and *ashak* means "to defraud." The Bible also uses the verb "to take" (*lakach*) in the sense of stealing. Taking spoils during war (Deut. 2:35, 3:7, 20:14), acquiring items from hunting (Lev. 17:13), or taking back one's own property (II Sam 3:15ff.) is not considered stealing in the Bible.

Some scholars, both ancient and modern, have argued that the original intent of the Eighth Word was to punish the kidnapper of a human being, and only later on was the scope of the law enlarged to cover many cases of misappropriation. To prove this point, they point out that in the Bible the verb *ganav* is often used to refer to kidnapping individuals. Thus, for instance, Joseph tells his jail mates, "I was stolen [*gunov gunavti*] from the land of the Hebrews" (Gen. 40:15). Similarly, one law in the Book of the Covenant reads, "One who kidnaps a person [*v'goneiv ish*]—whether having sold or still holding the victim—shall be put to death" (Exod. 21:16; cf. Deut. 24:7). This is also the way some of the Rabbinic texts understand the meaning of this verb (see, for example, *M'khilta, Bachodesh* 8; BT *Sanhedrin*

86a; *Sefer HaChinukh*, #36). Other commentators, however, argue that in the Eighth Word, stealing at large is banned, thus affirming the right of possession, because the verb *ganav* is also used in reference to animals (as in Exod. 22:11) and other stolen goods (as in Exod. 22:6). We simply do not know the original intent of the commandment.

Theft in Ancient Times

Ever since the nineteenth century, modern societies have made a distinction between civil and criminal law. In civil law, a private party files a lawsuit, whereas in criminal law, the litigation is initiated by governmental authorities. This difference was not known in ancient times. In Rome, for example, the *ius civile* referred to the entire system of law that the empire had established for itself.

In the ancient Near East, theft was broadly defined, and the penalties varied depending on the circumstances. Thus, for example, according to the laws of Lipit Ishtar (Sumer, ca. 1930 BCE), "If a man enters the orchard of another man, and is seized there for thievery, he shall weigh and deliver 10 shekels of silver" (#9).[1] On the other hand, in the Laws of Hammurabi, "If a man commits robbery and is then seized, that man shall be killed" (#22).[2] In the Qur'an, the penalty for stealing is severe: "As for the thief, both male and female, cut off their hands" (5:38).

Outside of the Decalogue, there are many references to stealing in the Bible, but they are scattered throughout different legal compendia. On the other hand, in Rabbinic texts, we see an attempt to systematize the laws of theft, with the best arrangement found in Maimonides's *Mishneh Torah* (in book 11, *Hilkhot G'neivah*) and in the codes (such as the *Shulchan Arukh* by Joseph Caro).

The Punishment for Theft

The Decalogue does not include a penalty clause associated with thievery. Leviticus 19:11 states, "You [pl.] shall not steal" (*lo tignovu*), but it, too, fails to deal with the question of punishment. In order to find out how the thief was penalized in biblical times, we need to look for special categories of stealing that are highlighted in other parts of the Bible. In surveying these examples, we note that in comparing our biblical laws on stealing with their counterparts in the ancient Near East, Jewish law appears to be much more lenient in punishing the thief. Thus, for instance, though Mesopotamian law at times imposes capital punishment for offenses against property, biblical law does not. As Moshe Greenberg aptly puts it, "In biblical law life and property are incommensurable."[3] Biblical legislators seem to be more interested in the return of the property to its lawful owner; thus they punish the thief with a small fine payable to the aggrieved party.

Types of Stealing in the Classic Jewish Texts

Both biblical legislators and Rabbinic scholars struggled with the concept of stealing by attempting to balance the rights of the original owner, the intention of the thief, and the well-being of society. These texts often show compassion for the thief while strongly defending the property rights of all individuals. The interest of the legislators seems to be the return of the stolen object rather than the punishment of the thief. Thus, for instance, according to Maimonides, even though misappropriating property worth a penny is considered stealing, for which the penalty is paying the principal plus the fine (*Mishneh Torah, Hilkhot G'neivah* l), if a thief admits his guilt, he is exempt from paying the fine (1:5). Thieves who are minors do not pay a fine but are required to return the object (1:8) and are subject to physical punishment (i.e., lashes) only in proportion to their strength.

In an attempt to systematize the laws regarding theft, the ancient Rabbis set up some basic principles that would guide their thinking. For example, they argued that robbery, stealing, and embezzlement constitute civil wrongs rather than crimes in Jewish law; that land could not be "stolen," because it could not be carried away; that to constitute theft, there has to be an act of *chazakah* (taking possession), either through lifting up the object or drawing it away, with the intent of appropriating it; that certain acts viewed as stealing in the Bible were actually "like" stealing or part of a different type of transgression (see below for examples).[4] In modern times, because civil law takes precedence over Jewish law, all biblical and Rabbinic laws regarding theft have ceased to have practical application and represent only moral values worthy of study and emulation.

Given the fact that "stealing" is a wide category in the Bible and Rabbinic literature, Jewish law considers the following cases of misappropriation as part of the general prohibition against the eighth commandment.

Kidnapping

In biblical times, the act of stealing a person was primarily for purposes of slavery and carried the death penalty (Exod. 21:16; cf. Deut. 24:7). In early biblical times, it was the family of the aggrieved party that put the culprit to death, but slowly this right was transferred to local courts. The penalty for kidnapping in other Near Eastern societies was also severe. For example, according to the Laws of Hammurabi, "If a man should kidnap the young child of another man, he shall be killed" (#14),[5] and in Hittite Laws, this crime was punished by paying a high ransom to the family (see #19a–21).[6]

The Bible does not record any clear act of kidnapping. The closest we have is the case of Joseph's jealous brothers, who, as an act of revenge, throw him into a pit and then sell him to some merchants on their way to Egypt (Genesis 37). Yet, Joseph claims that he was "stolen [*gunov gunavti*] from the land of the Hebrews" (Gen. 40:15). There is also a reference to what could be considered an abduction of children in the story of Laban, who complains that his son-in-law, Jacob, in fleeing to his homeland, the land of Canaan, secretly took away (*vatignov*) his children and grandchildren without his knowledge and approval (Gen. 31:26–28).

Talmudic law, realizing that it is not easy to prove that an actual abduction had taken place, made the prosecution for kidnapping (*g'neivat nefesh*) more difficult and required that the detention, enslavement, and sale of the abducted person were necessary elements of the offense (BT *Sanhedrin* 85b–86a). In medieval times, people were stolen for purposes of slavery, and many individuals, especially blacks from Africa, were often kidnapped by pirates, including a few Jewish pirates, and sold in the open markets in Europe and the United States, until slavery was first abolished by Spain in 1542, and in the United States with the adoption of the Thirteenth Amendment to the U.S. Constitution in 1865. Presently, kidnapping is mostly done for purposes of human trafficking or in order to extract a ransom from the family of the abducted individual; it is considered a crime, and the culprit is severely punished, depending on what happened to the victim.

The most notorious case of kidnapping of our time was the abduction of Charles Lindbergh Jr. (the "Lindbergh baby") in 1932. The perpetrator, Bruno R. Hauptmann, was executed in April 1936, even though he proclaimed his innocence to the end of his trial. More recently, an Israeli soldier, Gilad Shalit, was captured in June 2006 by Hamas militants in a cross-border raid in Gaza, in order to force Israel to release about one thousand Palestinian prisoners. After five years in captivity, Shalit was finally freed in October 2011, as part of a prisoner exchange between Hamas and Israel.

Stealing a Religious Object

In ancient Babylonia the theft of valuables belonging to the gods or the palace carried the death penalty for the thief as well as for the person who received the stolen goods (Laws of Hammurabi 6).[7] A case of stealing a religious object is mentioned in the Bible with reference to Rachel. When Laban accuses Jacob of stealing his household idols (*t'rafim*), the patriarch Jacob, not knowing that his wife Rachel had taken them without her father's consent, denies his father-in-law's accusation and says, "The one with whom you find your gods shall not live!"(Gen. 31:32). They search everywhere but cannot find them. Rachel, in the meantime, has kept the idols in her camel's cushion and is sitting on them. Furthermore, she declines to come down, pretending that she has her period, and thus escapes without punishment. It is not known, however, whether this case reflects the legal practice in ancient Israel. The only biblical example of an Israelite being put to death for stealing items consecrated to God is Achan son of Carmi, who lived during the days of Joshua, and took (*lakach*) "a Shinar [perhaps from Babylonia] mantle, two hundred shekels of silver, and a wedge of gold weighing fifty shekels" (Josh. 7:21). He was pelted with stones by the entire community (Josh. 7:25).

In biblical law, stealing a sacred object is called *meilah* ("trespass," based on Lev. 5:15) and requires restitution plus a fifth and a guilt offering. In the Talmud, some of the Rabbis argue that the penalty is decreed by God, but others maintain that an admonition is enough (BT *Sanhedrin* 84a).

Stealing from religious institutions still continues to occur in our time. However, public opinion views it as morally reprehensible and as the lowest kind of thievery, whether it is done by stealing from the collection plate in a church or from the donations that members make to the institution. In 2013, when two friends were arrested after they were caught stealing supplies donated to Hurricane Sandy victims from a Staten Island church, the Reverend Dr. John Rocco Carlo, a retired NYPD captain said, "They're stealing from God, because God brought it in, so to speak, to give to people."[8]

Stealing Movable Objects

Living in an agricultural society, ancient Israelites bought and sold animals, legally or illegally. In this case, biblical law makes a distinction between small and large cattle. If a person steals a sheep, whether he slaughters it or sells it, he is punished by fourfold payment (Exod. 21:37; cf. II Sam. 12:6). The Book of Proverbs also refers to stealing, and most likely it has in mind the act of stealing small cattle. However, it punishes the culprit more harshly; if a thief is caught, we are told, "he must pay sevenfold" (Prov. 6:31). However, it is doubtful that a wisdom book such as Proverbs would give us a clear picture of legal practices in ancient Israel. As one commentator puts it, "'Sevenfold' in the present verse may be a way of saying 'greatly.'"[9] If, on the other hand, the thief steals large cattle, the penalty, according to biblical law, is fivefold (Exod. 21:37). But if the animal, whether an ox or a sheep, is found alive in his possession, the fine is only double (Exod. 22:3). In the ancient Near East, the punishment for stealing cattle was much higher. For example, according to Hittite Laws, if a person stole a two-year-old bull, he gave fifteen cattle in return; in former days, the law states, they used to give thirty (# 57).[10] If he stole a ewe, he had to pay six sheep (#68).[11]

The Rabbis were puzzled about the discrepancy of punishment between cattle and sheep. One midrash justifies the lesser charges for the sheep, arguing that a stolen ox has to be led away by the thief, whereas stolen sheep must be carried, which is a degrading act for a human being who has been created in the image of God (see Rashi, ad loc). According to the Mishnah (*K'tubot* 3:9), if a thief confesses, he must pay the value of the stolen object but does not have to make double, fourfold, or fivefold restitution.

Biblical and Rabbinic law considers in great detail other types of theft, such as stealing objects from safekeeping (Exod. 22:6–8) or receiving stolen goods (*Mishneh Torah, Hilkhot G'veivah* 5:1), but the same basic principles of punishment apply in these cases, too; namely, so long as the object stolen is intact, it is the duty of the thief to return it, and the punishment is secondary and rather mild.

Encroachment

A person who attempts to enlarge his land property by extending it into his neighbor's yard by stealth commits "encroachment," a form of stealing. This must have been a wide practice in the past because even the ancient Egyptian wisdom book *Amen-em-opet* (ca. tenth to sixth century BCE) contains a warning about it: "Do not carry off the landmark at the boundaries of the arable land, nor disturb the position of the measuring-cord" (6:1; *ANET*, 422). The Book of Proverbs, reflecting this teaching, similarly states, "Do not remove the ancient boundary stone that your ancestors set up" (22:28), for if you do, as written in the following chapter, "they [the original owners who are orphans] have a mighty Kinsman [i.e., God], and He will surely take up their cause with you" (23:11). In the Book of Deuteronomy encroachment is described in 19:14: "You shall not move your neighbor's landmarks, set up by previous generations." The Bible does not specify a punishment for this act, because these were often done in secret. But the law does attempt to protect the original owner by issuing a curse, "Cursed be the one who moves a neighbor's landmark" (Deut. 27:17). In spite of this teaching, these acts must have been carried out with impunity, for, as Job complains, "people remove boundary-stones" (Job 24:2) and get away with it.

Even though property encroachment is considered stealing in the Bible as part of the general prohibition against theft, the Rabbis view it as a distinct wrong (*g'zeilah*, "robbery") and connect it with the biblical law about removal of boundaries (Deut. 19:14). They, too, warn against entering someone else's property, even if one has a good reason: "Do not enter [stealthily] into your neighbor's courtyard to take what belongs to you, lest you appear to him as a thief" (BT *Bava Kama* 27b). According to Rabbi Solomon ibn Adret (Rashba, fourteenth century, Spain), a willful and intentional remover of boundary must be compelled to give up possession no matter how great the loss or damage to him.[12]

Today property encroachment exists when a structure is built in whole or in part on a neighbor's property. This may be the result of incorrect surveys or mistakes or miscalculations by builders and/or owners when erecting a building, and it may be corrected by giving or selling the encroaching party an easement or lease for the lifetime of the building or, in the case of small structures, actually moving it onto the owner's own property. Conscious encroachment is not only legally wrong, but it creates bad feelings among those who live next to one another and disrupts the community peace. It is better to reach an accommodation with your neighbor than to live in constant tension.

Scrumping

The expression "scrumping" in England originally meant stealing apples from someone else's tree or orchard but was enlarged to include entering a garden and eating all kinds of fruit to satisfy one's hunger. This act is permitted in the Book of Deuteronomy with some limitations: "When you enter a fellow's vineyard, you may eat as many grapes as you want, until you are full, but you must not put any in your vessel" (Deut. 23:25). The excess is considered stealing. Similarly, "when you enter a fellow's field of standing grain, you may pluck ears with your hand; but you must not put a sickle to your neighbor's grain" (Deut. 23:26). This act must have been very common then, because the New Testament records a conversation between Jesus and the Pharisees on this subject. It appears that the followers of Jesus went through the grain fields and, being hungry, began to pluck some heads of grain and eat them. The Pharisees objected, not to the act itself but because this was done on the Sabbath, a day of rest. The Mishnah condones the act within limits but restricts it to the harvest time (*Mishnah Bava M'tzia* 7:2–8).

Most legal systems are very tolerant about scrumping today. In fact, the Theft Act of 1968, for England and Wales, states, "A person who picks mushrooms growing wild on any land, or who picks flowers, fruit or foliage from a plant growing wild on any land, does not (although not in possession of the land) steal what he picks, unless he does it for reward or for sale or other commercial purpose." Unless a person tries to sell these fruits, it is doubtful that anyone would be prosecuted for this deed in our time.

False Measures and Balances

For purposes of honesty in the marketplace, the Bible requires that measures and balances must be correct. The Book of Leviticus states, "You shall not falsify measures of length, weight, or capacity. You shall have an honest balance, honest weights, and honest *eifah* [an Egyptian dry measure], and an honest *hin* [an Egyptian liquid measure]" (Lev. 19:35–36). The Book of Deuteronomy contains a similar law: "You shall not have in your pouch alternate weights, larger and smaller. You shall not have in your house alternate measures, a larger and a smaller. You must have completely honest weights and completely honest measures" (Deut. 25:13–15; cf. Prov. 11:1). The Egyptian wisdom literature reflects the same teaching: "Do not lean on the scales nor falsify the weights, nor damage the fractions of the measure" (*Amen-em-opet* 16; *ANET*, 423). As the *Sefer HaChinukh* recognizes, the purpose of this injunction is to establish "fairness and honesty and the avoidance of robbery and cheating among people" (#259).

Using false weights and measures must have been prevalent in the marketplaces of ancient Israel as a way of defrauding the poor, because we find many prophets speaking in very strong terms against these cheaters. Thus, for example, the prophet Amos accuses those who use "an *eifah* that is too small, and a shekel that is too big, tilting a dishonest scale" (Amos 8:5); the prophet Isaiah complains that in Jerusalem, "your wine is cut with water" (Isa. 1:22), and Micah speaks of those who use "short *eifahs*," "wicked balances," and "fraudulent weights" (Mic. 6:9–12).

The Bible does not tell us how to enforce the law about correct weights and balances, but based on Rabbinic teachings, the *Sefer HaChinukh* states, "The court is obligated to appoint officers in every single location, to go about and adjust the scale and weights, and they should have the right to impose a fine on property, and even physical penalty, on anyone who is found to have a short weight" (end of #259).

Using false weights and balances is still considered stealing in American law. In fact, according to Michigan Compiled Laws (section 750.561):

> Any person who shall offer or expose for sale, sell, or use or retain in his or her possession a false weight or measure or weighing or measuring device or any weight or measure or weighing or measuring device in the buying or selling of any commodity or thing or for hire or reward; or who shall dispose of any condemned weight, measure or weighing or measuring device contrary to law or remove any tags placed thereon by the sealer of weights and measures; or any person who shall sell or offer or expose for sale less than the quantity he or she represents, or sell or offer or expose for sale any such commodity in any manner contrary to law, or any person who shall sell or offer for sale or have in his or her possession for the purpose of selling any device or instrument to be used to, or calculated to, falsify any weight or measure, is guilty of a misdemeanor. Upon a second or subsequent conviction, he or she shall be guilty of a misdemeanor punishable by imprisonment for not more than 1 year or a fine of not less than $100.00 or more than $1,000.00.

In our time, the prosecution of those who use false weights and measures is more difficult, because most scales are digital, and customers are rarely in a position to verify the accuracy of the machines. Stealing, therefore, becomes much easier for the perpetrator who knowingly tampers with the equipment. However, it is not less of a moral crime when the cheater takes advantage of the situation and misleads the unsuspecting customer. Whether we deal with rigged devices in gambling casinos or in supermarkets, the result is the same—using false weights and measures is stealing, and stealing is wrong.

The Thief and the Robber

Robbery is usually defined as taking property by force or intimidation. A biblical law states, "You shall not defraud [*lo taashok*] your fellow. You shall not commit robbery [*v'lo tigzol*]" (Lev. 19:13). Maimonides describes the distinction between a thief and a robber as follows: "Who is a thief? One who takes a person's property secretly without the owner's knowledge, as when he puts his hand into someone's pocket and takes money out without the awareness of the owner, and so on. If, however, one took something openly, publicly, or forcibly, he is not deemed a thief but a robber" (*Mishneh Torah, Hilkhot G'neivah* 1:3). He also applies this distinction to encroachment: "He who removes his neighbor's landmark and encloses within his own boundary even a finger's breadth of land, if he does it with violence, he is a robber, but if he does it secretly, he is a thief" (*Mishneh Torah, Hilkhot G'neivah* 7:11; cf. *Shulchan Arukh, Choshen Mishpat* 376).

The difference between defrauding (*oshek*) and stealing is subtle. According to Rashi, *oshek* is, for example, illegally withholding the wages of a day laborer (see his comments on Deut. 24:14).

The biblical text does provide a penalty clause regarding robbery. This is found in Lev. 5:21–26 (cf. Num. 5:5–8), where a robber, who has misappropriated some goods given to him for safekeeping, is sued by the owner of the objects. The *gazlan* (the robber) first denies under oath any knowledge about it, but then comes forth on his own and admits to lying. In this case, his penalty is to bring a sacrifice to the Temple, make restitution of the stolen object, and pay a fine of 20 percent to the original owner.

The punishment for the robber is remarkably lenient in biblical law. It was very different in other law collections of the ancient Near East, where robbery was punished by death (e.g., Laws of Hammurabi 22). The ancient Rabbis justified less severe punishment by saying that while the robber treated human beings and God equally, the thief regarded human beings more than God by acting in stealth as if no heavenly eye saw or heavenly ear had heard (*Tosefta, Bava Kama* 7:1; cf. BT *Bava Kama* 79b). According to Moshe Greenberg, "The smallness of the penalty is probably to encourage voluntary surrender in these cases, where, owing to lack of evidence, or to the impotence of the victims—the victims of robbery and oppression are almost invariably poor and defenseless (Ps. 35:10; Isa. 3:14; Jer.7:6; Amos 4:1)—legal means of recovery were of little avail."[13] In Rabbinic law, the penalty for the robber is not too different from the punishment applied to a regular thief; both have to return the object and pay a fine if the object is damaged.

In U.S. law, robbery can be either "in the first degree" or "in the second degree." The first, a more serious crime, is considered a class A felony and carries a heavier penalty, whereas the second is a class B felony, which commands a lesser punishment.

The Wider Scope of the Eighth Word

The ancient Rabbis, by widening the scope of the Eighth Word, discussed ethical issues well beyond what the original biblical law covered in this area. Thus, for example, based on the principle that "the property of your fellow human being should be as precious to you as your own" (*Pirkei Avot* 5:10), Rabbi Yochanan (most likely Yochanan ben Zakkai, first century CE) taught, perhaps with a bit of exaggeration, that "when a person robs his fellow even the value of a *p'rutah* [i.e., a coin of little value], it is as though he had taken his life away from him" (BT *Bava Kama* 119a). Sh'muel (second century CE) went even further by stating that "even if a man misappropriates a beam and builds it into a palace, he must demolish the entire palace, all of it, and return the beam to its owners" (BT *Taanit* 16a). Stealing is prohibited, whether the victim is a Jew or gentile, says Rabbi Huna (third century CE; BT *Bava Kama* 113b).

The norm "You shall not steal" is similarly viewed by many modern commentators broadly and applied to situations the ancient Sages did not or could not have envisioned, such as stealing intellectual property, issues related to patents, stealing ownership rights to genetic material, and others. These cases are now being adjudicated in civil or criminal courts, following the principle of Jewish law of *dina d'malchuta dina* ("the law of the land is the law") (e.g., BT *N'darim* 28a; *Gittin* 10b). Following are some examples.

Stealing Ideas (G'neivat Daat)

The Hebrew Bible knows of a category of deceit called "stealing the heart/mind." One example is found in the Book of Genesis regarding the flight of Jacob from Laban. We are told that "Jacob stole the heart [*vayignov Yaakov et lev*] of Laban the Aramean, by not informing him that he was fleeing" (Gen. 31:20; cf. v. 26).[14] Similarly, Absalom, the son of King David, "won away [*vay'ganeiv*] the heart of the men of Israel" (II Sam. 15:6), deceiving his countrymen as he was preparing to revolt against his father and take over the kingdom.

The expression *g'neivat lev*, "stealing the heart," is equivalent to the Talmudic *g'neivat daat* ("stealing knowledge"). The *Tosefta* mentions seven kinds of thieves, the worst being "one who steals the knowledge [*goneiv daat*] of other people" (*Bava Kama* 7:8; *M'khilta, Mishpatim* 13). The Babylonian Talmud (*Chulin* 94a) discusses all kinds of misrepresentations and deceit—all related to "stealing the mind" (see Rashi)—and among others, it gives the following examples: "A man should not urge his friend to dine with him when he knows that his friend will not do so. And he should not offer him many gifts when he knows that his friend will not accept them." However, if these acts are carried out to show the guest or friend great respect, the Talmud adds, it is permitted. In a similar vein, the *Shulchan Arukh* (sixteenth century) points out that a seller is obligated to inform the buyer ahead of time if the merchandise he is selling is defective or not (*Choshen Mishpat* 228:6). The *Mei-am Lo-eiz* identifies seven types of *g'neivat daat*: (1) creating a false impression; (2) urging a friend to be a guest when one does not really want him; (3) giving another a gift, even though the giver knows that the other would not accept such a gift; (4) giving a barrel of wine to another as a special gift, even though the seller had already decided to sell it to another customer; (5) using a false measure when selling; (6) substituting a deficient weight for an honest one; (7) diluting the wine with water or vinegar.[15]

Hershey H. Friedman, in his article titled "*Geneivat Da'at*: The Prohibition against Deception in Today's World," applies these Rabbinic teachings to contemporary issues, such as deceptive offers, irregular merchandise, deceptive quality, advertising puffery, deceptive bargains, phony markdowns, deceptive credentials, deceptive testimonials, deception for charity, and deceptive accounting practices, and points out that, according to Jewish law, the original owner must disclose correct information before selling any item.[16]

Unfair Competition

Generalizing the biblical law against encroachment, the ancient Rabbis used this law to prohibit unfair competition in the business world. On this subject, two opposing points of view were discussed in the Rabbinic academy (see BT Bava Batra 21b). One position was defended by Rabbi Huna (third century), who argues that if a person wants to set up a store near another businessman who deals with the same type of product, the latter one can prevent the interloper from doing so on the basis that he could lose his livelihood. However, another point of view recorded anonymously states that free trade must prevail, and the established owner cannot stop the newcomer from setting up his business in the same area. During the Middle Ages, among Spanish Jews, this issue became more acute, and the doctrine of *maarufiyah* (from an Arabic word meaning "sale'") became operative. According to this principle, if a person has a gentile customer, a Jewish competitor cannot interfere in the original owner's business by taking away his trade with the gentile. In a more recent responsum, Rabbi Solomon B. Freehof dealt with a similar situation and decided as follows: "If it is an open field with room for many to enter and the more that enter it the better will be the service to the public, then the Talmudic spirit of free trade should prevail. If it is a limited field which in this special environment cannot support rival companies, and one must go to the wall, then the spirit of the medieval law should prevail, and one Jew has not the right to destroy the livelihood of another."[17]

Identity Theft

In many parts of the world it is a crime to misappropriate another person's identifying information to commit fraud. The Identity Theft Assumption Deterrence Act of 1998 defines this culprit as one who "knowingly transfers or uses, without lawful authority, a means of identification of another person with the intent to commit, or to aid or abet, any unlawful activity that constitutes a violation of Federal law, or that constitutes a felony under any applicable State or local law." This usually happens when someone, without authorization, gets hold of a social security number, credit card information, or other financial records in order to pass him- or herself as another individual. Victims then spend thousands of dollars repairing the damage to their good name and credit records. This is popularly called "identity theft," even though the name is not totally accurate, because personal identity is not an object that can be "stolen." A better term would be "identity fraud" or "impersonation."

Civil law usually makes a distinction between various types of identity fraud, including business or commercial fraud (using someone else's identity to obtain credit), criminal identity fraud (passing as someone else when apprehended committing a crime), and identity cloning (assuming someone else's identity in daily life). According to Federal Trade Commission records, 8.3 million Americans became victims of identity fraud in 2007.

The Bible records a dramatic scene of identity theft when the patriarch Jacob passes himself as his brother Esau in order to obtain Isaac's blessing before his father's death. The biblical text recognizes that this is wrong, because it has Isaac saying, "Your brother came with deceit [*mirmah*] and took away your blessing" (Gen. 27:35). Discussing the moral problem today, Rabbi W. Gunther Plaut rightfully asks, "Are the means Jacob employs to gain his ends morally justifiable? The answer must be no."[18] Trying to soften the blow of Jacob's reprehensible action, some critics stress the fact that the patriarch did what he did reluctantly, and only in order to obey his mother. Thus, after Rebekah asks Jacob to fetch the ingredients in order to prepare Isaac's favorite meal, the text adds, "He [Jacob] went and got them and brought [them] to his mother" (Gen. 27:14). These short and staccato-type expressions reflect the attitude of Jacob, who is carrying out his actions "with nervous haste."[19] *B'reishit Rabbah* (15) notes that he acts "under duress, bent and weeping," thus recognizing that impersonation is an immoral act.

There is hardly anything written in the classical Rabbinic texts on identity theft, most likely because it was not a grave issue during their time. Today, it is a great irritant and a crime. Most rabbinic scholars today would agree that impersonation is prohibited under the general rule of *g'neivat daat*. For example, Rabbi Chaim Kohn maintains that it is against Jewish law to practice medicine by fraudulently obtaining a license by pretending you are someone else. "Imagine," he writes, "a physician obtaining his diploma by collusion or copying and then diagnosing patients, or an engineer falsely presenting papers and then building airplanes! Their expertise has an impact on our lives, and lack of professionalism can endanger people's well-being."[20] On the other hand, Rabbi Kohn argues that sometimes identity theft may be condoned as a means of survival. As an example, he states that during the Holocaust period, many Jews obtained false papers in order to pass themselves off as Aryans, thus saving their lives. But surprisingly for me, he also defends Jacob's disguise as being "not an act of deception but a rescue operation similar to a spy in enemy territory whose information saves people's lives." I cannot agree with his interpretation, for I think Jacob wrongfully impersonated his brother, thus deceiving his father, and this is morally wrong.

Stealing and Copyright

In our highly developed technological age, it is becoming much easier to copy or reproduce works of art. Instead of the labor-intensive work of copying by hand, one can easily download the material from the Internet and have it for self-use or sell it to others. Obviously this infringes upon the financial rights of authors, painters, or musicians who produce original works. Modern civil law protects the rights of artists through copyright laws. Is this right recognized in Jewish law?

Questions about copyright do not appear in halakhic literature and did not become a legal issue in modern civil law until the invention of the printing press. Contemporary rabbis, therefore, are compelled to find some guidelines in the spirit of Jewish law to protect the rights of creative minds. As Rabbi Israel Schneider points out, sometimes commentators use the biblical principal against encroachment (*hasagat g'vul*), while others defend book authors on the basis of the norm *dina d'malchuta dina* ("the law of the land is the law") and even on the basis of the Jewish law that speaks of *shiur* (retention), whereby, for example, the creator or producer of a CD could stipulate that the purchaser can use the recording for his own use but the owner still "retains" the right to all copies.[21] George Horowitz points out that in many rabbinic books printed in modern times it is customary to find, after the title page, the following statement: "It is well known that *hasagat g'vul* is prohibited by the law of our holy Torah and the law of the government."[22]

The question of copyright was discussed by the CCAR Responsa Committee in the year 2000. The question was this: "According to Jewish law, is it right to download files (music, games, etc.) from the Internet without the creator's consent or monetary compensation?" Following the spirit of the Jewish law that defends the legal rights of the owner, the committee reached the following conclusion:

> If it is wrong to print a book or to copy a painting without obtaining the permission of its creator, it is just as wrong to download literary and artistic creations as files without the consent of those who authored them or who own the rights to them. It is true that the "Internet age" confronts us with fundamentally new realities. It may also be true that existing copyright laws are insufficient to respond to these new realities. But it is certainly true that we continue to shoulder a duty, under Jewish tradition as well under the law of the state, to honor, protect and safeguard the rights of authors and publishers to the words they create. It is, therefore, wrong, from the standpoint of Jewish law, to download files from the Internet unless one has obtained permission from the authors of those files to do so.[23]

Ponzi Scheme

In modern life stealing takes a number of forms, referring not only to taking illicitly an article from another person but also to all types of fraudulent financial transactions that hurt other individuals. One of them is called Ponzi Scheme.

A Ponzi scheme is a fraudulent investing scam that promises high rates of return with little risk to investors. It generates returns for older investors by acquiring new ones. This scam actually yields the promised returns to earlier investors, as long as there are more new investors. These schemes usually collapse when the new investments stop. It was named after Charles Ponzi, an Italian businessman and a US con artist, who died in Brazil in 1949.

Recently, the most notorious Ponzi scheme was set up by Bernard ("Bernie") Madoff, an American stockholder, who victimized thousands of people, including many major Jewish institutions in the United States and prominent Jewish individuals. On June, 2009, he was sentenced to 150 years in prison. Writing in the Jewish Week (Dec. 3, 2010), David E. Y. Sarna called Ponzi schemes "a crime like laundering money through charities to gain improper tax deductions," both being against Jewish law.

Stealing to Save Life

Jewish tradition gives priority to life over property through its insistence that "you shall keep My laws and My rules, by the pursuit of which human beings shall live" (Lev. 18:5). If that is so, can a person steal in order to save his or her life? In his article on this subject, Charles J. Harary gives two examples, one of which is this: H, a diabetic, loses his insulin in an automobile accident. Before H lapses into a coma, he rushes to the house of C, another diabetic. C is not at home, but somehow H manages to get into her house. After first assuring himself that he has left C enough insulin for her own daily dosage, H takes the insulin he needs to survive. Is this behavior condoned by Jewish law? Based on the teachings of the *Shulchan Arukh* (*Choshen Mishpat* 380:3) and Maimonides (*Mishneh Torah, Hilkhot Choveil U'mazik* 8:13), Harary states that one is allowed to steal in order to preserve his or her life on the basis of the principle of *pikuach nefesh* (saving life) but only on the condition that the property be returned or that the "thief" compensate the owner for the property's value.[24] It is the same when someone attempts to save the life of another, except that in this case, a rescuer is exempt from the damage he has caused during the attempted rescue. The Supreme Court of Vermont seems to feel similarly (see *Ploof v. Putnam*, 1908), for it stated that one can trespass onto the property or sacrifice the personal property of another to save one's life or the lives of one's fellows.

Comparing Jewish law and American law on this subject, Harary writes:

> American law is similar to Jewish law regarding the issue whether a person can steal or destroy property to save lives. Although the law does seem similar, American law is not as definite as Jewish law. The cases that have created the American legal precedent were cases where the act was approved by society. Trespassing onto land to save yourself during a storm, throwing baggage overboard to save the lives of others are examples of scenarios that the courts have faced in creating such precedent. One wonders what the law would be if the

cases that came before the same courts involved situations where society did not agree with the action. Would the law be so forgiving if it involved a homeless person stealing to eat, or a person infected with AIDS stealing medication to live? The precedent, although clear, is weak. Future cases will probably be decided on a case by case basis, and the law will depend on the discretion, and the compassion, of the presiding judge. In contrast, the Jewish law is far more definite. Since Jewish law stems from God, deciphered through the words of the Torah, less discretion is given to presiding authorities. Therefore to a larger extent the issue has been resolved and no matter what the case will be, the law will stay far more constant than American law.[25]

In Conclusion

Even though the original scope of "You shall not steal" is unclear, Jewish tradition has, over the centuries, defended the right of ownership and severely condemned acts of misappropriation. Rabbinic sages attempted to apply the spirit of the biblical laws to the needs of their time, but their decisions remained primarily as moral guidelines, inasmuch as Jews often resorted to civil courts to resolve their conflicts or were compelled to do so. In our time, biblical and Rabbinic laws on stealing and robbery have completely given way to the laws of the land in which Jews live, because these acts are considered crimes, and only governmental authorities have the power to adjudicate them. Yet the values of these traditional Jewish norms are still worth studying, because they represent ethical standards by which Jews ought to live in the modern society.

The Ninth Word: False Witness

False Witnesses and Perjury

Societies function harmoniously when people can rely on each other's words. Words have the power of action; they can uplift or destroy a person. That is why the Book of Proverbs says, "Death and life are in the power of the tongue" (Prov. 18:21). When there is a conflict between individuals and the matter is referred to the judiciary, the obligation of the court is to make sure that witnesses tell the truth. As the *Sefer HaChinukh* states, "The world endures through true testimony, for all types of dispute between people are resolved through true witnesses; false testimony [*eidut sheker*] constitutes a cause of ruin in a community" (#37).

In the overwhelming majority of legal systems around the world, the truth of a legal case has primarily been determined by interrogating reliable witnesses who tell the court exactly what they saw. Even with the proliferation of DNA testing and other sophisticated scientific methods of analysis, witness testimony remains one of the major methods used by judicial authorities in the United States as they investigate the events leading up to an illegal act. Witnesses are expected to tell the truth, and in order to substantiate their statements, they take an oath, the wording of which may change from state to state but generally follows this pattern: "Do you swear/ affirm that the evidence you shall give concerning this case shall be the truth, the whole truth and nothing but the truth, so help you God / upon penalty of perjury?" The answer is yes. Issuing a false statement under oath is perjury. According to the Model Penal Code (1962), three conditions are required for this to become actionable: (a) the false statement has to be made under oath during a judicial proceeding; (b) the statement has to be relevant to the proceeding; and (c) the witness must have a specific intent to deceive. A perjurer is punished by paying a fine, being imprisoned, or both. Jewish laws regarding witnesses were formulated over a long period of time. Rabbinic laws on this subject are more voluminous and better systematized than the biblical examples. Since the truthfulness of testimony is so crucial for the justice system in any society, almost all legal systems known to humanity have created different methods of witness investigation. In this chapter we shall not only study what the Bible and Rabbinic sages have to say about the role and duties of witnesses, but we will also discuss the ethical implications of perjury on the fabric of society today.

The Text of the Ninth Word

The Plaut Torah commentary (following NJPS) translates the Ninth Word of the Decalogue in Exod. 20:13 as follows: "You shall not bear [*taaneh*] false witness [*eid shaker*] against your neighbor." The literal translation would be "Do not answer against your neighbor as a false witness." (In biblical Hebrew, the expression *anah v-* means to "testify against"). Deut. 5:17 has a slight change: instead of referring to an *eid shaker* (lit. "witness of falsehood"), it calls the culprit an *eid shav*, "witness of nothingness, vain."[1] Both must mean something similar, unless, as John I. Durham argues, the Deuteronomic version intends "to broaden the application of the ninth commandment to include any evasive or worthless testimony."[2] There is no way to ascertain the original intention of the Deuteronomic legislator on this subject, and most likely a "vain witness" is the same as "a false witness." The Nash Papyrus (ca. second or first century BCE), which is the oldest biblical manuscript we have and contains a text considered to be a third version of the Decalogue, has *eid shav*. In the Bible, Exod. 23:1 speaks of an *eid chamas*, "malicious witness." Pseudo-Philo (ca. first century CE) has a longer text: "Thou shalt not bear false witness against thy neighbor, lest your watchmen [i.e., probably, angels] speak falsely against thee" (James, chap. 11).

The wisdom literature in the Bible condemns the false witness in a number of places, using different terminology for the culprit; for example, "A false witness [*eid shaker*] testifies lies" (Prov. 14:5); "A false witness [*eid sh'karim*] will not go unpunished" (Prov. 19:5); "A malicious witness [*eid b'liyaal*] scoffs at justice" (Prov. 19:28); "A false witness [*eid k'zavim*] is doomed" (Prov. 21:28).

The Ninth Word states that a person is not allowed to bear false witness against a "neighbor"(*rei-akha*).The Book of Proverbs reflects the same thinking: "Do not be a witness [*eid chinam*] against your fellow [*b'rei-ekha*] without good cause"(Prov. 24:28).

But who qualifies as a "neighbor"? The expression "neighbor" here most likely refers to someone who is on trial, a fellow human being (e.g., Lev. 19:18), whether a Jew or gentile (e.g., Lev. 19:34; *Mei-am Lo-eiz* 11).

Some critics have argued that that the Decalogue here prohibits not only false testimony before judicial authorities but general lying (cf. Prov. 6:16–19). Lying in general is covered specifically by Lev. 19: 11—"You shall not deal deceitfully or falsely [*t'shak'ru*] with one another"—and Exod. 23:7—"Keep far from a false matter [*d'var sheker*]." These represent broad moral teachings and are hard to prosecute.

There are plenty of examples in the Bible where, in a nonlegal setting, characters lie and get away with it. For instance, Cain lies when he refuses to tell God where his brother, Abel, is (Gen. 4:9). Sarah lies when she tells God that she did not laugh at the suggestion that she could give birth in her old age (Gen. 18:15). Rebekah instructs her son Jacob to tell a lie when he passes himself off to Isaac, her husband, as if he were Esau, Jacob's brother, in order to make sure that Isaac would bless her favorite Jacob first (Gen. 27:6–13). Rachel lies to her father, Laban, when she steals her father's household gods, hides them in her camel's saddlebag, and refuses to come down, pretending that she has her period (Gen. 31:34–35). Potiphar's wife falsely accuses Joseph of attempting to lie with her (Gen. 39:14) and even produces incriminating evidence against him. Rahab, an innkeeper/harlot, lies to protect the Hebrew spies who come to reconnoiter the Land of Canaan (Josh. 2:2–6).

The plain reading of the Ninth Word, however, suggests that the setting-in-life, namely, the social context of the commandment, is the legal court, which, in biblical times, often met at the gate of the town (e.g., Ruth 4). The commandment requires a witness to be truthful when giving testimony before the judges. It is possible, however, that the law that originated in a court setting was later on expanded to apply to other cases of lying as well.

The Bible records a famous case of two false witnesses who cause the death of an innocent man. When King Ahab of Israel (ninth century BCE) wants to buy a piece of land belonging to Naboth, his neighbor, the king is shocked to find out that Naboth refuses to sell it to him. So Queen Jezebel finds two scoundrels who falsely testify in court that Naboth has actually "cursed God and king," an act punishable by death (see Exod. 22:27 and Lev. 24:15–16).

Based on their false testimony, Naboth is put to death outside of the city by the whole community (I Kings 21).

Similarly, we find a brazen case of false witnessing in the story of Susanna, a short book that appears in the Apocrypha, which is a collection of Jewish writings outside of the Hebrew Bible (30 BCE–70 CE) but included in the Catholic Bible. According to this dramatic story, Susanna is falsely accused by two elders because she has refused their sexual advances. Finally, a young man by the name of Daniel is able to prove her innocence, and the elders receive the same penalty of death that would have been administered to Susanna.

Who Is a Witness?

In our modern legal system, a witness is a person who testifies under oath in a trial or a deposition in a lawsuit. Most contemporary legal codes allow the plaintiff or defendant to become a witness. A witness is one who has firsthand knowledge about matters relevant to the case, and that testimony is subject to the applicable rules of evidence. There are two main types of witnesses: lay witnesses are ordinary people who testify based upon their personal knowledge and life experiences; "expert witnesses," on the other hand, testify based upon their qualifications of expertise in their field.[3]

In Hebrew, a witness is called an *eid*.[4] In biblical and Rabbinic times, in principle, only men could testify in court. Just as in modern secular law, Rabbinic law, too, distinguishes eyewitnesses (*eid r'iyah*) from attesting witnesses (*eid kiyum*), experts or those who are present when a legal document is signed (e.g., a *ketubah*). The first can report only on what they know and see, and not on what they have heard; they also do not receive any remuneration. If they receive payment, their testimony is invalid (*Mishnah B'khorot* 4:6). Attesting witnesses, on the other hand, report on what they know and are usually paid for their services. In Rabbinic law, witnesses are rarely placed under oath.

In our secular legal system, too, eyewitnesses are not paid, but their personal expenses are often covered; expert witnesses are paid for their knowledge. Bribing a witness is punishable by law.

The Obligation to Testify

Over the centuries, Jewish law has placed an obligation on witnesses to come forward to testify for the benefit of justice, and the specifics of this duty, based on biblical law, have been refined in early and late Rabbinic teachings.

According to biblical law, a person who witnessed an unlawful deed is obligated to testify: "If a person incurs guilt: When one has heard a public imprecation [*kol alah*] but (although able to testify as having either seen or learned of the matter) has not given information and thus is subject to punishment" (Lev. 5:1). This idea is reinforced in the Book of Proverbs: "He hears the imprecation and does not tell" (Prov. 29:24). The reference to a "public imprecation" refers to someone who hears a proclamation placing under a curse those who have information but refuse to come forward and testify, either because they are not willing or simply because they are afraid. The law states that if you have information pertaining to the case, you have an obligation to testify. In a specific case, biblical law requires that when someone observes an enticement to idolatry, the witness is required to expose the culprit and, in fact, is obliged to throw the first stone (Deut. 13:7–12; Lev. 24:11–23).

Rabbinic law makes a distinction between criminal and civil cases. In criminal cases the witness must step forward to testify, but in civil cases the duty to testify comes up only when the witness is summoned to do so (*Mishneh Torah, Hilkhot Eidut* 1:1). In fact, in Rabbinic times an oath may be imposed on someone to tell whether he knows anything about a particular case, and a ban may be pronounced on him in the synagogue to compel him to testify. The Mishnah, however, excuses the king from this duty: "The king may neither...testify nor be testified against" (*Mishnah Sanhedrin* 2:2). If a person refuses to testify, Jewish law says, he is answerable to the Heavenly Court.[5]

Maimonides states that any witness who has testified in a capital case cannot turn around and become one of the judges dealing with the same issue. He cannot prosecute or defend the accused. However, in civil cases, the same person may defend or prosecute the defendant but cannot be included among the judges in the lawsuit, for no witness can be a judge in a civil case (*Mishneh Torah, Hilkhot Eidut* 5:8).

Reporting a crime to the authorities becomes more urgent when it deals with cases of abuse. The U.S. Code (Title 18, Part I, Chapter 1, Section 4) states that anyone who has knowledge of a crime and fails to report that crime (called "misprision of felony") may be fined, imprisoned for up to three years, or both. Most states have similar laws on misprision, even though this law is very rarely enforced. However, when it comes to abuse of children, senior adults, or incapacitated individuals, the law is unequivocal. Failure to do that is punishable by law.[6] When the sexual abuse cases by some Catholic priests were brought to light in the last part of the twentieth century, many church high officials, so it was reported in the media, preferred to cover up the abuse or chose to send away the culprits to lead other churches around the country. Today, the Catholic hierarchy is keenly aware of this grave mistake and is trying to remedy the situation by taking a zero-tolerance attitude. The Jewish community is not immune to this type of breach of trust, either. The Jewish press recently reported that Rabbi Hershel Schachter, a top rabbinic dean of Yeshiva University, has warned other rabbis about the dangers of reporting child sex abuse allegations to the police because it could result in a Jew being jailed with a black inmate who might want to kill him. He added that children can lie and ruin an innocent man's life.[7] This attitude, shocking as it is, is against Jewish law.[8] In July 2003, Rabbi Norman Lamm, president of Yeshiva University of New York resigned, apologizing that he did not report to the authorities sexual allegations that occurred at Yeshiva in the 70's and 80's.

In many contemporary societies, citizens also have an obligation to give testimony when needed, even if it is not convenient. Witnesses may volunteer to testify, or they can be ordered to do that by a subpoena. A witness who refuses may be held in contempt of court, which is an offense punishable by a fine, imprisonment, or both. Regrettably, in our time, some witnesses try to shy away from reporting what they saw and stay away from the court or other legal authorities, fearing that they will be physically or emotionally hurt by the offending party or simply because they do not wish to get involved in someone else's problems. Consequently, victims suffer and culprits get away with impunity. On the other hand, some defendants resort to witness intimidation to keep the truth from coming out in court. Our secular legal system provides some assistance to witnesses who are intimidated through different witness protection programs. To convince a potential witness to accept this type of protection is by no means easy and very often fails. However, in the spirit of Jewish as well as our secular law, we need to keep trying to convince witnesses to come forward in order "to establish justice in the gates" (cf. Amos 5:15) of our society.

The Number of Witnesses

How many witnesses are needed to convict someone? Even though the Decalogue does not specify the number of individuals who must testify in a case, the Book of Deuteronomy states that two witnesses represent the minimum in both capital and noncapital cases: "A single witness may not validate against a person any guilt or blame for any offense that may be committed;

a case can be valid only on the testimony of two witnesses or more" (Deut. 19:15; cf. 17:6). The priestly laws confirm this understanding: "The testimony of a single witness against a person [who commits murder] shall not suffice for a sentence of death" (Num. 35:30). Rabbinic law has identified many exceptions to this two-witness rule. For example, in the case of a woman who wishes to remarry after her husband disappears or is dead (in Hebrew, *agunah*), the Mishnah allows for the testimony of one single witness (*Mishnah Y'vamot* 16:7; *Mishnah Eduyot* 6:1).

Similarly, Solomon Ganzfried states, "The testimony of one witness is admissible only when a monetary transaction is involved, when his testimony may result in requiring the administration of an oath. Likewise, if a person is about to commit an illegal act, one witness may testify in order to prevent him from committing it."[9]

The Qualification of Witnesses

Over the centuries, Jewish law has identified various individuals who could not be called upon to testify. Biblical law does not list any qualifications for becoming a reliable witness. It appears that any Israelite who witnessed a crime was eligible to testify. In the first century, the historian Josephus stated that the credibility of the witnesses was established by their past life and that women were not allowed to testify "on account of the levity and boldness of their sex" (*Ant.* IV, 8:15).

During Rabbinic times, the Mishnah disqualified a number of people from becoming a witness or a judge, because they could not be relied upon to issue sound judgment. These included dice players, usurers, pigeon flyers (i.e., those who engage in a certain type of gambling), traffickers in Sabbatical-year produce, close relatives, and enemies (see *Mishnah Sanhedrin* 3:3–5). The tractate *Rosh HaShanah* added slaves and women (*Mishnah Rosh HaShanah* 8). In medieval times, Maimonides listed ten classes of people who are not competent to testify in court, namely, women, slaves, children, the insane, the deaf-mute, the blind, the wicked, the despised (*b'zuyin*, i.e., uncouth, shameless), relatives, and the interested parties (*Mishneh Torah, Hilkhot Eidut* 9:1). For all practical purposes, by removing all these people who are not competent to appear in court, we are left with the following individuals, as George Horowitz notes: "To be competent, a witness must be a free, male, Israelite of full age (i.e., more than 13 years old), a 'law-abiding' person, respectable, of sound mind, and possessing normal sight, speech and hearing."[10]

In contemporary Jewish life, some Rabbinic rules of competency have been challenged by many liberal thinkers. The fact that women are not allowed to be witnesses in Rabbinic law does not sit well with our contemporary thinking that favors equality between the sexes. We do not know if women were able to testify in biblical times. Even though the Bible does not record any restriction about women witnesses, the Mishnah specifically does: "The (law about) the 'oath of testimony' [*sh'vuat eidut*, cf. Lev. 5:1] applies to men only, not to women" (*Mishnah Sh'vuot* 4: 1). This understanding is confirmed by the *Sifrei* on Deut. 19:17, which states that only men can testify. Maimonides includes women among those who are not eligible to act as witnesses. This is still the position of Orthodox Jews today.

Why were women disqualified? Various rationales have been advanced for this Rabbinic rule: that the Bible uses the masculine form when speaking about witnesses, the levity and boldness of women's sexuality (Josephus, above), or that the proper place for women is in the home and not in the court or marketplace. In spite of this Rabbinic rule, even the ancient Rabbis accepted a number of exceptions; for example, women were admitted as competent witnesses with regard to women's issues of purity (BT *K'tubot* 72a). This ruling obviously reflected the inferior status of women in many countries during Rabbinic times.

With the advance of women's rights in our time, however, this Rabbinic restriction, which some claim is even of biblical origin, cannot be maintained. The Reform Movement, as early as 1846, attempted to eliminate all legal discrimination against women. In a report to the Breslau Conference, the delegates maintained that "the Rabbinical Conference shall declare the female sex as religiously equal with the male, in its obligations and right."[11] This was restated in 1912 at the Posen Conference: "The participation of women in religious and communal life is indispensable. They should receive their equal share in religious duties as well as rights."[12] In the American Reform Movement, this practice was accepted as given: "The Reform Movement declares women equal in all legal religious matters to men."[13] In the Conservative Movement, Rabbi Myron Geller, in his paper entitled "Woman Is Eligible to Testify" and approved by the Committee on Jewish Law and Standards of the Rabbinical Assembly in 2001, writes:

> The ancient *takkanah* of the *Tannaim* establishing a woman's right to testify in limited circumstances, when she had knowledge of the facts and was not excluded for social reasons, is a paradigm permitting us to eliminate

restrictions on women serving as *edim* because there is no reason to doubt their *ne-emanut* [trustfulness] at this time. Women as a class are today the legal and social equals of males and are competent and reliable to serve as witnesses. Any residual impediment to *edut nashim* [testimony of women] is inoperative. An otherwise qualified woman is eligible to serve as a witness in all matters equally with a man, for **kiddushin** [wedding], *gittin* [divorce documents], *giyur* [conversion] or in any capacity governed by halakhah, evidentiary or affective.

In spite of this opinion, some Conservative rabbis currently affirm this only as a theoretical option. In modern Israel, the disqualification of women as witnesses was abolished by the Equality of Women's Rights Act of 1951.

Another issue with regard to witness incompetence has to do with some physical impairment, such as blindness. Even though Maimonides excluded the blind from being valid witnesses, the Reform Movement decided otherwise. In a responsum titled "A Blind Person as a Witness" (CCAR Responsa, 5759.8), the CCAR Responsa Committee argued:

> As Reform Jews, we regard it a positive duty to include the blind and all others who are physically disabled in the activities of our congregations and communities. We base this affirmation, in part, upon the traditional insight that to exclude the blind from the *mitzvot* is to exclude them from Jewish experience altogether. Our movement's historic commitment to the cause of social justice transforms this insight into a call to action: it is our obligation to do whatever we can to remove barriers that prevent the disabled from participating as fully as possible in Jewish life. In this case, since Jewish text and tradition *can* be understood so as to permit the blind to serve as witnesses to a wedding, we must adopt that understanding as our own. So long as a blind person, through the use of the senses of hearing and touch, can identify the bride and the groom and can testify that the act of *kiddushin* has taken place, we must permit them the opportunity to do so.

The Interrogation of Witnesses

The witness must speak the truth. But the truth is elusive and highly subjective. Therefore, the witness must share with the court only personal knowledge about an event or a fact. The biblical text is primarily concerned about the false witness, *eid sheker/shav*. If the witness heard the information from another individual, no matter how trustworthy the source may be, and irrespective of the fact that the witness may be convinced of the validity of the friend's observation or knowledge, the witness's testimony is not acceptable. Hearsay evidence is not valid in court (*Mishnah Sanhedrin* 3:6; cf. *Mei-am Lo-eiz* 11).

The Decalogue does not tell us how the witnesses are to be interrogated to ascertain that their testimony is reliable. Biblical law only states that the judges will make "a thorough investigation" (*v'dar'shu . . . heiteiv*) (Deut. 19:18). Similarly, the Mishnah urges the judges to "examine the witnesses thoroughly" (*Pirkei Avot* 1:9). During the Rabbinic period, the Sages went to considerable lengths to specify the interrogation method that judges ought to use. This involves *chakirah* (investigation) as to the time and place of the act and *d'rishah* (examination) regarding the substance of the case; at times, it may even involve *b'dikah* (cross-examination). At first this process was used for both capital and noncapital cases (*Mishnah Sanhedrin* 4:1), but later on the rules were relaxed regarding cases of tort (BT *Sanhedrin* 3a).

The Mishnah gives an example about the method the judges used in admonishing the witnesses in capital cases:

> They brought them in and admonished them saying, perhaps you will say what is a supposition, or hearsay, or secondhand information, or say to yourself that I heard it from a person who is trustworthy, or you do not know that we [judges] shall prove [the truth] by examination and inquiry. Know therefore, that capital cases are not like noncapital cases: in noncapital cases, a person can pay money and make atonement, but in capital cases the witness is answerable for the blood of him [that is wrongly condemned] and the blood of the posterity [that should have been born to him] to the end of time. (*Mishnah Sanhedrin* 4:5)

An interesting legal and ethical question has recently emerged in Jewish law with regard to a witness who turns state's evidence. This witness is offered lenience or even immunity from punishment for his own crimes in exchange for testifying against another defendant. Is this acceptable in Jewish law? According to the Mishnah (*B'khorot* 6:4), a witness is not supposed to benefit from his testimony. Receiving immunity or even leniency would appear to contradict this rule, and consequently, his testimony should not be considered valid.[14]

The Punishment for Being a False Witness

In the ancient Near East, the penalty for being a false witness was severe, but a distinction was made between capital and noncapital cases. For example, according to the Laws of Hammurabi, "If a man comes forward to give (false) testimony but cannot bring evidence for his accusation, if that case involves a capital offense, that man shall be killed (#3)."[15] However, "if he comes forward to give (false) testimony for (a case whose penalty is) grain or silver, he shall be assessed the penalty for that case" (#4).[16]

In the Qur'an, "those who defame honorable women and cannot produce four witnesses shall be given eighty lashes" (The Light 24:4).

The Ninth Word does not specify the punishment to be applied to the false witness. The Book of Proverbs states, "A false witness will not go unpunished" (19:5), but does not identify the penalty. The penalty clause is found in the Book of Deuteronomy, usually dated to the seventh century BCE. According to the instructions found in this book, talion law applies in cases of false testimony:

> If someone appears against another to testify maliciously [*eid chamas*] and gives incriminating yet false testimony, the two parties to the dispute shall appear before the Eternal, before the priests or magistrates in authority at the time, and the magistrates shall make a thorough investigation. If the one who testified is a false witness [*eid sheker*], having testified falsely against a fellow Israelite, you shall do to the one as the one schemed to do to the other. Thus you will sweep out evil from your midst; others will hear and be afraid, and such evil things will not again be done in your midst. Nor must you show pity: life for life, eye for eye, tooth for tooth, hand for hand, foot for foot. (*Deut. 19:16–21*)

This law makes a number of important points. The punishment is carried out, not as in earlier times by the aggrieved party, but by the courts. The penalty is applied only after a careful examination of the witnesses. Adjudicating the law may require either an ordeal ("appear before the Eternal"), where the punishment is decided (perhaps through a self-curse) and applied by God, or a judgment by those in authority, namely "priests or magistrates in authority at the time." Even though talion is invoked in this case, in Rabbinic law this was changed to compensation (see "The Sixth Word: Homicide" see page 123). The clause "as the one schemed" was differently understood by the Sadducees and the Pharisees. The former maintained that the death penalty was applied only if a person against whom a false witness testified had already been executed, whereas the latter taught that it was applied only if he were still alive (*Mishnah Makot* 1:6; cf. BT *Makot* 5b).

Often, however, society is defenseless against malicious witnesses, and victims can only hope that God will not leave this evil unpunished (Prov. 19:5). The Aramaic *Targum* called Pseudo-Jonathan (also known as *Targum Y'rushalmi*; ca. eighth century CE?) maintains that "because of the guilt of perjury the clouds go up and the rain does not come down, and drought comes upon the world."[17]

In our legal system, the punishment for perjury under federal law is the imposition of a fine, imprisonment, or both.

The Wider Application of the Ninth Word

In Jewish tradition the Ninth Word is often interpreted widely to include general lying. For example, in his commentary on the Pentateuch, Joseph H. Hertz states that this commandment "embraces all forms of slander, defamation and misrepresentation, whether of an individual, a group, a race, or a faith."[18] Rabbi Obadiah Sforno (1475–1550) adds to this list talebearing too (see his comment on Exod. 20:13).

In dealing with harmful and frivolous speech, the Rabbis make a distinction between *r'khilut* (talebearing), *lashon hara* (gossip), and *motzi shem ra* (defamation); one is worse than the others.

R'khilut—Talebearing

Talebearing is a type of gossip when one passes on hurtful statements that one person has said about another and is severely condemned in Rabbinic literature. The term *r'khilut* comes from the noun *rakhil*, which in the Bible most likely means "merchant" and is found in Lev. 19:16. The Plaut Torah commentary translates this verse, "Do not deal basely [*rakhil*] with members of your people." Others prefer an older translation, "Thou shalt not go up and down as a talebearer among thy people" (Soncino). In Jewish tradition, the word *rakhil*, whose exact meaning is unknown, is related to *r'khulah*, "merchandise" (see Ezek. 26:12). Therefore, a person who is engaged in *r'khilut* is considered like a merchant who deals in hurtful information, rather than goods. The Rabbis teach that even if the information that is passed around is not derogatory, it is still *r'khilut* and is prohibited by the Ninth Word.

Lashon HaRa—Gossip

When people use true speech for wrongful purposes, the Rabbis say, they engage in gossip, *lashon hara* (lit. "evil tongue"). Some call this type of speech "mean-spirited truth." *Lashon hara* is a Rabbinic expression and is not found in the Bible. The closest we have to it is the statement in the Book of Psalms *N'ztor l'shonkha meira*, "Guard your tongue from evil" (Ps. 34:14), which most likely became the source for the Rabbinic expression. According to a Talmudic teaching, "Four classes of people will not receive the presence of God [*Shekhinah*]: the class of scoffers, the class of flatterers, the class of liars, and the class of gossipers [*m'sap'rei l'shon hara*]" (BT *Sotah* 42a). According to a midrash, Moses doubted that the Hebrews deserved deliverance from Egypt. This happened after he had killed an Egyptian who was beating a fellow kinsman. When he confronted the two men fighting one another, one said to Moses, "Do you mean to kill me as you killed the Egyptian?" (Exod. 2:14). At that point, Moses realized that "gossip [*lashon hara*] is prevalent among them." Adds the midrash, "How can they ever be worthy of deliverance?" (*Sh'mot Rabbah* 1:30).

Motzi Shem Ra—Defamation

"Defamation" is issuing a false statement about another person that causes harm. It can take two forms: "slander," when a defamatory communication is done via the spoken word, and "libel," when it is done in writing. According to the U.S. Supreme Court (1964), the harmful statement must be made with actual malice. In our legal system, a person who has been defamed can seek actual and punitive damages.

Jewish law condemns the person who defames (*motzi shem ra*, lit. "spreads a bad name") another individual and does not make a distinction between slander and libel. Whoever makes a habit of speaking slander, say the Rabbis, acts as though he has denied the existence of God (BT *Arakhin* 15b). One rabbi said that the slanderer deserves to be stoned (ibid.). A slanderous tongue, adds the midrash, is called *sh'lishi* (third), because it harms three people: the slanderer, the person who hears the slander, and the person about whom the slander is uttered (*B'midbar Rabbah* 19:2). Using a wordplay, the midrash states that those who are afflicted with *tzaraat* (traditionally "leprosy," but real meaning unknown, maybe some kind of plague) are those who *motzi shem ra*, act as slanderers (*B'midbar Rabbah* 1:2). Is there a cure for slander, asks the Talmud? If the slanderer is a scholar, let him engage in Torah study, and if he is an ignorant, let him become humble (BT *Arakhin* 15b).

White Lies

Telling the truth is a biblical and Rabbinic mandate. At times, however, telling the truth can harm another individual, because, as noted above, words often have power of action; they can heal or do damage. Especially when we attempt to reprove another individual, as the Bible says we must (Lev. 19:17), we need to pay special attention to what we say and how we say it. What happens when truth and peace collide? Often the Rabbis seem to give priority to peace over truth. The midrash, commenting on the biblical passage "Love and truth meet; justice and peace kiss" (Ps. 85:11),[19] states that God chooses peace over truth (see *B'reishit Rabbah* 8:5).

Even though the Rabbis urge people to speak the truth, under some circumstances, they did allow "white lies," which are well-intentioned untruths uttered in the interest of tact, politeness, or peace. Saying kind words, such as "Thank you for your lovely gift" or "Your new haircut really highlights your eyes," is a value rooted in Rabbinic ethics. The Talmud states, "One may modify a statement in the interest of peace" (BT *Y'vamot* 65b).

The Rabbis find justification for white lies in some biblical texts. For example, after Jacob's death, Joseph's brothers tell him, "Your father [Jacob] left this charge before his death, saying, 'Thus shall you say to Joseph: Please I beg of you, forgive the transgression of your brothers and their sin, though they inflicted harm upon you'" (Gen. 50:16–17), even though there is no such command by Jacob to his sons. They simply do it to save their lives and preserve family unity and peace. Even God, the Rabbis point out, resorts to white lies for the sake of family peace. Thus, when the three angels come to visit the elderly Abraham and Sarah, perhaps after Abraham's circumcision, and tell them that they will be blessed with a child, the biblical text informs us, "Sarah laughed inwardly, thinking: 'Now that I am withered, will I have pleasure, with my lord so old!' But the Eternal One said to Abraham, 'Why is Sarah laughing so, thinking: "Am I really going to bear a child, when I have grown so old?"'" (Gen. 18:12–13). Here, when God repeats Sarah's statement to Abraham, God changes the wording: instead of making Abraham "old," God makes Sarah "old," thus saving Abraham's pride.

The Rabbis allow white lies when a *ketubah*, a legal document where truthfulness counts, is written. Thus, in a discussion about the correct description of the bride, two schools of Rabbinic thought clash. The Talmud asks, "How does one dance [*m'rak'din*, i.e., sing or recite] before the bride? 'The bride as she is' [i.e., pretty or not]. This is the opinion of the House of Shammai. But the House of Hillel say: 'Beautiful and graceful bride'" (BT *K'tubot* 16b–17a). Thus, for the sake of family harmony, the House of Hillel maintained that all brides should be described as beautiful.

In Conclusion

According to Rabban Shimon ben Gamliel, truth is one of three foundations of society (the other two are justice and peace) (*Pirkei Avot* 1:18). In fact, in biblical teaching, "the Eternal is truth" (Jer. 10:10). The Rabbis agreed: "The seal of God is truth" (BT *Shabbat* 55a). We are urged to "speak the truth to one another, render true and perfect justice" (Zech. 8:16). For, as the Psalmist adds, "he who speaks untruth shall not stand before Me" (Ps. 101:7). The testimony of witnesses determines the fate of another individual. Therefore, their words must be reliable and true. The Ninth Word briefly establishes the principle that a witness has to tell the truth and cannot be a false witness. The Rabbis of the Mishnah and the Talmud created a legal system by which the integrity of the judicial system is maintained through different ways of interrogating those who appeared in court. Yet as the ancient Sages also recognized, sometimes, in nonlegal settings, in order to save a life and for the sake of peace, one may modulate the truth and formulate comments that are beneficial to all parties. Like many other commandments in the Decalogue, the Ninth Word, too, originally appears to have had a specific application in the court system, but in time, it has taken on a life of its own and is now applied to other interpersonal relations for the sake of justice and peace in society.

The Tenth Word: Coveting

Endless Desire

It is natural for a human being to have healthy desires, and that is commendable. For example, ambition, understood as a desire for personal achievement, is good; it propels us to work hard, reach our potential and fulfill our ultimate goal. The Psalmist expresses his gratitude to God by saying, "You lead me to a rock that is high above me" (Ps. 61:3). The motto of the Jewish-German philosopher Moses Mendelssohn (1729–1786) was "To see the true, to love the beautiful, to desire the good, and to do the best." However, when ambition turns to envy or greed, it can become destructive.

Some people are never happy with what they have. To them applies the observation that "the eye is never satisfied with seeing; endless are the desires of the heart."[1] Jewish ethics attempts to curb this inclination to envy by urging us to reconsider our priorities. The Tenth Word of the Decalogue enshrines this teaching into law by letting us know that it is illegal to "covet" something that belongs to another. However, by doing so, it goes a step further than the preceding injunctions in the Decalogue. The Tenth Word stands alone in the Ten Commandments with regard to the content of its mandate: whereas all other commandments deal with some type of action, such as making sculptures for worship, murder, stealing, or committing adultery, the Tenth Word concerns itself with the intention of the individual. How can this allegation be proved? How can it be prosecuted? How can it even be legislated? This chapter will deal with the legal as well as ethical implications of this special command in the Bible, Rabbinic law, and contemporary life.

The Uniqueness of the Tenth Word in Ancient Near Eastern Law

Coveting is usually understood as desiring what belongs to another. The Tenth Word of the Decalogue occupies a unique place in all the law collections of the ancient Near East. The closest parallel is found in the Laws of Hammurabi (eighteenth century BCE), which reads as follows: "If a fire breaks out in a man's house, and a man who came to help put it out covets [lit. "casts his eye on"] the household furnishings belonging to the householder, and takes household furnishings belonging to the householder, that man shall be cast into that very fire" (#25).[2] In a Babylonian hymn called "The Shamash Hymn" (date unknown), there is a line that reads, "A man who covets [lit. "casts his eye on"] his neighbor's wife will [text broken] before his appointed day."[3] Though we do not have a collection of laws from ancient Egypt, in the "The Protestation of Guiltlessness" (ca. sixteenth century BCE), found in the Egyptian "Book of the Dead," the deceased, in his testimony before a court, denies any guilt in various crimes, and among them, he states, "I have not been covetous" (*ANET*, 35). Similarly, in the Egyptian "Instruction of the Vizier Ptah-hotep" (ca. twenty-fifth century BCE) we find, "Do not be covetous against thy [own] kindred" (*ANET*, 143). Again in the Egyptian text, "The Protests of the Eloquent Peasant" (ca. twentieth to eighteenth century BCE), we have, "The covetous man is void of success. . . . Though thy heart is covetous, it is not [of avail] for thee" (*ANET*, 409). These, however, are wisdom texts, not legal documents, though they may well represent one of the few sources we have of ancient Egyptian social laws.

The Text of the Tenth Word

The text of the Tenth Word in Exod. 20:14 differs in a number of places from its parallel in Deut. 5:18. The Plaut Torah commentary translates Exod. 20:14 as follows:

> You shall not covet [*tachmod*] your neighbor's house: you shall not covet [*tachmod*] your neighbor's wife, nor male nor female slave, nor ox nor ass, nor anything that is your neighbor's.

The translation of Deut. 5:18 reads like this, with some differences highlighted:

You [men] shall not covet [*tachmod*] your neighbor's wife. Likewise, none of you shall **crave** [***titaveh***] your neighbor's house, **or field**, or male or female slave, or ox, or ass, or anything that is your neighbor's.

A number of observations can be made about these two texts.

Whereas Exodus uses "covet" for both parts of the statement, Deuteronomy has "covet" for the first but "crave" for the second. Do they mean the same thing? What would be the implication if they did not? (See below for discussion.) It is noteworthy that other related texts, such as the Samaritan Pentateuch as well as some Deuteronomic remnants and phylacteries found in the Dead Sea area, use only the verb "covet."

In the list of coveted items, Exodus places "house" first and then "wife." In Deuteronomy, however, "wife" comes first, before "house." Deuteronomy refers to "field"; Exodus does not. It appears that the items are listed in both texts in decreasing order of importance. Nahum Sarna maintains that in Exodus "house" means "household."[4] So the list in Exodus identifies the major components of a typical Israelite household, with wife occupying the highest place. In Deuteronomy, on the other hand, as Jeffrey Tigay writes, "house" means a "dwelling,"[5] and "wife" is not part of one's belongings. She stands outside of the property list. It is interesting to note that in Pseudo-Philo (ca. first century CE) "wife" is not mentioned at all; only household goods are included (11:13). The words "ox or ass" stand for domesticated animals used by the family. Furthermore, the text in Exodus appears to reflect a seminomadic society. Deuteronomy, on the other hand, by adding the word "field," reflects a sedentary life. In both texts, "neighbor" most likely means "anyone."[6]

Jewish tradition considers both sections of the commandment as being part of the same law. Catholics and Lutherans, however, consider the second half an independent command. According to the Catholic catechism, "the ninth commandment [i.e., "You shall not covet your neighbor's house," in Exod. 20:14a] forbids carnal concupiscence; the tenth forbids coveting another's goods" (#2514). Jewish tradition, in line with the content of the commandment, does not limit the text of Exodus and Deuteronomy to sexual matters and views it much more broadly.

Within a legal context, another occurrence of the verb form *chamad* (to covet) is found in a small collection of laws in Exodus 34, which some scholars view as a shorter version of the Decalogue. Here a promise by God is added to the law dealing with the Three Pilgrimage Festivals: "I will drive out nations from your path and enlarge your territory, no one will covet [*lo yachmod*] your land when you go up to appear before the Eternal your God three times a year" (Exod. 34:24). As Nahum Sarna points out, this promise was most likely written in post-Mosaic times, when the Israelites were already living in Canaan, and "presupposes the future existence of some central or, at least, regional sanctuary that, for many, will be far from home."[7]

According to some commentators, the Tenth Word reads like a conclusion to the Decalogue. Just as the words "house" and "slaves" are mentioned in the First Word (Exod. 20:2; Deut. 5:6), so are they used in the last (Exod. 20:14; Deut. 5:18). Similarly, the Tenth Commandment, which refers to "neighbor" (Exod. 20:14; Deut. 5:18), parallels the First Word, "I am the Eternal," for as a Rabbinic source puts it, "everything depends on these two things.[8] The second commandment prohibits the worship of other gods, and the Tenth Word prohibits coveting other people's goods. Umberto Cassuto writes, "The basic principle of the First Word is the Love of and Loyalty to God, whereas the last Commandment asks us to love our neighbors."[9] And, this love (better: "loyalty to") is at the foundation of the entire Decalogue.

"Covet" and "Crave"

As indicated above, whereas the law in Exod. 20:14 mentions only *tachmod* (from the verb *chamad*) for "coveting" in both parts of the law, the text in Deut. 5:18, has *tachmod* in part a, but *titaveh* (from the verb *hitaveh*) meaning "crave" in part b. What is the difference between the two? The question revolves around this issue: does the Bible here forbid mere mental activity, or does the transgression also require that this thought be translated into concrete action? Both positions have been advocated throughout the centuries. Some commentators maintain that "coveting" can be considered a transgression only when it leads to an illegal or unethical action. To justify this position, they point to a number of biblical texts where "coveting" is followed by an act of "taking"; for example, "You shall not covet [*tachmod*]) the silver and gold on them [the images of the gods of the idolaters] and keep it [*velakachta*] for yourselves" (Deut. 7:25); "I coveted them [*va-echm'deim*] and took them [*va-ekacheim*]" (Josh. 7:21); "They covet [*v'chamdu*] fields, and seize them [*v'gazalu*]" (Mic. 2:2). We find the verb *chamad* in a non-Israelite text with the same meaning: "If the [enemy desires [*ychmd*] this city and tears it down [*v'yisa*]."[10] This seems to be the understanding in the *M'khilta* as well, saying at first, "Perhaps the commandment prohibits coveting through words?" But quoting Deut. 7:25, it concludes, "Just as there [in Deut. 7] the carrying out of one's desire into practice is forbidden, so also here it is forbidden to carry out the desire into practice [*ad sheyaaseh maaseh*]" (*Bachodesh* 10, end). In the medieval period, Maimonides argues that the Torah prohibits "coveting" only when we act out our covetousness, stating, "He is not liable until he actually takes possession of the article he coveted" (*Mishneh Torah, Hilkhot G'zeilah* 9). *Sefer HaChinukh* also maintains that this law is operative when "some action is taken about it" (#38). For Bekhor Shor, a medieval commentary of thirteenth-century France, not coveting means "you shall not trick him into giving you what is his, either gratis or for payment."[11] So, the argument goes, the verb *chamad* originally referred to a reprehensible mind-set that inevitably leads to an illegal or unethical action.

Other critics, however, argue that "coveting" is simply a mental desire and does not require action. One is punished for thinking evil thoughts. They marshal, among others, the following examples. The Book of Proverbs uses the verb *chamad* in 6:25, as meaning "desire": "Do not lust [*al tachmod*] for her [i.e., an evil woman's] beauty in your heart." The idea that there can be obsessive desires without necessarily leading to action is found in the Septuagint's translation of our commandment, where the Greek verb *epithumia*, used for *lo tachmod*, is understood as "longing," "desire," or "crave." That also is the interpretation of Philo (first century), who most likely used the Septuagint as his source. Commenting on "coveting," he writes:

> Of all the passions there is not one so grievous as a covetous desire of what one has not got, of things which are in appearance good, but not in reality; a desire which produces grievous anxieties which are hard to satisfy; for such a passion puts the reason to flight, and banishes it to a great distance, involving the soul in great difficulties, while the object which is desired flies away contemptuously, retreating not with its back but with its face to one; for when a person perceives this passion of covetousness after having started up rapidly, then resting for a short time, either with a view to spread out its alluring toils, or because it has learnt to entertain a hope of succeeding in its object, he then retires to a longer distance uttering reproaches against it." (*Special Laws* 4:14, C. D. Yonge)

Moreover, those who argue that "coveting" does not necessarily require a specific action point to the Deuteronomic addition of the verb *titaveh*, in the second half of the command, which clearly means only "desire." According to Tigay, "The grammatical form of *titaveh* implies continuous or repeated action, in other words, constant craving."[12] So, "you shall not crave" may simply be an interpretation of "you shall not covet." In fact, Moshe Greenberg maintains that "crave" is the same thing as "covet."[13] Plaut sees *titaveh* as a stylistic variance of *tachmod*."[14] Thus, by placing both expressions in parallel, the commandment's intention is, according to these critics, to teach us that we must control even our inner thoughts.

Other commentators disagree and say that "coveting" is different from "craving." Maimonides, for example, maintains that *taavah* ("craving" or "desire"), the noun form of the verb *hitaveh*, means just that: "Desire [*taavah*] is only in the heart" (*Mishneh Torah, Hilkhot G'zeilah* 10). The nineteenth-century Russian Jewish rabbinic commentator Malbim distinguished between "coveting" and "craving," not as the *M'khilta* does as degrees of emotional intensity, but with regard to imagination and sight. "Coveting" (*chemdah*), he says, refers to a physical experience, like seeing with the eye, whereas "craving" (*taavah*) refers to a desire even for something that is not present or perceived by the senses. Thus, he adds by way of example, we do not "covet" our neighbor's wife as a result of our imagination but only when we see that person in the flesh. But we can easily "crave" our neighbor's wealth by imagining what it would be like to have what he has without actually experiencing that sensation. A modern critic, B. Childs, summarizes the distinction between *chamad* and *hitaveh* as follows: "The emphasis of *chamad* falls on an emotion which often leads to a commensurate action, whereas the focus of *hitavveh* rests much more on the emotion itself."[15] In this respect, Deuteronomy 20 went a step farther than Exodus 20 by internalizing the concept of "coveting." As Alexander Rofe points out, "The Deuteronomic author, in using the words, 'you shall not crave,' went beyond the original prohibition against coveting, adding even longing thoughts for the property of one's fellowman."[16]

Between these two interpretations, one saying that "coveting" requires action, and the other arguing that it does not, I prefer to view the command "You shall not covet" in line with the dominant Jewish tradition and many modern scholars who maintain say that the prohibition "You shall not covet" refers to an obsessive desire leading to an illegal or unethical action, whereas "You shall not crave" represents an extension and, perhaps, an internalization by Deuteronomy of the commandment in Exodus.

Biblical Narratives about Coveting

There are a few biblical texts that deal with the idea of coveting (using the verb *chamad*) and the results that ensue because of it.

The Case of Achan

During the invasion of Canaan, God tells Joshua, Moses's successor, that he will be successful in capturing the city of Jericho (Josh. 6). Consequently, Joshua commands his soldiers, under penalty of death, to put everything in the city under "proscription" (*cheirem*), namely, to consecrate it to God and to place it into God's treasury at the local sanctuary, save a woman by the name of Rahab, the innkeeper/harlot who hid the Israelite spies in her home (Josh. 6:17). However, on the way, the people of the city of Ai, just eight miles north of Jerusalem, rout the Israelites and defeat them. God tells Joshua that this tragedy happened because one person took some items from the proscribed booty for his own use. The culprit, Achan[17] son of Carmi of the tribe of Judah, is identified, most likely by casting lots. Upon interrogation, he confesses, "It is true, I have sinned against the Eternal, the God of Israel. This is what I did: I saw among the spoils a fine Shinar [i.e., from Babylonia] mantle, two hundred shekels of silver, and a wedge of gold weighing fifty shekels, and I coveted them and took them [*va-echm'deim va-ekacheim*]" (Josh. 7:21). Consequently, he and his family, including his animals, are all put to death by the whole community. Afterwards, the text informs us, "The anger of the Eternal subsided. That is why that place was named the Valley of Achor—as is still the case" (Josh. 7:26).

There are some historical problems with this episode, especially because the city of Ai was uninhabited at the time of the alleged Israelite invasion. Furthermore, this story, emerging from the early Israelite conception of community solidarity, was most likely written to explain the reason why the "Valley of Achor" (a play on the word "Achan") was named as such. The moral of the narrative also seems to be that one person can, because of envy and greed, jeopardize the well-being and security of the whole people.

Eve and the Fruit

According to the biblical narrative, Adam and Eve are placed in a Garden in Eden (not "of" Eden), which contains all kinds of trees, including the "Tree of Life" and the "Tree of All Knowledge." Eve tells the serpent that God has forbidden them to eat or touch "of the fruit of the tree in the middle of it [the

Garden]" (Gen. 3:3). (Here Eve seems to identify "the tree in the middle of the Garden" with the "Tree of All Knowledge.") When the serpent assures her that she will not die, she, realizing "how good to eat the tree's fruit would be, and how alluring to the eyes [*taavah hu la-einayim*] it was, and how desirable the insight was that the tree [*nechmad ha-eitz l'haskil*] would bring" (Gen. 3:6), takes of its fruit and eats it. She also gives some to Adam, who eats it, too. As a result, both open their eyes, and noticing that they are naked, they cover themselves with fig leaves (*aleih t'einah*) (Gen. 3:7).

Here the serpent is called *arum* (cunning), most likely a play on the word "naked," *arumim*, which describes the status of the first two human beings, Adam and Eve, just one verse before our episode. The serpent is not yet the "evil personified," as he would become much later in postbiblical times. The type of fruit that the first couple eats is left unidentified in the text. The Rabbis imagine that it could be grapes, a citron, figs, even wheat (*B'reishit Rabbah* 15:7). I surmise the fruit is probably a fig, because, right after they eat from the fruit, they cover themselves with "fig leaves."[18] It is interesting to note that in this text the two expressions *taavah* (alluring) and *chamad* (desirable) are used in parallel, which would indicate that they mean the same thing, thus strengthening the argument of those who say that "coveting" and "craving" are similar. Yet, it should be noted that Adam and Eve not only covet the fruit, but also take it and eat it. It is also possible that by the time this passage was written, most likely post-Deuteronomy, when the word *taavah* (craving) internalized the action-oriented concept of "coveting," the two were considered synonymous. Besides, our narrative is not a legal document and cannot be used against those who transgress the prohibition of *lo tachmod*.

The story of Adam and Eve's eating from the forbidden fruit has been interpreted in a variety of ways throughout history and gave rise to the belief that Eve was a seductress and their disobedience represents the "Fall of Mankind." In some respect that is the position of many Christians. *Paradise Lost*, the epic poem by John Milton (seventeenth century), clearly reflects this belief. There is, however, another way of reading the biblical story. As Harold S. Kushner points out, the story of the Garden of Eden "is a tale, not of Paradise Lost but of Paradise Outgrown, not of Original Sin, but of the Birth of Conscience."[19] And that is a good thing. After eating from the fruit, Adam and Eve "graduated" (Kushner's word, p. 30) from the uncomplicated world of animal life to a more sophisticated one where Good and Evil are in tension with one another, and people need to learn how to make proper ethical decisions for the common good. How to avoid greed is one of them.

Other Biblical Stories of Coveting

In addition to these two texts where the verb *chamad* is clearly mentioned, the biblical text, aware of the human propensity of wanting more, provides other examples where individuals envy each other, are jealous of their neighbors, and commit acts of violence against them, mainly because their eyes are not satisfied. In these narratives, other Hebrew verbs similar to *chamad* are used, or the context makes it clear that we are dealing with situations involving envy or jealousy. For example, Cain kills his brother Abel because he is envious of the fact that God has paid heed to Abel's sacrifice and not to the one he himself has offered (Gen. 4:3–8). The Pharaoh desires and takes Sarai as his wife because his courtiers praise her to him, and he does not know that she is already married to Abram (Gen. 12:15). Rachel is envious (*vat'kaneih*) of her sister, Leah, who has already borne children for their common husband, Jacob, and she is still barren (Gen. 30:1). Joseph's brothers become jealous of him (*vayisn'u*, lit. "they hated," "they rejected") when they realize that Jacob, their father, consider him a favorite son (Gen. 37:4). Aaron and Miriam become envious of their brother, Moses, because they realize that God prefers to speak only through him (Num. 12:2). King Saul keeps "a jealous eye [*oyein*] on David" (I Sam. 18:9) because he is becoming more popular among the people. King Ahab desires and forcibly obtains the field of his neighbor, Naboth (I Kings 21; see "The Sixth Word: Homicide" see page 116). King David desires and lies with Bathsheba (II Sam. 11), thus committing adultery (see "The Seventh Word: Adultery" see page 139). Gehazi, the servant of the prophet Elijah, covets the belongings of Naaman, a military commander of the Arameans, for which he is punished with leprosy (II Kings 5:20–27). So, the biblical narrator was acutely aware of the destructive effects of evil desires and the consequences that ensue because of them. Each story is a warning to the reader not to follow the example of the main character.

The Punishment

The Tenth Word does not specify any punishment for violating this command. Nor is it possible to prosecute a person for it, for as many critics have pointed out, human beings' desires and thoughts cannot be controlled. People are penalized only when they take an illegal action. Yet, even harmful thoughts have an emotional impact on individuals, and this impact cannot be easily ignored. Some individuals who fall to coveting—or, worse, craving—need to learn how to curb their desires; others must confront the guilt that ensues because of them. Let me elaborate.

Some thinkers argue that "evil thoughts" constitute a transgression and deserve punishment. Thus, for example, according to the New Testament, "Everyone who looks at a woman lustfully has already committed adultery with her in his heart" (Matt. 5:28). Here the sin is committed only in one's thought, and no action was taken by the person who desired the other woman. The thirty-ninth president of the United States (1977–1981), Jimmy Carter, has spoken about this type of sin. In his 1976 interview with *Playboy* magazine, he stated, "I've looked on a lot of women with lust. I've committed adultery in my heart many times.... This is something that God recognizes, that I will do and have done, and God forgives me for it." In Jewish tradition, this type of behavior would not be considered a sin, because no action followed it.

Rabbinic sages, realizing that thoughts cannot be controlled and that individuals who harbor such thoughts cannot be punished for them, deal with the human propensity for transgression by invoking the categories of *yetzer tov* (the inclination to do good) and *yetzer ra* (the inclination to do bad). The Rabbis teach that every individual is born with these two inclinations (BT *B'rakhot* 61a). However, *yetzer ra*, which is the aggressive instinct for creativity and achievement, is not, in and of itself, "evil," for as Rabbi Sh'muel ben Nachman taught, "Were it not for the impulse to do bad, a person would not build a house, take a spouse, beget children, or engage in commerce" (*B'reishit Rabbah* 9:7). The Talmud tells that Ezra and the Men of the Great Assembly, wanting to destroy the *yetzer ra*, once put it in jail for three days, but then, when they looked for a new-laid egg, they could not find any (BT *Yoma* 69b). The lesson is this: it is not possible to eliminate totally the aggressive impulse that motivates a human being. The best that can be done is to control it and eliminate its excesses by rechanneling its energies for the common good. Thus Rabbi Levi ben Chama taught, "If he prevails against it [i.e., *yetzer ra*], it is well; but if not, he should occupy himself with Torah [study and practice]" (BT *B'rakhot* 5a). One is called "a *gibor* [mighty]" when "he subdues his impulse [*yitzro*]" (*Pirkei Avot* 4:1).

From a Rabbinic perspective, therefore, one cannot be punished for bad thoughts or desires, but as Nehama Leibowitz points out, "it is possible to train oneself not only not to commit adultery or not to steal, but also not to covet and desire things not his own."[20] We should be able to internalize the command of *lo tachmod* and desist from envying a particular item, such as a house, a car, or a watch, that belongs to someone else. But this takes conviction and discipline. In the Apocrypha, Ben Sira teaches, "God gave us power over our will" (15:14). With goodwill and determination, we can straighten our paths and curb our inclination to do bad. Joseph Telushkin suggests a few ways of reducing envy: realizing that a certain level of envy is natural, a person ought to focus on the good someone is doing or has done; one must love the other person, instead of feeling hostility and envy toward that individual; when envying the other person, you must also consider the suffering and the problems that this individual has gone through in order to achieve what her or she has done; it is important to think about the positive things you have instead of concentrating on the other person, who may not have enjoyed these blessings.[21] By applying these rules, one can curb the negative impact of bad thoughts and reorient them toward healthy desires.

Curbing desires requires strong will and determination. Even if nothing is done about them, another deeper consequence ensues. Psychologists often argue that one of the negative impacts of evil thoughts is a sense of "guilt," and that in itself is a great source of self-punishment for many individuals. Guilt, broadly defined as a feeling of responsibility or remorse, real or imagined, of having violated a moral standard, can lead to emotional depression and paralysis. The realization of coveting can, at times, lead to guilty feelings, and though these are hardly prosecutable, people who feel guilt, shame, or remorse find themselves stuck and unable to move forward. However, these individuals, if they wish to and find the personal strength to do it, can turn their life around through self-love and forgiveness or by turning the negative experiences into positive ones by doing charitable work or seeing a competent therapist.

Coveting and Greed

Jewish tradition interprets the prohibition *lo tachmod* widely and approves of healthy desires while condemning the unhealthy ones, such as ambition leading to greed. This affects both the individual as well as groups of people.

The original meaning of the word "ambition" (from the Latin *ambitio*) referred to going around soliciting votes, or striving for favor, courting, and flattery. Today ambition or aspiration is viewed positively and as worthy of pursuit. "Ambition," said the philosopher Friedrich Nietzsche (1844–1900), "is the path to success; persistence is the vehicle to arrive in." Some people have high hopes for themselves and stay the course with hard work and tenacity. It is good for people to aim high and to work toward the achievement of better things for themselves, their family, and their community. We admire these people, and they become our role models. Author Karen Ravn states, "Only as high as I reach can I grow; only as far as I seek can I go; only as deep as I look can I see; only as much as I dream can I be."

Ambition, pursued with imagination, ethical means, and hard work, is a healthy desire. That is not where the problem lies. It is our unhealthy desires that cause us problems, and they often lead us from bad to worse. Maimonides warns us, "Desire leads to covetousness and covetousness to robbing" (*Mishneh Torah*, *Hilkhot G'zeilah* 11). A modern application of this slippery slope is provided by Lisa G. Lerman, who, in her article "The Slippery Slope from Ambition to Greed to Dishonesty," discusses the decreasing professional integrity among some lawyers today. Stating that "there is substantial evidence that lawyer dishonesty is on the rise,"[22] she gives the following reasons for this phenomenon: the desire for money, the desire for status, the declining loyalty to law firms, the opportunities open to attorneys and lack of oversight at many law firms, and firm culture that imposes enormous pressure on all lawyers to bill huge numbers of hours. This matter is not limited to practicing attorneys. Some professionals in other fields, too, fall under the influence of their unhealthy desires and resort to illegal means to achieve their goals.

Most people recognize that of all the human traits, greed is the absolute worst, because it implies resorting to any means necessary to reach one's goal. In 1985, a stock speculator, Ivan Boesky, during a commencement address at the University of California, Berkeley, declared, "Greed is healthy. You can be greedy and still feel good about yourself." Similarly, in a particularly moving scene in *Wall Street* (1987), Gordon Gekko (played by Michael Douglas) addresses the Teldar Paper stockholders and tells them, "Greed is good. Greed is right. Greed works. Greed, in all of its forms, greed for life, for money, for love, knowledge, has marked the upward surge of mankind. " However, greed, as an unhealthy desire, ultimately consumes the individual. It is excessive and selfish. The psychoanalyst Erich Fromm writes, "Greed is a bottomless pit which exhausts the person in an endless effort to satisfy the need without ever reaching satisfaction."[23] In 2002, Alan Greenspan, the Federal Reserve chairman, told Congress that "infectious greed" was the reason for business crises.

There is doubt that the *yetzer hara* of coveting and greed is imprinted in our souls. Consciously or unconsciously, people desire what others have—a car, a house, even a wife. It seems to me that, what the Tenth Word prohibits is when a person "covets" another object and goes out and obtains it without permission; and, in the case of "craving," when an individual not only desires a house, but as Arnold Jacob Wolf argues, when he wants a particular object, namely *his* car, *his* house, *his* wife.[24]

Human beings are not the only ones who are motivated by greed. There is also corporate greed, which is as destructive, if not more so. In corporate greed, which often leads to crime, an entire group of employees or even a town is sacrificed in the name of illegal financial gain by owners or corporate executives. No one denies that corporations are often set up to obtain financial gain for their owners and shareholders. The question is how far can this go? It is institutional greed that motivates some telemarketers who use aggressive methods to push their products, and according to Aaron Levine, these pressure tactics constitute a technical violation of the command *lo tachmod*.[25] Recently, some examples of corporate crime have even been turned into popular movies reflecting actual events in our country: *Norma Rae* (1979) dramatizes the effort of an individual who combated unsafe working conditions of workers; *Silkwood* (1983) tells the story of a nuclear facility in Oklahoma, which contaminated many people by wrongfully using plutonium; *Erin Brockovich* (2000) fought a nuclear company in California for polluting the city's water supply. In the spirit of biblical law, these companies, too, are to be considered as having broken the Tenth Word.

Envy, Jealousy, and Greed

Modern psychology teaches us that unhealthy desires come in different varieties, some stronger than others. There is envy, jealousy, coveting, and greed. Envy is the mildest, and greed the worst. Coveting is often the end result of envy and jealousy. The latter two are similar, but one is usually envious of another person but jealous of more than one. Joseph Telushkin gives the following example: "a man who is jealous of his wife because he fears she is cheating on him is also jealous of the man he suspects is her lover."[26] Coveting is similar to greed, except that with greed, one often uses illegal and unethical means to attain the coveted desire.

Biblical teachers condemn excessive wants, without distinguishing between envy, jealousy, and greed. The prophet Micah, for example, clearly speaks against greed: "They covet [*v'chamdu*] fields, and seize them; houses, and take them away" (Mic. 2:2). Similarly, the prophet Isaiah cries out, "Ah, those who add house to house and join field to field, till there is room for none but you"

(Isa. 5:8). In the same vein, the prophet Habakkuk laments, "Ah, you who have acquired gains to the detriment of your own house, who have destroyed many peoples in order to set your nest on high to escape disaster!" (Hab. 2:9). For the biblical wisdom sages, envy (*kinah*) "is rottenness in the bones" (Prov. 14:30). In the New Testament, covetousness is compared to idolatry (Eph. 5:5). For Rabbi Elazar HaKapar, "Envy [*hakinah*], lust [*hataavah*], and pursuit of honor will ruin a person's life" (*Pirkei Avot* 4:28).

On the other hand, envy, like ambition, can have its positive side, too. For example, the ancient Rabbis teach that one should try to envy another person's wisdom. The Talmud says, "The envy of the scribes [*kinat sof'rim*] increases wisdom" (BT *Bava Batra* 21a). The reason is because this type of envy leads one to study and increase one's knowledge. And that is good for the individual and, often, for the society as a whole, if it is put to good use and for the benefit of humanity. One can and should admire the good qualities of another person and try to be like that individual. There is nothing wrong with trying to emulate the beneficial actions of our neighbor, such as being honest in business, hardworking in our endeavors, and generous toward the downtrodden, while not harboring ill will toward that person. This attitude leads to peace of mind and contentment of soul.

In life, we need to pursue not happiness but contentment. The first is illusory and vain, the second is possible and often gives you peace of mind, and may even yield happiness as a result. In the best of all worlds, one is born and, through hard work, persistence, and ethical means, accomplishes one's basic dreams, and leaves the earth saying, "I am happy with what I have done in my life." When Abraham became old, the Bible states, he "breathed his last and died in good old age, full of age [*zakein v'savei-a*, lit. "old and content"], and was gathered to his people" (Gen. 25:8). Some Rabbinic commentators add, "He died content that he was able to accomplish all his desires during his lifetime" (Ramban, S'forno, on Gen. 25:8).

A contented person is one who has learned how to appreciate what he or she has here on earth, for there is no end to wanting more. At some point, one should say, *dayeinu*, "I am content." The author of the Book of Ecclesiastes writes, "I got myself more wealth than anyone before me in Jerusalem" (Eccles. 2:9), but all that proved to be nothing but "futile and pursuit of wind" (2:11). Similarly, the Rabbis say, "Nobody departs from the world with half his desires gratified. Whoever possesses one hundred, desires two hundred; whoever possesses two hundred, desires four hundred" (*Kohelet Rabbah* 1:13). But greed has its limits and ultimately becomes a turnoff for many social observers. That is one of the reasons why people with a sense of propriety are revolted when rich people get richer by illegal means, when high-level executives receive huge bonuses at a time when most individuals are working hard to make a living, or when athletes and entertainers command big salaries at a time when the economy of the country is suffering.

The Rabbinic ideal of contentment is clearly expressed by a second-century sage, Shimon ben Zoma, who rhetorically asks, "Who is rich?" The expected answer would be, a person who possesses lots of things. But this is not what the sage teaches. For him a person is "rich" (*ashir*) "when he is happy with his lot [*hasamei-ach b'chelko*]," and quoting the Psalmist, he adds, "When you eat from the labor of your hands, happy will you be and all will be well with you" (*Pirkei Avot* 4:1). This idea of contentedness is also reflected in a famous saying by the Roman philosopher Cicero (106–43 BCE): "If you have a garden and a library, you have everything you need."

Some critics state that the concept of *hasamei-ach b'chelko* may hinder progress in the world. It is only through aggressive behavior that progress is possible, they say. Considering these two positions, other sages suggest moderation as the middle ground. Rabbi Meir teaches that one ought to balance business with Torah study (*Pirkei Avot* 4:12). Writing in medieval times, Maimonides, too, advocates moderation:

> Every human being is characterized by numerous moral dispositions which differ from each other and are exceedingly divergent.... One is so greedy that all the money in the world would not satisfy him.... Another so curbs his desires that he is content with very little.... The right way is the mean in each group of dispositions common to humanity.... He will only desire that which the body absolutely needs and cannot do without.... He will only labor at his occupation to obtain what is necessary for his sustenance.... He will not be tight-fisted nor yet a spendthrift.... This is the way of the wise.[27]

For me, this seems to be the best approach. If envy and jealousy lead to something positive, to personal improvement, and without negative impact on others, it is acceptable as a motivator in life; when they turn into coveting, craving, and greed, they become destructive and should be avoided, curbed, and eliminated.

In Conclusion

The Tenth Word comes to warn us against excessive and destructive desires. No wonder that many thinkers have believed that it encapsulates the highest goals toward which we must all strive. Thus, the *P'sikta Rabbati*, a sixth- or seventh-century Rabbinic text in the Land of Israel, states that "to covet is to violate all the Ten Commandments" (21:107a). The Tenth Word, functioning like a conclusive statement to the Decalogue, urges us not to resort to unhealthy desires, because it often leads us to use illegal and unethical means to reach our goals, and that can be the source of our downfall. On the contrary, the Rabbis encourage us to avoid its pitfalls by training ourselves to rise above our petty thoughts and learn how to live with moderation, within our means, contentedly and gratefully.

Legislation and Commandment

In this book we have studied the biblical context within which the Ten Words were placed, distilled the format and structure of the Decalogue, and analyzed the meaning and ethical implications of each commandment separately. Now is the time and place to formulate some conclusions and, in particular, to see how these norms can be internalized. The Decalogue often uses the pronoun "you" in the singular. Each commandment is addressed to you and me individually, not to corporate Israel. The only way these injunctions can motivate us to work for the common good is if we are willing to open our hearts and minds to each one of them and accept them as guideposts.

In ancient times, the Ten Words represented a basic religious and ethical teaching. Most likely, some of them existed in small clusters and were combined by some editors at a time that can no longer be determined. Ultimately, they were attributed to God, who is viewed as the primary source and formulator of the law in the Bible. Thus, they became divine words carrying legal force. The Rabbis who inherited these commandments considered them as the foundation of the Jewish faith, for, as they claimed, they contained all of the 613 commandments (Rashi, on Exod. 24:14). The Sages also enlarged the scope of each law and tried to adapt them to the needs of their own time. Medieval and modern commentators followed suit. And even today these basic principles of law and morality are being used as the primary springboard for the discussion of many legal and moral issues that were unimaginable in early biblical times.

Because of their brevity and broad scope, these Ten Words have always set high goals for every individual. These goals are often difficult to achieve, yet, ancient sages and contemporary thinkers urge us to do our best in making them our own. A story: It is told that once on Shavuot, before the reading of the Decalogue, Rabbi Menachem of Riminov (1745–1816) ordered his assistant to announce that anyone who had not fulfilled the Ten Commandments should leave the synagogue during the reading. Almost everyone left the sanctuary. So Rabbi Menachem said to his assistant, "Go and tell them that if they undertake to fulfill them in the future, they can come back in." They did and the rabbi read the Decalogue.[1]

Many people today look at the Ten Commandments as a collection of moral imperatives that have universal appeal. How can these instructions affect an individual and impact behavior in our own time?

According to one Rabbinic midrash, when the Israelites gathered around Mount Sinai, they accepted the Torah without asking any questions. They simply said, *Naaseh v'nishma*, "We will do and we will listen" (Exod. 24:7) (*M'khilta, Yitro* 5). Yet, according to another source, at Mount Sinai, God lifted up the mountain, held it over the heads of the families of Israel like an open casket, and said, "If you accept the Torah, it will be well. But if you do not, this will be your burial place" (BT *Shabbat* 88a). The first text implies that the Torah is good and worthy of keeping, even if we do not always understand everything in it; whereas the second text, perhaps written at a time of persecution, views the Torah as a burden that can be kept only under duress. In our time, no one can be coerced to observe the covenantal obligations. They have to be assumed freely. How so?

The answer can be found in the distinction that the German Jewish philosophers Martin Buber (1978–1965) and Franz Rosenzweig (1986–1929) made between "legislation" and "commandment." According to these two thinkers of the past century, "legislation" is something we find in the books. However, legislation can be elevated to the level of "commandment" when it is felt that it is addressed to you personally. This is done when a person studies the set of instructions, is convinced of its validity and importance, and considers each of them so valuable and so compelling that they feel as though it has been directed to him or her on a personal level. As Jakob Petuchowski writes, "Only the Jew who can lift a given 'law' from the level of 'legislation' to that of a 'commandment' addressed to him personally, only he can really re-enact the moment of Revelation, and only he can experience God as the "Giver of the Torah."[2] Similarly, Martin Buber maintains that "the Soul of the Decalogue is to be found in the word 'thou." ...Only those persons really grasped the Decalogue who literally felt it as having been addressed to themselves; only those, that is, who experienced that original state of being addressed as an address to themselves. Thanks to its 'thou' the Decalogue means the preservation of the divine voice."[3] The ancient Rabbis, too, stressed that one of the most important words in the Decalogue is "you." They asked: Why are the Ten Commandments addressed in the singular? So that each person would think that he or she alone, in the whole word, was responsible for studying, performing, and upholding all the words of the Torah.[4]

Now that we have examined the intricacies of the Ten Words, the challenge for all of us is whether we are willing to assume them as our guiding lights and moral imperatives, which, once imprinted in our conscience, require a change in our attitude toward God and humanity in our everyday life. I hope the present study has cleared the way for such a transformation.

Notes

Preface

1. Samuel Sandmel, *The Hebrew Scriptures* (New York: Knopf, 1963), 3.
2. Ian Burrell, "Clergy Forget Commandments," *The Independent* (UK), Jan. 27, 1997, http://www.independent.co.uk/news/clergy-forget-commandments-1285406.html.
3. "Americans Know Big Mac Better Than Ten Commandments," *Reuters*, Oct. 12, 2007, http://www.reuters.com/article/2007/10/12/us-bible-commandments-idUSN1223894020071012.
4. David Flusser, "The Ten Commandments and the New Testament," in *The Ten Commandments in History and Tradition*, ed. Ben-Zion Segal (Jerusalem: Magnes Press, Hebrew University of Jerusalem, 1990), 219.
5. Geerhardus Vos, *Biblical Theology: Old and New Testament* (Edinburgh: Banner of Truth Trust, 2000), 132.
6. *M'norat HaMaor*, an ethical compendium by Yitzchak Aboab, Spain, fourteenth century. Quoted in S. Y. Agnon, *Present at Sinai: The Giving of the Law*, trans. Michael Swirsky (Philadelphia: Jewish Publication Society, 1994), 250.
7. Quoted by P. Goodman, *The Shavuot Anthology* (Philadelphia: Jewish Publication Society, 1974), 77.

Torah and Law in Judaism

1. Jacob Milgrom, *Numbers*, The JPS Torah Commentary (Philadelphia: Jewish Publication Society, 1990), 486.
2. "Divining the Meaning of Yale's Insignia," *Biblical Archaeology Review*, March/April 2005, 37.
3. For the full list of the thirteen *midot*, see *Encyclopaedia Judaica* (2007), 9:25–29; Philip Birnbaum, *Encyclopedia of Jewish Concepts* (New York: Hebrew Publishing, 1979), 331–35.
4. *Encyclopaedia Judaica*, 20:41.
5. *Gates of Prayer*, ed. Chaim Stern (New York: CCAR Press, 1975), 424.
6. *Gates of Repentance*, ed. Chaim Stern (New York: CCAR Press, 1978), 100.
7. *Mishkan T'filah*, ed. Elyse Goldstein (New York: CCAR Press, 2007), 375.
8. For the problem of identifying what is law in the Bible, see Rifat Sonsino, "Toward a Definition of Law in the Pentateuch," *Journal of Reform Judaism*, Summer 1979, 117–23.

Text and Context

1. See the discussion in John I. Durham, *Exodus*, Word Biblical Commentary (Waco, TX: Word Books, 1987), 458–59.
2. On the Samaritans, see *The Anchor Bible Dictionary* (New York: Doubleday, 1992), 5:940–47.
3. On the Nash Papyrus, see Marvin A. Sweeney, "The Nash Papyrus," *Biblical Archaeology Review*, July/August 2010.
4. The *M'khilta* is an old midrash, perhaps of tannaitic origin. See *Mekhilta de-Rabbi Ishmael*, 2nd ed., trans. Jacob Z. Lauterbach, 2 vols. (Philadelphia: Jewish Publication Society, 2004).
5. S. Y. Agnon, *Present at Sinai: The Giving of the Law*, trans. Michael Swirsky (Philadelphia: Jewish Publication Society, 1994), 243.
6. *Sefer HaHinnuch:* The Book of [Mitzvah] Education, trans. Charles Wengrov (Jerusalem: Feldheim, 1992), vol. l, no. 25, 143.
7. Leviticus 11–12. Quoted by Agnon, *Present at Sinai*, 235.
8. Agnon, *Present at Sinai*, 221.
9. Moshe Weinfeld, "The Uniqueness of the Decalogue and Its Place in Jewish Tradition," in *The Ten Commandments in History and Tradition*, edited by Ben-Zion Segal (Jerusalem: Magnes Press, 1990), 3.
10. *Encyclopaedia Judaica* (2007), 5:1443–44.
11. H. W. E. Saggs, *The Greatness That Was Babylon* (New York: Hawthorn Books, 1962), 366.

12. H. Cazelles, "Ten Commandments," in *Interpreter's Dictionary of the Bible*, supplementary vol. (Nashville: Abingdon, 1976), 875–77.
13. Weinfeld, "Uniqueness of the Decalogue," 20.
14. For more details, see Rifat Sonsino, *Did Moses Really Have Horns?* (New York: URJ Press, 2009), 70–96.
15. Nahum Sarna, *Exploring Exodus* (New York: Schocken Books, 1986), 132.
16. By the end of the biblical period, however, the name was changed to "Nisan" (see Esther 3:7). It is thus known in the calendar finalized by the Rabbis as well.
17. How the "third" day can correspond to the sixth of Sivan is a problem in itself. Various interpretations have been offered.
18. See "Ark of the Covenant," in *The Anchor Bible Dictionary*, 1:390–91.
19. Lawrence A. Hoffman, ed., *My People's Prayer Book*, vol. 4, *Seder K'riat Hatorah (The Torah Service)* (Woodstock, VT: Jewish Lights, 2000), 125.
20. E. E. Urbach, "The Role of the Ten Commandments in Jewish Worship," in *Ten Commandments in History and Tradition*, 179.

The First Word: God

1. Joseph Albo, *Sefer Ha-'Ikkarim*, trans. Isaac Husik (Philadelphia: Jewish Publication Society, 1946), 1:14, 128.
2. Umberto Cassuto, *The Book of Exodus* [in Hebrew] (Jerusalem: Magnes Press, 1969), 106.
3. *Sefer HaHinnuch: The Book of [Mitzvah] Education*, trans. Charles Wengrov (Jerusalem: Feldheim, 1992), vol. 1, no. 25.
4. Rabbi Moshe ben Asher, "The Yoke of the Kingdom of Heaven," 2007, Khevra shel Kharakim, www.gatherthepeople.org.
5. For more details, see Rifat Sonsino, *Did Moses Really Have Horns?* (New York: URJ Press, 2009), 17–20; or Rifat Sonsino, "God Doesn't Need a Name," *CCAR Journal*, Fall 2010, 108–15.
6. How can that be? We really do not know. Perhaps, being considered too sacred, the name was avoided, fearing that it could be used in magic.
7. For more details, see Sonsino, "God Doesn't Need a Name."
8. Nahum Sarna, *Exodus*, The JPS Torah Commentary (Philadelphia: Jewish Publication Society, 1991), 18.
9. *Wall Street Journal*, Sept. 12, 2009.
10. W. Gunther Plaut, ed., *The Torah: A Modern Commentary*, rev. ed. (New York: CCAR Press, 2005), 1201.

11. For more details, see Rifat Sonsino and Daniel B. Syme, *Finding God*, rev. ed. (New York: URJ Press, 2002); and Rifat Sonsino, *The Many Faces of God* (New York: URJ Press, 2004).
12. For other arguments, see Sonsino, *Finding God*, 97–98.
13. On various views about the source of ethics, see, e.g., Daniel Kolak and Raymond Martin, *The Experience of Philosophy* (Belmont, CA: Wadsworth Thomson Learning, 2002), 598–647, or other standard books on ethics.
14. Menachem Kellner, *Must a Jew Believe Anything?* (London: Littman Library of Jewish Civilization, 1999), 71–82.

The Second Word: Idolatry

1. "Monolatry" is related to "henotheism." For some, henotheism is similar to but less exclusive than monolatry, because, even though "monolators" worship only one god and deny that other gods are worthy of worship, "henotheists" worship anyone within the list of gods depending on circumstances, although they usually will worship only one throughout their life.
2. We know that King Jeroboam of Israel (ninth century BCE) dedicated two calves in the Northern Kingdom (I Kings 12:28). It is not known which of these two incidents influenced the other or if there is even a relationship between the two.
3. Jeffrey H. Tigay, *You Shall Have No Other Gods*, Harvard Semitic Studies 31 (Atlanta: Scholars Press, 1986), 37.
4. See Hershel Shanks, "The Persisting Uncertainties of Kuntillet Ajrud," *Biblical Archaeology Review* 38, no. 6 (November/December 2012), 29–37.
5. Hans Wildberger, *Isaiah 1–12*, trans. Thomas H. Trapp (Minneapolis: Fortress Press, 1991), 264.
6. Solomon B. Freehof, *Modern Reform Responsa* (Cincinnati: Hebrew Union College Press, 1971), 187.
7. Solomon B. Freehof, *Contemporary Reform Responsa* (Cincinnati: Hebrew Union College Press, 1974), 130.
8. Walter Jacob, ed., *American Reform Responsa* (New York: CCAR Press, 1983), 70.
9. Nehama Leibowitz, *Studies in Shemot: Exodus* (Jerusalem: World Zionist Organization, 1986), 320.
10. Ibid.
11. Ibid., 321.
12. Erich Fromm, *The Art of Loving* (New York: Harper, 1956), 98.
13. Rachel S. Mikva, ed., *Broken Tablets* (Woodstock, VT: Jewish Lights, 1999), 23.

The Third Word: Misuse of God's Name

1. Mary Pemerton, "Jessica Beagley, Alaska woman, Convicted of Child Abuse After Squirting Hot Sauce Into Adopted Son's Mouth." http://www.huffingtonpost.com www.huffingtonpost.com, Aug. 23, 2011.
2. This is the Bible's popular etymology. In reality, the name *Yaakov*, coming from the Semitic root *k-v*, "to protect," means "May *El* protect."
3. On curses, see the article and references in *Anchor Bible Dictionary*, 1:1218–19.
4. Umberto Cassuto, *The Book of Exodus* [in Hebrew] (Jerusalem: Magnes Press, 1969), 168.
5. Solomon B. Freehof, *Recent Reform Responsa* (Cincinnati: Hebrew Union College Press, 1963), 53.
6. Walter Jacob, *Questions and Reform Jewish Answers* (New York: CCAR Press, 1992), 230.
7. Ibid., 231.
8. Ibid., 233.
9. Ibid., 229.
10. John I. Durham, *Exodus* (Waco, TX: Word Books, 1987), 288.
11. Nahum Sarna, *Exodus*, The JPS Torah Commentary (Philadelphia: Jewish Publication Society, 1991), 111.
12. Dr. C Matthew McMahon, "Taking the Name of God in Vain," "http://www.apuritansmind.com" www.apuritansmind.com.
13. Nehama Leibowitz, *Studies in Shemot: Exodus* (Jerusalem: World Zionist Organization, 1986), 331.
14. Joseph Telushkin, *Jewish Literacy* (New York: William Morrow, 1991), 57.

The Fourth Word: The Sabbath

1. *The Biblical Antiquities of Philo*, trans. M. R. James, 1917, http://www.sacred-texts.com/bib/bap/index.htm.
2. Nahum Sarna, *Exodus*, The JPS Torah Commentary (Philadelphia: Jewish Publication Society, 1991). 111.
3. Gen. 2:2, states, "On the seventh day, God completed [*vay'khal*] the work that had been done, ceasing then on the seventh day. . . ." Did God work on the seventh day, a day of rest? Some critics say "seventh day" is an error for "six" (see the Septuagint). Others try to understand *vay'khal* ("he finished") as "brought to a close" or "declared finished."
4. Sarna, *Exodus*, 90.

5. Florentino Garcia Martinez, *The Dead Sea Scrolls Translated* (Leiden: Brill, 1994), 42.
6. John I. Durham, *Exodus*, Word Biblical Commentary (Waco, TX: Word Books, 1987), 413.
7. Moshe Greenberg, "Crimes and Punishments," in *The Interpreter's Dictionary of the Bible* (New York: Abingdon Press, 1962), 1:735.
8. David N. Laband and Deborah H. Heinbuch, *Blue Laws* (Lexington, MA: Lexington Books, 1987).
9. Jeffrey H. Tigay, *Deuteronomy*, The JPS Torah Commentary (Philadelphia: Jewish Publication Society, 1996), 69.
10. See Yossi Braun, "Saving Lives on Shabbat," http://www.chabad.org/library/article_cdo/aid/1113745/jewish/Saving-Lives-on-Shabbat.htm.
11. Mark Dov Shapiro, *Gates of Shabbat: A Guide for Observing Shabbat* (New York: CCAR Press, 1991), 113.
12. *Catechism of the Catholic Church* (Ottawa: Canadian Conference of Catholic Bishops, 1994), no. 2190.
13. Samuele Bacchiocchi, "How It Came About: From Saturday to Sunday," *Biblical Archaeology Review*, September/October 1978, 32–39.
14. *Catechism of the Catholic Church*, no. 2185.
15. For more details about the Sabbath in a Reform context in America, see, W. Gunther Plaut, *The Growth of Reform Judaism* (New York: World Union for Progressive Judaism, 1965), 269–83.
16. Abraham Chill, *The Commandments and Their Rationale* (Jerusalem: Urim Publications, 2000), 37.
17. Erich Fromm, *You Shall Be As Gods* (New York: Fawcett Premier, 1969), 164.
18. Peter Knobel, *Gates of the Seasons: A Guide to the Jewish Year* (New York: CCAR Press, 1983), 23.
19. "Ask the Rabbi," Schechter Institutes, http://www.schechter.edu/askRabbiCatagory.aspx?ID=15.
20. Ibid.
21. Ibid.
22. Solomon B. Freehof, *Reform Responsa and Recent Reform Responsa* (New York: Ktav, 1973), 25.
23. Ibid., 170.
24. Walter Jacob, *American Reform Responsa*, vol. 1 (New York: CCAR Press, 1983), no. 43.
25. Ibid., no. 46.

26. Walter Jacob, *Questions and Reform Jewish Answers* (New York: CCAR Press, 1992), 98.
27. Abraham Joshua Heschel, *The Sabbath* (New York: Farrar, Straus and Giroux, 1975), 10.
28. Lawrence A. Hoffman, "The Meaning of Shabbat: A Virtual Domain in Time," in *Broken Tablets*, ed. Rachel S. Mikva (Woodstock, VT: Jewish Lights, 1999), 51.
29. Mordecai M. Kaplan, *The Meaning of God in Modern Jewish Religion* (New York: Reconstructionist Press, 1962), 59.

The Fifth Word: Honoring Parents

1. Judith Viorst, *Necessary Losses* (New York: Simon & Schuster, 1986), 16.
2. In Latin, the verb *diligere* means "to respect, esteem, love." Whether the change from "honor" to "love" is deliberate or if *dilige* is used here in the sense of "honor" is not clear.
3. James F. Keenan, *Commandments of Compassion* (Franklin, WI: Sheed & Ward, 1999), 20.
4. Martin Noth, *Exodus*, The Old Testament Library (Philadelphia: Westminster Press, 1962), 165.
5. John I. Durham, *Exodus*, Word Biblical Commentary (Waco, TX: Word Books, 1987), 291.
6. Cornelis Houtman, *Exodus* (Leuven, Belgium: Peeters, 2000), 3:50.
7. On Ahikar, see, *ANET*, 427–30, and *The Anchor Bible Dictionary* (New York: Doubleday, 1992), 1:119–20.
8. CCAR Responsa Committee, "Adopted Children and Their Biological Parents" (April 1983), in *Contemporary American Reform Responsa*, ed. Walter Jacob (New York: CCAR Press, 1987), 59.
9. Joseph H. Hertz, *The Pentateuch and Haftorahs* (London: Soncino, 1971), 34, comment on Gen. 9:23.
10. Richard E. Address, *Seekers of Meaning* (New York: URJ Press, 2012), 83.
11. Ibid., 81.
12. Erich Fromm, *The Art of Loving* (New York: Harper, 1936), 26.
13. Quoted by Menachem Kellner, *Maimonides on Judaism and the Jewish People* (Albany: State University of New York Press, 1991), 51.
14. Leonard Fein, "I Was Young, and I Have Also Grown Older," in *Broken Tablets*, ed. Rachel S. Mikva (Woodstock, VT: Jewish Lights, 1999), 70.

15. Meir of Rothenburg, *Responsa*, 2:120ff., cited in CCAR Responsa, "Responsibility of Children to Their Parents" (1982), in *American Reform Responsa*, ed. Walter Jacob (New York: CCAR Press, 1983).
16. Michael Chernick, "Family Responsibilities to the Aged," Sh'ma 26, no. 497. Sheima, 26/497, September 15, 1995, 3–5
17. CCAR Responsa, no. 212, May 1990.
18. Walter Jacob, *Questions and Reform Jewish Answers* (New York: CCAR Press, 1992), no. 32.
19. Judy B. Shanks, "Whatever Happened to 'Honor Your Father and Your Mother?'," *Reform Judaism*, Summer 1999.
20. Walter Jacob, *Contemporary American Reform Responsa* (New York: CCAR Press, 1987), 45.
21. For this subject, see Rifat Sonsino, *Motive Clauses in Hebrew Law*, SBL Dissertation Series 45 (Chico, CA: Scholars Press, 1980).
22. Aaron HaLevi, *Sefer HaHinnuch: The Book of [Mitzvah] Education*, trans. Charles Wengrov (Jerusalem: Feldheim, 1992, no. 33.
23. Nahum Sarna, *Exodus*, The JPS Torah Commentary (Philadelphia: Jewish Publication Society, 1991), 113.
24. David Noel Freedman, *The Nine Commandments* (New York: Doubleday, 2000), 82.
25. Chernick, "Family Responsibilities."
26. Hertz, *Pentateuch and Haftorahs*, 299.

The Sixth Word: Homicide

1. See U.S. Code, at Title 18.
2. The Brown-Driver-Briggs biblical dictionary suggests the Arabic *radaka* (meaning "to break or smash") as a possibility.
3. The literal translation of the expression "the murderer may be executed" is, "[one] shall murder the murderer," most likely by the "blood-avenger" (see Jacob Milgrom, *Numbers*, The JPS Torah Commentary (Philadelphia: Jewish Publication Society, 1960), 295.
4. Wilma Ann Bailey, in her book *You Shall Not Kill" or "You Shall Not Murder"?* (Collegeville, MN: Liturgical Press, 2005), opts for "You shall not kill."
5. Cf. Gen. 1:27.
6. Nahum Sarna, *Genesis*, The JPS Torah Commentary (Philadelphia: Jewish Publication Society, 1989), 12.
7. *The Jewish Study Bible*, ed. Adele Berlin and Marc Zvi Brettler (Oxford, UK: Oxford University Press, 1999), 25 (notes).

8. R. E. Friedman suggests that the reason is because the high priest's death had an expiatory value in biblical times. See Richard Elliot Friedman and Shawna Dolansky, *The Bible Now* (Oxford, UK: Oxford University Press, 2011), 129.
9. B'reishit Rabbah 22:5 says, it was "of the inferior crops."
10. Claus Westermann, *Genesis* (Grand Rapids, MI: W.B. Eerdmans, 1987), 33.
11. Sarna, Genesis, 33.
12. Daniel Polish, "Judaism and the Ultimate Punishment," *Reform Judaism*, Summer 2003, 33.
13. See the details in Louis Ginzberg, *The Legends of the Jews* (New York: Simon & Schuster, 1961), 546.
14. Promised in I Kings 21:20–24.
15. On judicial hanging around the world, see http://www.capitalpunishmentuk.org/hanging2.html.
16. "Capital Punishment," *Encyclopaedia Judaica* (2007), 5:144.
17. Yaakov Culi, *Me'am Lo'ez*, trans. Aryeh Kaplan (New York: Moznaim Publishing, 1979), 6:405.
18. The Committee on Jewish Law, Proceedings of the Committee, 192–7, 1970, Vol. 2, 1537-8.
19. 45th Council, November 1959, Miami Beach, FL
20. deathpenaltyprocon.org
21. Quoted by Immanuel Jakobovits, *Jewish Medical Ethics* (New York: Bloch Publishing, 1975), 123.
22. American Reform Responsa, Edited by Walter Jacob. NY: CCAR: NY, 1969, No. 77, 121).
23. *Gates of Mitzvah*, ed. Simeon J. Maslin (New York: CCAR Press, 1979), 50.
24. American Reform Responsa, No. 79, p. 273.
25. Culi, *Me'am Lo'ez*, 403.
26. Solomon Ganzfried, *Code of Jewish Law (Kitzur Shulchan Arukh)*, trans. Hyman E. Goldin (New York: Hebrew Publishing, 1963), 4:201, #3.
27. On Jewish martyrdom, see "Martyr, Martyrdom," in *Anchor Bible Dictionary* (New York: Doubleday, 1992), 4:574–79; and *Encyclopaedia Judaica* (2007), 12:141ff.
28. "Declaration on Procured Abortion," November 18, 1974, no. 14.
29. Rabbi Solomon B. Freehof allows abortion to safeguard the mother's well-being, including her mental anguish now and in the future, and states that Rabbi Ben Zion Uziel permitted abortion even to prevent "permanent deafness." See Freehof's responsum in *Recent Reform Responsa* (Cincinnati: Hebrew Union College Press, 1963), 188–93, originally published in the *CCAR Yearbook* in 1958.
30. *Gates of Mitzvah*, 12.

The Seventh Word: Adultery

1. Martha T. Roth, *Law Collections from Mesopotamia and Asia Minor*, 2nd ed. (Atlanta: Scholars Press, 1997), 18.
2. Ibid., 158.
3. Ibid., 105.
4. Though both concubines are called "wife" (*ishah*) in Genesis 30, Bilhah is clearly called "a concubine" (*pilegesh*) in Gen. 35:22.
5. *The Anchor Bible Dictionary* (New York: Doubleday, 1992), 4:565.
6. Roth, *Law Collections*, 18.
7. George Horowitz, *The Spirit of Jewish Law* (New York: Central Book, 1963), 219.
8. On the "sister-wife" motif, see, S. Greengus, "Sisterhood Adoption at Nuzi and the 'Wife-Sister' Motif in Genesis," *Hebrew Union College Annual* 46 (1975): 5–31; or the short discussion online, "My Wife, My Sister," by Dan Judson at www.myjewishlearning.com.
9. Louis Ginzberg, *The Legends of the Jews* (New York: Simon & Schuster, 1961), 101.
10. Jeffrey Tigay, *Deuteronomy*, The JPS Torah Commentary (Philadelphia: Jewish Publication Society, 1996), 476.
11. Jacob Milgrom, *Numbers*, The JPS Torah Commentary (Philadelphia: Jewish Publication Society, 1990), 350.
12. W. G. Lambert, *Babylonian Wisdom Literature* (Oxford, UK: Clarendon Press, 1967), 119.
13. Moshe Greenberg, "Some Postulates of Biblical Criminal Law," reprinted in *The Jewish Expression*, ed. Judah Goldin (New York: Bantam Books, 1970), 23.
14. *Encylopaedia Judaica* (2007), 1:314.
15. Moshe Greenberg, "The Decalogue Tradition Critically Examined," in *The Ten Commandments in History and Tradition*, ed. Ben-Zion Segal (Jerusalem: Magnes, 1990), 105.
16. Yaakov Culi, *Me'am Lo'ez*, trans. Aryeh Kaplan (New York: Moznaim, 1979), 408.
17. J. H. Hertz, *The Pentateuch and Haftorahs*, 2nd ed. (London: Soncino Press, 1971), 299.
18. On grounds of divorce, see list in George Horowitz, *The Spirit of Jewish Law* (New York: Central Books, 1963), no. 152.
19. Mark Washofsky, *Jewish Living: A Guide to Contemporary Reform Practice* (New York: URJ Press, 2001), 175.

20. CCAR Ad Hoc Committee on Human Sexuality, "Marital Sexual Infidelity," *CCAR Journal*, Fall 2001.
21. Similarly, in the TV series *Downton Abbey*, season 3, 2013, Lady Edith Crawley, second daughter of the 7th Earl of Grantham, Robert Crawley, falls for a handsome editor, whose wife is in a mental institution and therefore cannot be divorced by law. Though Edith seems to be alright with this situation, her family objects as not being socially acceptable in early nineteenth-century England.
22. Richard F. Address, "Till Death Us Do Part?," *Generations*, Fall 2011.
23. Richard F. Address, "Is It Still Adultery if the Spouse Has Alazheimer's?" The Jewish Daily Forward August 15, 2007
24. According to Lev. 21:7, a *kohein* (priest) "shall not take a woman that is a harlot [*zonah*], or profaned [*chalalah*]; neither shall they marry a divorced woman [*g'rushah*]; for he is holy unto his God."
25. Ephraim Oshry, *Responsa from the Holocaust* (New York: Judaica Press, 1983), 193–94.
26. Peter S. Knobel, "Sacred Boundaries," in *Broken Tablets: Restoring the Ten Commandments and Ourselves*, ed. Rachel S. Mikva (Woodstock, VT: Jewish Lights, 1999), 91.
27. Ibid., 88–89.

The Eighth Word: Stealing

1. Martha T. Roth, *Law Collections from Mesopotamia and Asia Minor*, 2nd ed. (Atlanta: Scholars Press, 1997), 28.
2. Ibid., 85.
3. Moshe Greenberg, "Some Postulates of Biblical Criminal Law," in *Jewish Expression*, ed. Judah Goldin (New York: Bantam, 1970), 27.
4. For details, see George Horowitz, *The Spirit of Jewish Law* (New York: Central Book, 1963), 601–18.
5. Roth, *Law Collections*, 84.
6. Ibid., 220.
7. Ibid., 82.
8. Kate Kowsh and Rebecca Harshbarger, "Stealing from God," *New York Post*, January 27, 2013.
9. Adele Berlin and Marc Zvi Brettler, eds., *The Jewish Study Bible* (Oxford, UK: Oxford University Press, 1999), 1459.
10. Roth, *Law Collections*, 226.
11. Ibid., 227.

12. Horowitz, *Spirit of Jewish Law*, 616.
13. Moshe Greenberg, *The Interpreter's Dictionary of the Bible* (New York: Abingdon Press, 1962), 1:741.
14. The *JPS Hebrew-English Tanakh* (Philadelphia: Jewish Publication Society, 1999) translates the expression "stealing the heart/mind" as "kept in the dark," whereas *The Torah: A Modern Commentary*, rev. ed., ed. W. Gunther Plaut, Genesis trans. Chaim Stern (New York: URJ Press, 2005), more appropriately, states that Jacob "deceived" Laban.
15. Yaakov Culi, *Me'am Lo'ez*, trans. Aryeh Kaplan (New York: Moznaim, 1979), chap. 10.
16. Hersey H. Friedman, "*Geneivat Da'at*: The Prohibition against Deception in Today's World," *Jewish Law*, August 2002, <http://www.jlaw.com/Articles/geneivatdaat.html>.
17. Solomon B. Freehof, *Modern Reform Responsa* (Cincinnati: Hebrew Union College Press, 1971), no. 285.
18. Plaut, *The Torah*, 184.
19. Nahum Sarna, *Genesis*, The JPS Torah Commentary (Philadelphia: Jewish Publication Society 1989), 191.
20. Chaim Kohn, "Identity Theft," *Hamodia*, June 14, 2006, http://www.businesshalacha.com/articles/identity-theft.
21. Israel Schneider, "Jewish Law and Copyright," *Jewish Law*, http://www.jlaw.com/Articles/copyright1.html.
22. Horowitz, *Spirit of Jewish Law*, no. 327, 617.
23. "Copyright and the Internet," CCAR Responsa 5761.1, http://ccarnet.org/responsa/rr21-no-5761-1/.
24. Charles J. Harary, "Stealing to Save Someone's Life," Jewish Law, March 13, 2003, http://www.jlaw.com/Articles/ch_stealsavelife.html.
25. Ibid.

The Ninth Word: False Witness

1. See my discussion on *shav* and *sheker* in "The Third Word: Misuse of God's Name."
2. John I. Durham, *Exodus*, Word Biblical Commentary (Waco, TX: Word Books, 1987), 296.
3. See "Witness," in U.S. Legal Definitions, http://definitions.uslegal.com/w/witness/
4. See "Witness," in *Encyclopaedia Judaica* (2008); also quoted online in Jewish Virtual Library under the same title.

5. Solomon Ganzfried, *Code of Jewish Law (Kitzur Shulhan Arukh)*, trans. Hyman E. Goldin (New York: Hebrew Publishing, 1963), 4:69, no.12.
6. "Duty to Report Child Abuse," Michigan Education Association, http://www.mea.org/legal/duty_to_report.html.
7. Paul Berger, "Yeshiva Condemns 'Offensive' Racial Remarks by Rabbi Hershel Schachter," *The Jewish Daily Forward*, March 15, 2013. See also, his article in the March 21, 2013 issue.
8. Steven H. Resnicoff, "Jewish Law and the Tragedy of Sexual Abuse of Children," *Rutgers Journal of Law and Religion* 13, no. 2 (2012).
9. Ganzfried, *Code of Jewish Law*, 4:69, no. 13.
10. George Horowitz, *The Spirit of Jewish Law* (New York: Central Book, 1963), 683.
11. W. Gunther Plaut, *The Rise of Reform Judaism* (New York: World Union for Progressive Judaism, 1963), 254.
12. W. Gunther Plaut, *The Growth of Reform Judaism* (New York: World Union for Progressive Judaism, 1965), 72.
13. Solomon B. Freehof, *Reform Jewish Practice* (New York: Union of American Hebrew Congregations, 1963), Vol. 1, 52.
14. See the comments by Yuval Sinai in "Witness," *Encyclopaedia Judaica* (2008).
15. Martha T. Roth, *Law Collections from Mesopotamia and Asia Minor*, 2nd ed. (Atlanta: Scholars Press, 1997), 81.
16. Ibid.
17. Quoted by S. Goldman, *The Ten Commandments*: Phoenix Books: Chicago and London, 1956, 184.
18. J. H. Hertz, *The Pentateuch and Haftorahs*, 2nd ed. (London: Soncino Press, 1971), 300.
19. The midrash understands "meet" as "meeting to fight," and "kiss," taken from the Hebrew word *neshek*, "weapon," as "took arms."

The Tenth Word: Coveting

1. *Gates of Repentance*, ed. Chaim Stern (New York: CCAR Press, 1978), 480, based on Prov. 27:20 and Eccl. 1:8.
2. Martha T. Roth, *Law Collections from Mesopotamia and Asia Minor*, 2nd ed. (Atlanta: Scholars Press, 1997), 85.
3. W. G. Lambert, *Babylonian Wisdom Literature* (Oxford, UK: Clarendon Press, 1967), 131.
4. Nahum Sarna, *Exodus*, The JPS Torah Commentary (Philadelphia: Jewish Publication Society, 1991), 115.

5. Jeffrey Tigay, *Deuteronomy*, The JPS Torah Commentary (Philadelphia: Jewish Publication Society, 1996), 72.
6. W. Gunther Plaut, ed., *The Torah: A Modern Commentary*, rev. ed. (New York: URJ Press, 2005), 479.
7. Sarna, *Exodus*, 219.
8. S. Y. Agnon, *Present at Sinai: The Giving of the Law*, trans. Michael Swirsky (Philadelphia: Jewish Publication Society, 1994), 257.
9. Umberto Cassuto, *The Book of Exodus* [in Hebrew] (Jerusalem: Magnes Press, 1969), 172–73.
10. In the inscription by Azitawadda of Adana, Phoenician, ca. eighth century BCE.
11. Agnon, *Present at Sinai*, 242.
12. Tigay, *Deuteronomy*, 72.
13. Moshe Greenberg, "The Decalogue Tradition Critically Examined," in *The Ten Commandments*, ed. Ben-Zion Segal (Jerusalem: Magnes Press, 1990), 108.
14. Plaut, *Torah*, 1199.7
15. Brevard S. Childs, *The Book of Exodus*, Philadelphia: Westminster, 1974, 127.
16. Alexander Rofe, "The Tenth Commandment in the Light of Four Deuteronomic Laws," in Segal, *Ten Commandments*, 54.
17. In I Chron. 2:7, his name appears as *Achar*. Cf. "Valley of Achor."
18. See, for more details, "Did Eve Eat an Apple?" in Rifat Sonsino, *Did Moses Really Have Horns?* (New York: URJ Press, 2009), 38–46.
19. Harold S. Kushner, *How Good Do We Have to Be?* (Boston: Little, Brown, 1966), 21.
20. Nehama Leibowitz, *Studies in Shemot: Exodus* (Jerusalem: World Zionist Organization, 1986), 350.
21. Joseph Telushkin, *A Code of Jewish Ethics* (New York: Bell Tower, 2006), 306–10.
22. Lisa G. Lerman, "The Slippery Slope from Ambition to Greed to Dishonesty: Lawyers, Money and Professional Integrity," *Hofstra Law Review*, May 22, 2002.
23. Erich Fromm, *You Shall Be as Gods* (New York: Fawcett Premier, 1969), 115.
24. Arnold Jacob Wolf, in *Broken Tablets: Restoring the Ten Commandments and Ourselves*, ed. Rachel S. Mikva (Woodstock, VT: Jewish Lights, 1999), 135.
25. Aaron Levine, "Ethical Dilemmas in the Telemarketer Industry," *Tradition* 38, no. 3 (2004): 1–39.
26. Telushkin, *Code of Jewish Ethics*, 304.

27. *Mishneh Torah, Sefer HaMada* 1:1–4, quoted in I. Twersky, *A Maimonides Reader* (New York: Behrman House, 1972), 51–52.

Legislation and Commandment

1. S. Y. Agnon, *Present at Sinai: The Giving of the Law*, trans. Michael Swirsky (Philadelphia: Jewish Publication Society, 1994), 265.
2. Jakob J. Petuchowski, *Ever Since Sinai* (New York: Scribe Publications, 1961), 79.
3. Martin Buber, *On the Bible* (New York: Schocken Books, 1968), 106.
4. Agnon, *Present at Sinai*, 243.

Bibliography

Address, Richard F. *Seekers of Meaning: Baby Boomers, Judaism, and the Pursuit of Healthy Aging*. New York: URJ Press, 2012.

Agnon, S. Y. *Present at Sinai: The Giving of the Law*. Translated by Michael Swirsky. Philadelphia: Jewish Publication Society, 1994.

Albo, Joseph. *Sefer Ha-'Ikkarim*. Translated by Isaac Husik. Philadelphia: Jewish Publication Society, 1946.

The Anchor Bible Dictionary. Edited by David Noel Freedman. New York: Doubleday, 1992.

Bacchiocchi, Samuele. "How It Came About: From Saturday to Sunday." *Biblical Archaeology Review*, September/October 1978, 32–39.

Bailey, Wilma Ann. *"You Shall Not Kill" or "You Shall Not Murder"?* Collegeville, MN: Liturgical Press, 2005.

Berlin, Adele, and Marc Zvi Brettler, eds. *The Jewish Study Bible*. Oxford, UK: Oxford University Press, 1999.

Birnbaum, Philip. *Encyclopedia of Jewish Concepts*. New York: Hebrew Publishing, 1979.

Buber, Martin. *On the Bible*. New York: Schocken Books, 1968.

Cassuto, Umberto. *The Book of Exodus* [in Hebrew]. Jerusalem: Magnes Press, 1969.

Cazelles, H. "Ten Commandments." In *The Interpreter's Dictionary of the Bible: Supplementary Volume*, edited by Keith R. Crim, 876. Nashville: Abingdon Press, 1976.

Chernick, Michael, "Family Responsibilities to the Ages," *Sh'ma* No. 26/497, 1995.

Chill, Abraham. *The Mitzvot: The Commandments and Their Rationale*. Jerusalem: Urim Publications, 2000.

Culi, Yaakov. *Me'am Lo'ez*. Translated by Aryeh Kaplan. New York: Moznaim, 1979.

Durham, John I. *Exodus*. Word Biblical Commentary. Waco, TX: Word Books, 1987.

Fein, Leonard. "I Was Young, and I Have Also Grown Older." In *Broken Tablets:*

Restoring the Ten Commandments and Ourselves, edited by Rachel S. Mikva. Woodstock, VT: Jewish Lights, 1999.

Flusser, David. "The Ten Commandments and the New Testament." In *The Ten Commandments in History and Tradition*, edited by Ben-Zion Segal, 219–46. Jerusalem: Magnes Press, 1990.

Freedman, David Noel. *The Nine Commandments*. New York: Doubleday, 2000.

Freehof, Solomon B. *Contemporary Reform Responsa*. Cincinnati: Hebrew Union College Press, 1974.

———. *Modern Reform Responsa*. Cincinnati: Hebrew Union College Press, 1971.

———. *Recent Reform Responsa*. Cincinnati: Hebrew Union College, 1963.

———. *Reform Responsa and Recent Reform Responsa*. New York: Ktav, 1973.

Friedman, Richard E., and Shawna Dolansky. *The Bible Now*. Oxford: Oxford University Press, 2011.

Fromm, Erich. *The Art of Loving*. New York: Harper & Brothers, 1936.

———. *You Shall Be As Gods*. New York: Fawcett Premier, 1969.

Ganzfried, Solomon. *Code of Jewish Law (Kitzur Shulhan Arukh)*. Translated by Hyman E. Goldin. New York: Hebrew Publishing, 1963.

Ginzberg, Louis. *The Legends of the Jews*. New York: Simon & Schuster, 1961.

Goodman, P. *The Shavuot Anthology*. Philadelphia: Jewish Publication Society, 1974.

Greenberg, Moshe. "Crimes and Punishment." In *The Interpreter's Dictionary of the Bible*, edited by George Arthur Buttrick, vol. 1. New York: Abingdon Press, 1962.

———. "The Decalogue Tradition Critically Examined." In *The Ten Commandments in History and Tradition*, edited by Ben-Zion Segal, 83–119. Jerusalem: Magnes Press, 1990.

———. "Some Postulates of Biblical Criminal Law." Reprinted in *The Jewish Expression*, edited by Judah Goldin, 18–37. New York: Bantam Books, 1970.

HaLevi, Aaron. *Sefer HaHinnuch: The Book of [Mitzvah] Education*. Translated by Charles Wengrov. Jerusalem: Feldheim, 1992.

Hertz, Joseph H., ed. *The Pentateuch and Haftorahs*. 2nd ed. London: Soncino Press, 1971.

Heschel, Abraham Joshua. *The Sabbath*. New York: Farrar, Straus and Giroux, 1975.

Hoffman, Lawrence A. "The Meaning of Shabbat: A Virtual Domain in Time." In *Broken Tablets: Restoring the Ten Commandments and Ourselves*, edited by Rachel S. Mikva. Woodstock, VT: Jewish Lights, 1999.

———, ed. *Seder K'riat Hatorah (The Torah Service)*. Vol. 4 of *My People's Prayer Book*. Woodstock, VT: Jewish Lights, 2000.

Horowitz, George. *The Spirit of Jewish Law*. New York: Central Books, 1963.

Houtman, Cornelis. *Exodus*. Leuven, Belgium: Peeters, 2000.

Jacob, Walter, ed. *American Reform Responsa*. Vol. 1. New York: CCAR Press, 1983.

———. *Contemporary American Reform Responsa*. New York: CCAR Press, 1987.

———. *Questions and Reform Jewish Answers*. New York: CCAR Press, 1992.

Jakobovits, Immanuel. *Jewish Medical Ethics*. New York: Bloch Publishing, 1975.

Kaplan, Mordecai M. *The Meaning of God in Modern Jewish Religion.* New York: Reconstructionist Press, 1962.

Keenan, James E. *Commandments of Compassion.* Franklin, WI: Sheed & Ward, 1999.

Kellner, Menachem. *Must a Jew Believe Anything?* London: Littman Library of Jewish Civilization, 1999.

Knobel, Peter S. "Sacred Boundaries." In *Broken Tablets: Restoring the Ten Commandments and Ourselves,* edited by Rachel S. Mikva. Woodstock, VT: Jewish Lights, 1999.

Kushner, Harold S. *How Good Do We Have to Be?* Boston: Little, Brown, 1966.

Lambert, W. G. *Babylonian Wisdom Literature.* Oxford, UK: Clarendon Press, 1967.

Leibowitz, Nehama. *Studies in Shemot: Exodus.* Jerusalem: World Zionist Organization, 1986.

Lerman, Lisa G. "The Slippery Slope from Ambition to Greed to Dishonesty." *Hofstra Law Review,* May 22, 2002.

Levine, Aaron. "Ethical Dilemmas in the Telemarketer Industry." *Tradition* 38, no. 3 (2004): 1–39.

Martinez, F. Garcia. *The Dead Sea Scrolls Translated.* Leiden: Brill, 1994.

Maslin, Simeon J., ed. *Gates of Mitzvah: A Guide to the Jewish Life Cycle.* New York: CCAR Press, 1979.

Meir of Rothenburg, *Responsa,* 2:120ff. Cited in CCAR Responsa, "Responsibility of Children to Their Parents" (1982), in *American Reform Responsa,* edited by Walter Jacob, New York: CCAR Press, 1983.

Mikva, Rachel S., ed. *Broken Tablets: Restoring the Ten Commandments and Ourselves.* Woodstock, VT: Jewish Lights, 1999.

Milgrom, Jacob. *Numbers.* The JPS Torah Commentary. Philadelphia: Jewish Publication Society, 1990.

Noth, Martin. *Exodus.* The Old Testament Library. Philadelphia: Westminster Press, 1962.

Oshry, Ephraim. *Responsa from the Holocaust,* 193–94. New York: Judaica Press, 1983.

Petuchowski, Jakob J. *Ever Since Sinai.* New York: Scribe Publications, 1961.

Plaut, W. Gunther. *The Growth of Reform Judaism.* New York: World Union for Progressive Judaism, 1965.

———. *The Rise of Reform Judaism.* New York: World Union for Progressive Judaism, 1963.

———, ed. *The Torah: A Modern Commentary.* Rev. ed. New York: URJ Press, 2005.

Polish, Daniel. "Judaism and the Ultimate Punishment." *Reform Judaism,* Summer 2002.

Resnikoff, Steven H. "Jewish Law and the Tragedy of Sexual Abuse." *Rutgers Journal of Law and Religion,* 2012.

Rofe, Alexander. "The Tenth Commandment in the Light of Four Deuteronomic

Laws." In *The Ten Commandments in History and Tradition*. Edited by Ben-Zion Segal. Jerusalem: Magnes Press, 1990.

Roth, Martha T. *Law Collections from Mesopotamia and Asia Minor.* 2nd ed. Atlanta: Scholars Press, 1997.

Saggs, H. W. E. *The Greatness That Was Babylon.* New York: Hawthorn Books, 1962.

Sandmel, Samuel. *The Hebrew Scriptures.* New York: Alfred A. Knopf, 1963.

Sarna, Nahum. *Exodus.* The JPS Torah Commentary. Philadelphia: Jewish Publication Society, 1991.

———. *Exploring Exodus.* New York: Schocken Books, 1986.

———. *Genesis.* The JPS Torah Commentary. Philadelphia: Jewish Publication Society, 1989.

Segal, Ben-Zion, ed. *The Ten Commandments in History and Tradition.* Jerusalem: Magnes Press, 1990.

Shanks, Hershel. "The Persisting Uncertainties of Kuntillet Ajrud." *Biblical Archaeology Review* 38, no. 6 (November/December 2012), 29–37.

Shanks, Judy B. "Whatever Happened to 'Honor Your Father and Your Mother?'" *Reform Judaism*, Summer 1999.

Sonsino, Rifat. *Did Moses Really Have Horns? And Other Myths about Jews and Judaism.* New York: URJ Press, 2009.

———. "God Doesn't Need a Name." *CCAR Journal: The Reform Jewish Quarterly*, Fall 2010, 109–15.

———. *The Many Faces of God.* New York: URJ Press, 2004.

———. *Motive Clauses in Hebrew Law.* SBL Dissertation Series 45. Chico, CA: Scholars Press, 1980.

———. "Towards a Definition of Law in the Pentateuch." *Journal of Reform Judaism.* Summer 1979, 117–23.

Sonsino, Rifat, and Daniel B. Syme. *Finding God.* Rev. ed. New York: URJ Press, 2002.

Telushkin, Joseph. *A Code of Jewish Ethics.* New York: Bell Tower, 2006.

———. *Jewish Literacy.* New York: William Morrow, 1991.

Tigay, Jeffrey. *Deuteronomy.* The JPS Torah Commentary. Philadelphia: Jewish Publication Society, 1996.

———. *You Shall Have No Other Gods.* Harvard Semitic Studies 31. Atlanta: Scholars Press, 1986.

Urbach, E. F. "The Role of the Ten Commandments in Jewish Worship." In *The Ten Commandments in History and Tradition*, edited by Ben-Zion Segal, 161–90. Jerusalem: Magnes Press, 1990.

Van Harn, Roger E. *The Ten Commandments for Jews, Christians, and Others.* Grand Rapids: Wm. B. Eerdmans, 2007.

Viorst, Judith. *Necessary Losses.* New York: Simon and Schuster, 1986.

Vos, Geerhardus. *Biblical Theology—Old and New Testament.* Finland: Banner of Truth Trust, 2000.

Washofsky, Mark. *Jewish Living: A Guide to Contemporary Reform Practice*. Rev. ed. New York: URJ Press, 2010.

Weinfeld, Moshe. "The Uniqueness of the Decalogue and Its Place in Jewish Tradition." In *The Ten Commandments in History and Tradition*, edited by Ben-Zion Segal, 1–44. Jerusalem: Magnes Press, 1990.

Westermann, Claus. *Genesis*. Grand Rapids, MI: Wm. B. Eerdmans, 1987.

Wildberger, Hans. *Isaiah 1–12*. Translated by Thomas H. Trapp. Minneapolis: Fortress Press, 1991.

Zimmels, H. J. *Ashkenazim and Sephardim*. London: Marla Publications, 1976.